READING CHARACTER AFTER CALVIN

Reading Character
after Calvin

SECULARIZATION, EMPIRE, AND
THE EIGHTEENTH-CENTURY NOVEL

David Mark Diamond

UNIVERSITY OF VIRGINIA PRESS
Charlottesville and London

UNIVERSITY OF VIRGINIA PRESS

© 2024 by the Rector and Visitors of the University of Virginia

All rights reserved

Printed in the United States of America on acid-free paper

First published 2024

1 3 5 7 9 8 6 4 2

Library of Congress Cataloging-in-Publication Data

Names: Diamond, David Mark, author.
Title: Reading character after Calvin : secularization, empire, and
the eighteenth-century novel / David Mark Diamond.
Description: Charlottesville : University of Virginia Press, 2024. |
Includes bibliographical references and index.
Identifiers: LCCN 2023052270 (print) | LCCN 2023052271 (ebook) | ISBN 9780813950884
(hardcover) | ISBN 9780813950891 (paperback) | ISBN 9780813950907 (ebook)
Subjects: LCSH: Characters and characteristics in literature. | Calvinism in
literature. | English fiction—18th century—History and criticism. | Calvin,
Jean, 1509–1564—Influence. | BISAC: HISTORY / Modern / 18th Century
Classification: LCC PR448.C52 D53 2024 (print) | LCC PR448.
C52 (ebook) | DDC 823/.509353—dc23/eng/20240102
LC record available at https://lccn.loc.gov/2023052270
LC ebook record available at https://lccn.loc.gov/2023052271

Cover art: Frontispiece from *The Life and Death of Mr. Badman*, John Bunyan.
(Cambridge University Press, 1905 / Project Gutenberg)

To Andi, who believed

CONTENTS

ACKNOWLEDGMENTS

In the years it took me in to write this book, I accumulated many intellectual debts. Small repayment though it may be, I offer my enthusiastic thanks to the brilliant scholars whose work and conversation has sustained this project though several iterations. James Chandler, Heather Keenleyside, Richard Rosengarten, Tim Campbell, Tristan Schweiger, Elaine Hadley, and Frances Ferguson, among others at the University of Chicago, were generous interlocutors when this book was a dissertation of narrower scope. Peter Coviello, still my teacher, elucidated what we really mean when we talk about secularism. His thinking was a guiding light. The incomparable Julie Orlemanski provided incisive feedback and much-needed encouragement at several pivotal moments in the book's development. In convening their 2019 NEH Summer Seminar (Religion, Secularism, and the Novel) at the University of Iowa, Lori Branch and Mark Knight created an ideal environment in which to explore the theoretical and political stakes of my literary analyses. It was in Iowa City that I met James Reeves and Matthew Wickman, whose kind attention to my arguments honed them. In conference panels, hotel bars, and Zoom windows, I learned from David Alvarez, Dwight Codr, Alison Conway, Sarah Ellenzweig, Jacob Sider Jost, and Dustin Stewart.

I will be forever grateful to the teachers who set me down the path to writing this book. At Bowdoin College, before graduate school was on the horizon, Ann Kibbie introduced me to eighteenth-century studies, Aaron Kitch suggested that I might be a good fit for the "contemplative life" of teaching and scholarship, and Pete helped me find the joy in exacting reading and argumentation. Before that, at Mansfield High School, John Pontes presented long, difficult books to skeptical tenth-graders and won us all over.

My students at the University of Colorado–Colorado Springs, Haverford College, and the University of Georgia have enlivened the work of research, writing, and revision. At UCCS, Ann Amicucci, Steve Carter, Helen Davies, Andrea Herrera, Rebecca Laroche, Katherine Mack, Suhaan Mehta, Susan Taylor, and Jeff Scholes were exemplary colleagues. Gus Stadler and Jill Stauffer offered ballasting friendship during a year on the Philadelphia Main Line. My new colleagues in the UGA Department of English and Institute for African American Studies provided advice and conviviality as I revised my manuscript and prepared it for publication. For their hospitality, for their mentoring, and for their collaboration on various endeavors related to the themes and texts in my book, I wish to thank Sujata Iyengar, Miriam Jacobson, Aruni Kashyap, Elizabeth Kraft, Isiah Lavender, Casie LeGette, Barbara McCaskill, Richard Menke, Channette Romero, and Esra Santesso. Cody Marrs and Carolyn Medine helped me find my place in English and IAAS, respectively. The late and much missed John Lowe was a beacon of warmth and intellectual vivacity, and I feel lucky to have known him.

I am grateful to the reviewers for the University of Virginia Press for their perceptive comments and genuinely helpful suggestions. My editor at the Press, Angie Hogan, was a pleasure to work with and an indispensable resource—knowledgeable, transparent, supportive. Indeed, everyone at the Press has my deep appreciation for the work they have done to help this book move from proposal to reified objecthood. Parts of several chapters have appeared previously in academic journals. Copyright © 2015 Johns Hopkins University Press. The opening paragraphs and the first section of chapter 1 appeared in earlier form as "Sinners and 'Standers-by': Reading the Character of Calvinism in *The Pilgrim's Progress*" in *Eighteenth-Century Studies* 49, no. 1 (Fall 2015): 1–15. Copyright © 2018 Johns Hopkins University Press. Several short passages in the Introduction and a section of Chapter 3 appeared as "Secular Fielding" in *ELH* 85, no. 3 (Fall 2018): 691–714. Both articles are published with the permission of Johns Hopkins University Press.

Much of this book was written during the early years of the COVID-19 pandemic, in fits and starts and between carefully negotiated parenting shifts. My little family was remarkably gracious and patient as I navigated between those responsibilities. Gabriel's effervescence continually drew me out, made me more a part of the world, and I have needed that. Andi's generosity, love, and occasional cheerleading enabled me to write this book. I dedicate it to her.

READING CHARACTER AFTER CALVIN

In Good Faith

I N "THE AUTHOR'S APOLOGY FOR HIS BOOK" for *The Pilgrim's Progress* (1678), John Bunyan defends his use of "Types, Shadows, and Metaphors" on the grounds of biblical precedent.[1] Lest he transgress against the "highest Wisdom," the ideal reader does not find "fault" with such figures when they appear in the gospel:

> No, he rather stoops,
> And seeks to find out what by pins and loops,
> By Calves, and Sheep; by Heifers, and by Rams;
> By Birds and Herbs, and by the Blood of Lambs,
> God speaketh to him. (7)

Bunyan prompts readers of *The Pilgrim's Progress* to adopt the same approach, to ask "what by" various emblems and personifications he "speaketh" to them. He argues further that the mode of representation he shares with the author of revelation only veils its "solidness," and he uses a series of metaphors to explain how his figures convey valuable knowledge: like a "Toads-head," an "Oister-shell," or a "cabinet," they enclose "pearls" and "gold." Bunyan's animal and inanimate figures yield meaning by revealing their insides to the reader who "stoops" to interpret their initially opaque surfaces. Introducing two-dimensional "figures" that "call for one thing, to set forth another," Bunyan asks his readers to bridge literal and figurative planes of meaning (9). He instructs them to discover the truth of an object by lifting the veil of figurative language and matching its double meanings, substituting one quantity (the thing called for) for another (the thing set forth). This is the ideal of two-dimensional reading.

Human characters in *The Pilgrim's Progress* would seem, at first, to operate according to a similarly doubled logic, exhibiting a consonance of name and nature. The apostate Turn-away turns away from God, Ready-to-halt embraces every opportunity to suspend his pilgrimage, and Hopeful's optimism buoys Christian's spirits while the two languish in the dungeon of Doubting Castle. One of the convoy of Christiana's fellow pilgrims in part 2, Mr. Honest, invokes this consonance when he proclaims his own representational status, explaining that he is "Not Honesty in the Abstract, but Honest is my Name, and I wish that my Nature shall agree with what I am called" (194). His self-introduction hints at the surprising complexity of Bunyan's characters. On the one hand, Mr. Honest tells readers of and within the text exactly what kind of character he is: not quite a personified abstraction, he is nevertheless two-dimensional and wholly intelligible. He illustrates E. M. Forster's definition of "flat" characters, adhering to the moral pattern conveyed by his surname and, thus, to readers' expectations.[2] Specifically, Mr. Honest exemplifies a familiar ethical type, a "Cock of the right Kind" to join a company of pilgrims, as their guide, Great-heart, puts it (193). On the other hand, Mr. Honest complicates the two-dimensionality of Bunyan's characters by implying that names might not match inner or essential natures, or that their correspondence is a matter of aspiration rather than a matter of fact. Such a disjunction is not the only or even the most likely contingency, but it is a contingency—one that haunts interactions between professed coreligionists throughout *The Pilgrim's Progress*. Since it is "Honest" who proclaims the possibility of discordance, the passage implies that the only honest understanding of character is one that doubts the coincidence of name and nature.

As Bunyan ushers his pilgrims and his readers through a series of encounters with fellow religious professors, he underscores the urgency of their efforts to distinguish between a "Cock of the right kind" and a false friend, to read religious character correctly. With such efforts, Bunyan's pilgrims respond to an imperative of Congregational ecclesiology, which restricted communion to "visible saints" who could give credible testimony to their faith.[3] The ministers and lay members of gathered churches vetted applicants for admission, assigning salvific categories established by the Calvinist doctrine of double predestination.[4] The doctrine attributes salvation to God (as opposed to good works) and organizes all persons into two mutually exclusive classifications, the elect and the reprobate. Taken in the abstract, then, Calvinist doctrine promotes a "rigidly dualistic" concept of character: everyone we meet is defined, in advance, by an ostensibly fixed spiritual status.[5] They belong to the race either of the saved or the damned.

For all the simplicity of this taxonomy, the task of assigning would-be pilgrims to prescribed genera proves difficult for Christian and his peers. Confronted by the religious hypocrite Talkative in part 1, Faithful hits upon the underlying problem: "How doth the saving Grace of God discover it self, when it is in the Heart of man?" (P, 164). In keeping with his commitment to gathered church ecclesiology, Bunyan insists that outward signs of grace—markers of one's spiritual status or character—are accessible to "him that hath it, or to standers by." But, in *The Pilgrim's Progress,* he presents the interpretation of such signs as a fraught and uncertain process. Ways of reading depicted and required by *The Pilgrim's Progress* affirm the doctrinal orthodoxy of Calvinism. At the same time, Bunyan's careful application of that doctrine produces strangely inscrutable characters. They are "flat" and underpsychologized, gestural more than interiorized, yet they resist easy interpretation.

This book argues that similar two-dimensional characters populate the worlds of British fiction from the Restoration through the Romantic era. They represent Calvinism's bequest to the novel as a form. The fate of Calvinism in Britain after the seventeenth century has been much studied. Because they focus on its aftermath or afterlives, though, existing conversations tend to elide the breadth of relations available to Calvinism throughout the period. Early novels demonstrate this breadth by appealing not to the predestinarian soteriology typically identified with Calvinism—the conviction that our spiritual fates are fixed, unalterable—but to a method of characterological interpretation and its corresponding idea of self. Calvinism survives in the pages of the novel as a portable set of heuristics rather than a totalizing system of faith. The need to police the borders of the community of saints, to know whether other people are in good faith, yields protocols for discerning religious hypocrisy—and, eventually, for rendering recognizable the distinctions of imperial race-making. In Calvin's teachings, every person has an outward face and an inward, spiritual condition. The outward face ideally makes the inward condition intelligible from without: we can discover another person's salvific state by interpreting extrinsic evidence. Even in its most orthodox elaborations, however, this method of interpretation is haunted by the possibility of incongruence between the two dimensions of the self, outer and inner, this-worldly and ultimate.

Like the Calvinist subject, characters in early novels are two-dimensional—that is, they posit a hermeneutics of correspondence, between inside and outside, gesture and morality, sign and spirit. In literary terms, two-dimensionality is a system of reference that "call[s] forth one thing, to set forth another," as Bunyan puts it when describing his method (P, 8–9). Symbolic associations may operate on the scales of individual character (e.g., metonym and physiognomic description), form (as in Bunyan's allegorical schema), or intertextuality (allusion and typology). In practice, however, the correspondence of the thing called for to the thing set forth tends to strain or fail, and the result is less a stable referential relation, like the one that subsists between Bunyan's figures and their meanings, than a hermeneutical problematic. We might describe this problematic as the semiotics of character.

Here, and throughout my study, I invoke the dynamic and unpredictable process theorized by Umberto Eco and applied to cultural identity by William Boelhower. Eco stresses that signs are multivocal and contingent, complicating earlier theories in which the sign corresponds to a single, static referent.[6] Boelhower adapts Eco's theory of semiosis as an explanatory frame for the "spatial problematics" of reading ethnicity in American literature.[7] What seems like a simple matter of matching superficial markers of difference to core identities—a practice that Boelhower calls "ethnic facework"—turns out to involve readers in an always unfinished labor of putting external signs and internal signifieds into relation.[8] This is the model of semiotic activity that Calvinist doctrine demands of its adherents and that *The Pilgrim's Progress* enacts through its allegorical method. The appeal of the model's explanatory potential extends its influence beyond the culture of Protestant dissent during the eighteenth century, affiliating the Calvinist Bunyan with (among others) committed Anglicans like Laurence Sterne and supposed freethinkers like Aphra Behn. In particular, the semiotics of character furnishes these disparate writers with a frame of response to the material, social, and institutional conditions of empire.

Early novelists' efforts to think with and beyond Calvinism's system for decoding the signs of religio-ethical character clarify the place of the novel in a larger, often occluded historical dynamic—that, I argue, is the project of imperial secularism. Long taken to be synonymous with the diminution or displacement of religion, "secularization" has been made newly legible in recent years thanks to queer and anticolonialist scholarship.[9] By the light of this work, secularization appears as a process by which a fundamental distinction between good and bad belief ramifies into an extensible chain of oppositions: disenchantment and enchantment, reason and faith, volition and coercion, modernity and tradition, public and private, religion and zealotry, West and East. The machinery of secularist distinction assigns the falling term of each dyad to Euro-Christendom's imperial rivals and colonized subjects while legitimizing, as real religion, a form of Protestant belief that has been liberalized, or released from its doctrinal moorings.

Through the migration of Calvinist semiotics from its originary, sectarian contexts to the imperial and cosmopolitan worlds of eighteenth-century British fiction, I propose, we glimpse the discourse of secularism at the beginning of its arc toward consolidation. The persistence and complexity of two-dimensionality reveals novelistic character as the formal site of Calvinism's liberalization and, through that, its accommodation to colonialist thought. There are two steps, or phases, to this secularizing process, each registering through a different kind of characterological instability. The first consists of the loosening of doctrinal propriety as late seventeenth- and early eighteenth-century writers adapt Calvinism's semiotics as a way to represent racial and cultural difference. The characters in their books are strange because Calvinism's construction of the self is already strange, a function of the shifting inside-outside relation that defines it. In the next phase of secularization, mid- and late eighteenth-century authors take doctrinal latitude further by positioning the Calvinist semiotics of character within larger matrices of formal and theological possibility. Writers like Henry Fielding and Sterne enact a phenomenon that the philosopher Charles Taylor calls the "nova effect."[10] Taylor names the process by which religion is redistributed within a pluralized marketplace of belief, the result of which is a "mutual fragilization of all the different views in presence" during modernity.[11] Their novels present Calvinist semiotics and its literary concomitant, two-dimensionality, as one fragilized option among many: insufficient but ultimately compatible with positions once antithetical to it. The strangeness of their characters derives from the variety of techniques used to compose them, a multiplicity that replicates formally the expanding horizon of possibility for belief. Their incipiently secularized Protestantism gathers normative force through its paradoxical gesture toward openness. Fielding and, especially, Sterne represent a putative doctrinal fluidity, even pluralism, that in fact deepens the cleavage between it and what is cast as the dogmatic systematicity of, for instance, Islam or Catholicism.

Eighteenth-century secularism differs from the fully eventuated, contemporary iterations described by scholars like Talal Asad and Gil Anidjar in that it does not perform semantic masking; although it propagates divisions between true and false beliefs, the real religion of the early novel has not yet come to rename itself "secularity" and its others "religion."[12] Another significant difference between these historical formations of the secular consists in the ways they relate bodies and beliefs. Secularism today "conjugates what flesh it encounters," Peter Coviello explains, inscribing religious difference onto the bodies of its subjects.[13] Corporeal differences of sex and race "are made to appear, are invested with heft and significance, in and through secularism" and, in turn, the violence of empire is made to appear justified.[14] The disciplinary valence of eighteenth-century secularism is less stable. Secularized in the ways I've just explained—whether simply abstracted and made newly flexible, or more thoroughly pluralized through the nova effect—Calvinism offers novelists a characterological logic through which to perpetuate the division between true and false religion. What is for Bunyan a model of difference within a religious community becomes a tool for differentiating religious traditions. Islam, Obeah, Latitudinarian Anglicanism, Christian skepticism, natural theology, West African animism, Roman Catholicism, the syncretic belief of the white "Nabob": all are arranged in dyadic pairs at various points in this literary history. The novel's secularized Calvinism does not, perforce, overlay the good/bad belief binary onto the distinction between viable and errant forms of life, however. Calvinism's play of two-dimensionality, its ultimately withheld promise of semiotic or symbolic coherence, enables certain writers to hold apart or reinterpret religious meanings assigned to the gendered and racialized subjects of empire. Novels like Behn's *Oroonoko* (1688) and the anonymously published *The Woman of Colour, A Tale* (1808) represent theo-racial "Others" in ways that trouble the secularist equation of bad beliefs and racialized bodies, sometimes even celebrating spiritual excesses and insufficiencies. They do so for the most part in view of an amelioration; while not reaching to the standard of anticolonialism, they nevertheless advocate for more equitable models of colonization or colonial management. These are appeals within and to empire, collectively elaborating a human semiotics of reading after Calvin.

The Characters of Reformed Theology

Histories of English Calvinism after the Restoration tend to describe a self-contained theology that was either pushed to the fringes of Protestant dissent by more progressive religious forms or assimilated by them. Gerald R. Cragg and Isabel Rivers support the displacement model, reconstructing a zero-sum contest between Calvinist predestinarian grace and Arminian free will.[15] They argue that Arminianism's rise to hegemony in the Anglican church was a precursor to enlightenment. Where Calvinists privileged faith as the felt experience of divine grace, Anglican Arminians stressed "the capacity of human reason and free will to cooperate with Grace" in achieving salvation.[16] On this account, the elevation of reason set the stage for the eventual triumph of skepticism over religious belief. The outcome of the Calvinism-Arminianism controversy had characterological implications, as well. Calvinists imagined the world as divided into mutually exclusive classifications, the elect and the damned. The individual believer was passive, only indirectly responsible for the qualifying faith of election and deeply anxious about which feelings might indicate the operations of grace. Extending the possibility of—and responsibility for—salvation to all human beings, Anglican Arminians asserted the preeminence of rational choice in earning or forfeiting grace. On this account of religious history, rationalist self-determination superseded providential determinism on its way toward a fully realized modern subject.

Another perspective, elaborated in twentieth-century literary history, eschews the logic of displacement for that of persistence and transformation. This body of scholarship seeks to illuminate the broad cultural relevance of a vital question raised by the doctrine of double predestination: How do I know whether I am saved? Scholars agree that this "question of assurance" outlived Calvinism's direct influence, shaping forms of social, spiritual, and economic identity in the eighteenth century and beyond.[17] They are divided, however, as to how it did so. Developing the link between the privatization of faith and the evolution of capitalist ideology proposed by Max Weber, Ian Watt and George Starr argue that Calvinism bequeaths to eighteenth-century fiction an idiom of self-analysis that would serve as the foundation for psychological realism in the modern novel.[18] More recent work shows how the question of assurance became a project of collective accreditation. Sarah Rivett historicizes the outward turn of Calvinist thought on both sides of the Atlantic, arguing that congregations developed empirical protocols to authenticate potential members' conversion narratives.[19] Such applications of Calvin's teachings "transformed the parameters of human knowledge so substantially that subsequent philosophical changes, including Baconian empiricism, natural theology, and mechanical philosophy, would also bear its mark."[20]

My book builds on these contributions, devoting attention to Calvinism's social orientation while carrying forward the more fundamental insight that it cannot be reduced to a sectarian or doctrinal crux. But my claim about the British novel's Calvinist leanings differs from existing scholarship in two crucial ways. First, where commentators from Watt to Rivett portray Calvinism as a kind of trace or residuum—the "mark" of an earlier paradigm that has been reshaped by the currents of modernity—I argue that Calvinism appears in early novels as a vital resource available throughout the long eighteenth century, and available not as counter-vailing a fully solidified sectarian discourse but as a flexible technics of character that was being taken up into secularist practices of narrative. Second, I emphasize that, in doing so, eighteenth-century writers lend the problematics of character a new valence: racial theodicy.

Calvinism's binary reduction is highly conducive to racial thinking. The wild variety of allegorical character supposedly reduces to a simple distinction, "saved or damned," just as the variety of the human species supposedly reduces to antitheses like white or nonwhite, self or other, us or them, human or subhuman. Although not yet fully operationalized in *The Pilgrim's Progress,* the race-making potential of Calvinism's charac-ter system is already present in Bunyan's corpus. *The Holy War* (1682), a crusader allegory published between the two parts of *The Pilgrim's Prog-ress,* attributes the misfiring of empirically reliable signs of character to miscegenation. "Unlawful mixtures" between Diabolonians, glossed in the margins as "Blacks or Negroes," and natives of the city of Mansoul make it harder to detect and purge reprobates.[21] In *The Holy War,* Bunyan intertwines Calvinist soteriology and racial hierarchy, insisting upon a simple referential correspondence between black skin and sinfulness.[22] A century later, however, another Calvinist author deploys the semiotics of character in a challenge to the same symbolic relationship.

Writing at the peak of the Atlantic slave trade, Quobna Ottobah Cugo-ano attempts to reconcile Christian aesthetics to the racial politics of lib-eration. The "different colors and complexions among men," he argues in *Thoughts and Sentiments on the Evil of Slavery* (1787),

were intended for the very purposes of instructive language among men. And by these extreme differences of colour, it was intended to point out and shew to the white man, that there is a sinful blackness in his own nature, which he can no more change, than the external blackness which he sees in another can be rendered otherwise; and it likewise holds out to the black man, that the sinful blackness of his own nature is such, that he can no more alter, than the outward appearance of his colour can be brought to that of another. And this is imported by it, that there is an inherent evil in every man, con-trary to that which is good; and that all men are like Ethiopians (even God's elect) in a state of nature and unregeneracy, they are black with original sin, and spotted with actual transgression, which they cannot reverse.[23]

Cugoano imbues skin color with metaphysical import, applying a conventional aesthetics in which blackness refers, in the abstract, to sinfulness and whiteness to "that which is good." But he also reconceptualizes the relationship between aesthetic and racial meanings of blackness by routing them through the Calvinist Protestant doctrine of salvation.[24] Corporeal difference comes to convey a universal spiritual condition, reprobation. "External blackness" and whiteness signify alike human nature's essential sinfulness, the inherited blight of original sin redoubled by the "actual transgressions" of the particular person. What's more, the immutability of racial difference figures the abrogation of free will. Because the process of spiritual awakening and regeneration requires prevenient grace, it is not in the power of individuals, however muscular their piety, to change salvific states—no more than it is in their power to change the color of their skin.

In order to promote race as a vehicle of divine instruction without reifying the fundamental cleavage of Calvinist theology—without, in other words, overlaying black/white and saved/damned dyads—Cugoano imagines a complicated relay of gazes. A couple of pages later, he suggests that, in an extension of the scriptural mode of "emblematical representation," white and black skin "hold out" a value beyond their materiality.[25] Spiritually neutral in and of itself, racial difference nevertheless carries figurative spiritual meaning. Although he does not quite "sever" the "matter of race" from the "sin of blackness," as Stefan Wheelock argues, Cugoano does hold these quantities apart, in the precisely calibrated distance between semiotic terms.[26] The effect is to make two, contradictory statements about race true at the same time. Black and white skin are "incidental," innocent as to "the things themselves," and yet under the proper epistemic conditions they function as signs of depravity.[27] Cugoano places the material and the spiritual dimensions of racial character, the "thing itself" and the meaning it "holds out," in productive tension.

Cugoano's account of the "instructive language of race" exemplifies Calvinist semiotics in its full complexity. As in Boelhower's theory of ethnic semiosis, somatic signs in this imagined scenario do not affix to one frozen referent. Neither the sign of blackness nor the sign of whiteness signifies properly except in proximity to its dialectical other. For Cugoano, racial blackness maintains a direct symbolic association with "inherent evil," and that coupling threatens to harden into damning ontology without the sign of whiteness present. Meanwhile, the association between racial whiteness and spiritual evil is indirect. For white skin to impart the same truths as black skin—that we are all stained with sin, and that expiation is above our ability—it must be triangulated with blackness. Because whiteness itself also holds its place in the Christian aesthetic hierarchy, white people must learn to recognize their own inward fallenness in the exteriorized spiritual state of "Ethiopians." Boelhower's statement about ethnic semiosis is apt here, as well: "The sign gaze did not establish a series of semantic correspondences, but offered instead an inferencing context. The gaze, the sign, is above all an interpretive relation, a putting into relation."[28] As interpreters of racial difference, Cugoano's exemplary "black man" and "white man" share the work of putting racial signs into the proper, triangulated relation. As bearers of those signs, though, they carry the burden of representation unequally. When the white man looks at the black man, he sees a projection of his own spiritual depravity. When the black man looks at the white man, he sees a spiritual ideal unachievable through his own will or works. This asymmetry reflects the difficulty of articulating a spiritually neutral theory of race through Christian aesthetics. That Cugoano manages to do this attests to his conceptual agility, of course, but also to the pliability of Calvinist semiotics. His recourse to this idea of character suggests an overlooked affinity, between early black Atlantic writing and the eighteenth-century British novel, to which I return at several points in my argument. I hope to show how these bodies of writing, together, define religious character under the conditions of racialized empire.

Redescribing Flatness

By recovering the persistence and complexity of the novel's Calvinist heuristics, I aim to give a fresh account of how early novelistic character functions. Historians of the novel tend to regard the flat characters in precursors and early exempla of the form as vestiges of a symbolically replete past. This is true not only of Ian Watt's thesis but also its most influential revisions. In *Rise of the Novel*, Watt adapts Weber's narrative of disenchantment explicitly: the arch individualism and psychological depth supposedly constitutive of the novel derives from a Protestant model of human character that has been emptied of genuine spiritual content. Deidre Shauna Lynch refutes Watt's argument, demonstrating the interest that surfaces (e.g., the face of a person, a printed page, a coin) held for early eighteenth-century writers and readers.[29] But Lynch in other ways follows Watt, positing a gradual movement in British culture away from an ideal of legibility and toward one of indeterminacy. Once signifying in the manner of typeface or the face of a coin, reflecting a view of the world as imbued with almost sacramental meaning, fictional characters lose their symbolic charge as they begin to reproduce rather than compensate for experiences of the new economic order. In another oft-cited corrective to Watt, Catherine Gallagher identifies "fictionality" with the realist novel's idiosyncratic system of literary reference—that is, its reference to "nonexistent persons" with real-seeming names—and places its emergence in mid-eighteenth-century Britain.[30] "Novelistic fictionality" is coeval with modern subjectivity, which Gallagher defines as "ironic credulity," a knowing assent to nonactual persons and situations that allows us to speculate in a variety of markets.[31] Julie Orlemanski's recent appraisal of Gallagher's periodizing definition of fiction is applicable to Lynch's argument, as well; in each we see a "repetition of the ideologies of secularism and disenchantment, those widespread narratives of historical difference that recount modernity's emergence from a credulous past."[32]

Reading Character after Calvin joins a small but distinguished body of scholarship that resists the progressivist instinct of novel studies. Srinivas Aravamudan proposes that, by expanding the archive of novel studies beyond domestic fiction and across borders of national parochialism, we might recuperate an enlightenment mode of earnest comparative inquiry not yet foreclosed by nineteenth-century discourses of race and empire.[33] John Frow not only refutes teleological narratives—including those, like Watt's, that present personhood as a "continuously developing entity which reaches its fullest form in modernity" and its fullest expression in the psychologizing interiority of the modern novel—but also demurs from giving a unitary thesis or theory of his key concepts, character and person.[34] Frow provides, instead, a repository of loosely connected insights about the interdependence of the formal category of character and "particular forms of life" at different times and in different genres.[35] Stephanie Insley Hershinow also eschews "development" as a model for describing fictional characters and literary history. Through bravura readings of mid- to late eighteenth-century novels and contemporary popular culture, Hershinow instead shows the influence of the archetype of "the novice," a character who, rather than maturing, enjoys the perspectival advantage of durable inexperience or "unworldliness."[36] The prevalence of this type, as Hershinow explores, unsettles standard assumptions about the relationship between plot and character in early realist fiction.

The present study applies, combines, and modifies insights from each of these scholars. I share Frow's aim of provincializing supposedly universal concepts, while at the same time working toward a more affirmative and historically particular account of novelistic character.[37] Like Hershinow, I argue for the enduring cultural relevance of character types. Whereas she centers a type illustrative of realist form, however, I examine the logic of type more generally. And where Hershinow tends to bracket form, looking to "carve out a way of thinking about consistently inexperienced characters on their own terms," I proceed from the conviction that character is not a blank, formal concept.[38] Rather, it is imbricated with the histories of religion, race, and empire. This book aspires to show not only how early novelistic character works, but also how it works to normalize, question, or reinflect the sexualizing and racializing logics of imperial secularism. I, thus, follow Aravamudan in relating literary genre to cultural encounter. But where Aravamudan sees an enlightenment mode of encounter worth recuperating, I see ambivalence toward a secularist ideology in formation. In the genre-promiscuous body of writing that Aravamudan calls "Enlightenment orientalism," culturally alien characters and settings set the irrationality and corruptions of European societies in sharp relief. The depictions of theo-racial others discussed here reflect a variant of orientalism closer to Edward Said's original definition.[39] Even where they serve as vehicles of European autocritique, as in Behn's *Oroonoko* and William

Earle's *Obi; or, The History of Three-Fingered Jack* (1800), such characters are interpolated within asymmetrical systems of reference. They testify, sometimes through straightforward normalization and sometimes through back-formation, to the recursive processes of self-legitimation by which imperial secularism extends its circumference and renews its civilizing mission.

Toward a Postsecular History of the Novel

Surveying the field of eighteenth-century studies, Alison Conway and Corinne Harol "raise the question as to whether or not the secular tools we bring to eighteenth-century texts blind us to important dimensions of the literary objects before us."[40] The early history of novelistic character suggests that they do, and that one thing secularizing logic occludes is a defining feature of early eighteenth-century fictional characters: their tension between two-dimensionality and inscrutability. They simultaneously invite and frustrate efforts, by readers of texts and readers inscribed within them, to assign straightforward meanings. By foregrounding that tension, we might extricate a vital critical category from the self-created myth of secularization—the story, retold in different ways by Watt and then Lynch and Gallagher, of progressive disenchantment. In place of that myth, I offer a revisionist literary history of secularization.

Although I take a different tack than most, my readings have been enabled by recent scholarship that has helped to move eighteenth-century studies away from disenchantment stories and toward responsiveness to the religiosity of the period. Misty G. Anderson, Dwight Codr, Jacob Sider Jost, Jordy Rosenberg, and Courtney Weiss Smith, among others, have successfully challenged the mainline secularization thesis, finding the sacred in unexpected places: natural and moral philosophy, financial markets, theories of desire, and aspirations to literary fame.[41] This is a significant contribution to a field that has been slow to divest from the secularizing premises of "enlightenment." Codr's *Raving at Usurers* offers the additional insight that such premises are embedded within our historical narratives and critical methods, obscuring continuities

between the premodern and the modern. As he challenges the consensus notion that an autonomous, "secular economic sphere" emerged at
the end of the seventeenth century, Codr observes that religious and
extrareligious domains appear separate and distinct only because "an
economistic model of human motivations and desires influences most
accounts of eighteenth-century literature and culture, even those that
do not expressly aim to address economic history."[42] The "economistic"
perspective that Codr criticizes is, by definition, secularist: it presumes
the ascendancy of *Homo economicus,* a "need-satisfying, acquisitive, and
rational individual" who is liberated from an earlier, and recognizably
Protestant, ethical framework.[43] I argue the point with reference to a different history, that of empire rather than economics, but I concur with
Codr's general claim—namely, that secularization is a real historical process, but its contents are not what its own ideology says they are. It is not
the achievement of disenchantment (an impeded encounter with reality),
but, rather, the institutional, material, and disciplinary reorganization of
categories such that modernity can claim for itself a superiority in values.

My book differs methodologically from this body of criticism, specifically in the way I attempt to read the religiosity of eighteenth-century
literary texts. When literary critics challenge the metahistory of secularization, we tend to make what could be described as a religious turn.[44]
Existing scholarship attempts to excavate the spirituality embedded
within secular forms and institutions, as if religion were a discrete substance in the world, occluded and perhaps attenuated by forces of modernization but ultimately recoverable. By contrast, and following Asad,
I emphasize the constructedness of the categories of the religious and
the secular. Rather than probing eighteenth-century fiction for authentic
but heretofore neglected theological content, this book examines the role
that novels played in predicating the characters proper to true religion.

Reading Character after Calvin also proceeds from a different definition
of secularism than the one applied by literary critics who take this concept—as opposed to religion—as the primary object of analysis. Colin
Jager shows the capacity of Romantic-era literature to register discontent
with and, in some cases, imagine alternatives to new political and social
arrangements created through the privatization of religious belief.[45] He

defines secularism as a political doctrine leading to religion's sequestration. Kevin Seidel invokes a similar conception when he (justly) criticizes the secularizing premises of prominent accounts of the origins of the English novel.[46] Historians of the novel like Watt and McKeon, Seidel claims, perpetuate the narrative of religion's inevitable dislodgment or distortion by the forces of rational modernity. While Jager traces authors' responses to the material and social effects of secularist political doctrine, Seidel disclaims the critical corollary to that doctrine, which on his account obscures the religious foundations of the novel as a form. They disagree about its historical accuracy, then, but Jager and Seidel each describe secularization as the process of religion's alienation from other cultural domains. For me the valence of the term "secular" is first and foremost disciplinary. My book gives an account of the discursive operations and formal strategies by which "a corporate, plastic," Protestantized Christianity took initial shape and began, in Anidjar's words, "colonizing the world."[47]

The genealogy of character that unfolds over the five chapters of this book brings insights of "postsecular" critique to the study of eighteenth-century fiction. Introducing a special journal issue on American studies "After the Postsecular," Peter Coviello and Jared Hickman proceed from the conviction that "the secularization thesis is dead."[48] Weberian disenchantment stories no longer hold sway, they argue, and so it is time for postsecular criticism to look beyond the work of refutation. A casual survey of scholarship on eighteenth-century culture would confirm the need to qualify this pronouncement. To be sure, the secularization thesis has come under increasing scrutiny in the specific domains of sociology, cultural anthropology, and, from there, American literary studies, but it remains powerful in other literary-historical fields. There is sufficient interest, however, in the paradox of "enlightenment religion" to license a foray into the subjunctive.[49] If—or, rather, when—we finally lay to rest narratives of religion's dislodgment, what new vistas might resolve into clarity?

Postsecular critique charts two main paths forward. One, initiated by Charles Taylor and indebted to Heideggerian philosophy, reclaims sensibilities—ways of being in the world—only accessible through religion and contrary to the phenomenological conditions presumed by the myth of rational modernity.[50] A second path travels from Michel Foucault to

Asad and then to religious historians and literary critics like John Lardas Modern and Coviello. It requires us to describe and, wherever possible, reinflect the structures of power within which the very terms "religious" and "secular" are stipulated. To mark the differences between these approaches, and to convey my rationale for hewing more closely to the latter, Foucauldian analyses, I turn, briefly, to a provocative recent interpretation of *The Pilgrim's Progress* that runs contrary to the one that I sketch above and develop further in chapter 1.

Lori Branch diverges from the commonplace identification of Bunyan with vestigial religious intensity, arguing instead that his writings promote an almost postmodern understanding of faith. *The Pilgrim's Progress* advances an idea of faith as "believing within uncertainty," Branch writes.[51] Such faith exemplifies—"avant la lettre," as Branch puts it—religion as it has passed through modernity: necessarily reshaped by intellectual and material currents yet undiminished.[52] Consistent with the first version of postsecularity, Branch underscores the reparative potential of Christian faith that has survived first the instantiation and then the failure of secular reason. She recovers a faith attuned to the fundamental indeterminacy of language and consequent precarity of all knowledge production. For reasons I discuss in my first chapter, I think Bunyan is ultimately less resigned to the impossibility of objective truth than Branch suggests. But the more substantive, salient difference between Branch's reading and my own pertains to our methods of postsecular literary-critical practice. Branch's intentionally hopeful analysis not only highlights the complexity of past religious lives like Bunyan's but also projects a path forward, through critical sensibilities that derive from Bunyan's faith and balance critique with needful epistemic humility. This book is also concerned with the forms that Protestant Christianity takes as it collides with modern imperatives, but I foreground the particular imperative to planetary domination and, thus, the biopoliticizing tendencies of secularized Protestantism.

That is not to say that the roads to postsecularity never intersect, nor that Branch's objective of homeostatic criticism—her wish to balance attunement and rigorous critique—holds no value. Indeed, the textual analyses developed in the following pages often foreground eighteenth-century devotionalities that are generatively aslant of secularist ideology, such as erotic faith in Oroonoko's native Coromantien, Lady Matilda's good fetishism in *A Simple Story* (1791), or the efficacy of Obeah charms in *Obi*. The radical possibilities introduced through such alternatives come into full view only with reference to the material realities of slavery and colonialism, however. This is because the affordances and discontents of secular faith itself, of the religious forms that have been reshaped (though not attenuated) by modernization, do not operate in a vacuum but within histories of racialized violence.

Religion, Race, and Representation

Entanglements of secularized Calvinist Protestantism with slavery and colonialism arise through an uneven, ambivalent process. Secularization proceeds in a linear fashion if we measure it by Calvinism's unbinding from the doctrinal orthodoxies of Bunyan's gathered-church ecclesiology. The story begins with Behn's and Penelope Aubin's efforts to adapt Calvinism's idea of character without espousing the specific soteriology from which it originates. They make this paradigm more flexible, accommodating it to their imperial imaginaries, by detaching it from the doctrine of double predestination. The loosening of doctrinal propriety continues in the mid-eighteenth century, when Henry Fielding attempts to redefine religion as a fluid matrix of concepts, including Calvinism's semiotics of character, that is not governed by a specific theological tradition. Later fictions by Sterne and Elizabeth Inchbald witness the subsequent counter-codification of antiorthodoxy as liberal-rationalist sociability, a new Anglican hegemony that claims epistemic humility and resiliency for itself. In this formation of the secular, Calvinism takes on several roles: as one of the modes of Anglicanism's malleable epistemology or, alternately, as a closed system of beliefs juxtaposed to this one true religion. The mobilization of this conception of religion as a strategy of theo-racial domination does not follow the same unswerving trajectory. Eighteenth-century novels exhibit a dual relation to the emergent discourse of secularism. They tend to promote a version of Christianity similar to the one that Anidjar and others see operative today: notionally pluralized but held together by normative models of religious epistemology, subjectivity, and ethics. Just as often, though, the same texts abstract race from the semiotics of character, denying or reinterpreting the spiritual meanings attached to physical markers of difference, as Cugoano does in *Thoughts and Sentiments on the Evil of Slavery.*

As a result, cultural and somatic signifiers take on shifting relational values, revealing in the process the dynamic character of eighteenth-century race-making. Historians of race in the Atlantic world emphasize that constructions of corporeal meaning that predate the crystallization of nineteenth-century race "science" were variable, contingent on "historically specific social, economic, and cultural needs."[53] The relations of body and belief depicted in early novels confirm the social-constructivist view, while also pointing, contra scholars who adopt this perspective, to the role that religion plays in shaping constructions of human difference. Scholarship on the discursive origins of race tends to argue that race is produced through a mode of retroactive justification for the material conditions of slavery.[54] Understood as an ideology that reduces identity to skin color, race emerges in the nineteenth century; what precedes and establishes the conditions for its advent is a messier, denser, and more localized set of ideas about the meanings of physical difference.[55] But this understanding of race hinges on the assumption that culture (which contains religious practices among others) and corporeality belong to discrete ways of organizing the world. Based on the evidence of early novels, I argue for their intersection under imperial secularism and before the consolidation of nineteenth-century antiblack racism.

To do so, I apply Geraldine Heng's more capacious "hypothesis of race."[56] Race, Heng writes, names "a repeating tendency, of the greatest import, to demarcate human beings through differences among humans that are selectively essentialized as absolute and fundamental, in order to distribute positions and powers differentially to human groups. Race-making thus operates as specific historical occasions in which strategic essentialisms are posited and assigned through a variety of practices and pressures, so as to construct a hierarchy of peoples for differential treatment."[57] Heng dissociates race from modernity and affords religion a prominent role in its discursive origins. She explains that "the differences selected for essentialism" vary, and that, while they may attach to corporeal signs of "physiognomy and somatic attributes such as skin color," these differences may also consist of "social practices, religion, and culture" at other times and locations.[58] In fact, as Heng's history of medieval race illustrates, religion could "function both socioculturally and biopolitically: subjecting peoples of detested faith, for example, to a political theology that could biologize, define, and essentialize an entire community as fundamentally and absolutely different in an interknotted cluster of ways."[59]

Contributions to the new secular studies recognize just this phenomenon at work in nineteenth- through twenty-first-century America. Amplifying the arguments of Modern and the historian Joan Scott, Coviello has recently asserted that secularism has a body; it is a discipline that inscribes misfiring religiosity onto the surfaces of the body.[60] Heng's discussion of the European Middle Ages demonstrates that the racialization of religious others also operates in contexts more properly understood as *presecular*. It obtains, that is, to conflicts between religious cultures with self-contained doctrinal systems, before we can speak of the mutual fragilization of belief synonymous with secularization. Secularism does not invent race, but it counts as a strategy of essentialism specific to the historical and geographical purview of North Atlantic modernity.

Reading Character after Calvin addresses the gap between European premodernity and the ongoing secular age. Through the lens of an inchoate literary form, it views a crucial historical moment—the period in which secularism came to be grafted more and more fully onto the project of racialized dominion. If early novels witness this suturing of liberalized belief to British colonialism, they also suggest that their synonymy was not inevitable. Some writers rely on the codex of Calvinist soteriology to translate God's "instructive language" of race, to borrow Cugoano's phrase, assigning salvific meaning to embodied characteristics. But others offer the universalizing, doctrinally promiscuous Protestantism favored by eighteenth-century secularism as a bulwark against racial identification. In each case, novelists' adjudications between real/false belief and viable/errant forms of life manifest through techniques of character, and particularly through the complicated interplay of different dimensions of character: concrete and abstract, literal and figurative, inside and outside.

Chapter Summaries

In my discussion of *The Pilgrim's Progress* above, I suggested that Bunyan enacts the difficulty of discerning intrinsic truths according to extrinsic evidence. My first chapter provides further evidence for this claim and then builds on it in several ways. First, I argue that Bunyan's sequel insists on indirect revelation as a failsafe against the dislocation of exterior signs from interior religious character, requiring that characters and readers alike stand astride paradigms of prevenient grace and individual rational agency. Next, I consider the affinity between the Calvinist problematics of character and racial hierarchy, comparing *The Holy War* to James Albert Ukawsaw Gronniosaw's encounter with Bunyan's text nearly a century after its publication. *The Holy War* allegorizes personal spiritual struggle as a medieval crusade, identifying spiritual evil with blackness and characterological uncertainty to the threat of racial exogamy. The link between black skin and reprobation is strong enough in that work to have exacerbated the spiritual self-loathing of Gronniosaw, a formerly enslaved black Calvinist who records his conversion in *A Narrative of the Most Remarkable Particulars in the Life of James Albert Ukawsaw Gronniosaw, an African Prince, as Related by Himself* (ca. 1772). Yet it is also through Calvinist ways of reading that Gronniosaw becomes recognizable as a member of the elect to English Methodist and Reformed Dutch communities. Together, Bunyan and Gronniosaw illustrate the flexibility of Calvinism when it is applied as a religious hermeneutic of race.

Chapter 2 maps the first serious in-roads of secularization in fiction by Behn and Penelope Aubin. As they import Calvinism's typological, two-dimensional understanding of character to settings like British Suriname and Ottoman North Africa, these writers represent the collision of two categories of difference: religio-cultural variety and corporeality. In *Oroonoko*, tensions between critique and white supremacy appear as an overloading of types on the hero's countenance: personification of Stuart legitimacy, noble savage, self-liberating African-diasporan, Christ proxy. In Aubin's *The Noble Slaves* (1722), the possibility of religious conversion, the reducibility of Islam to a set of imitable cultural signs and performances, and the liminal status of African slaves all threaten to undermine the integrity of two religious types—the paragon of pan-European, ecumenically Christian virtue and the epitome of Islamic depravity—that are supposed to organize the narrative's global vision. Points of strain and rupture in Aubin's method of characterization appear, particularly, wherever the novel attempts to relate Christian/Muslim antimony to racial difference.

In Chapter 3, I examine the further liberalization of Calvinism through the nova effect. I argue that Fielding's *Tom Jones* (1749) and *Amelia* (1751) are "secular" in the precise sense that they are not in the thrall of any particular theological system. These novels perform the mutual fragilization of belief through a proliferation of ways of writing and reading character, each corresponding to a different religious concept. Calvinism appears in these works as one imperfect and incomplete option among many. Sterne's *Tristram Shandy* (1759–67), too, experiments with different systems of literary character, but with the effect of countercodifying antiorthodoxy as Anglican moralism. Sterne defines this ideal against the extremes of systematicity and mysticism that he sees in ancient philosophy, Calvinist Protestantism, Roman Catholicism, and Islam. *Tristram Shandy* embeds but cannot fully erase the malign orthodoxy that secularism carries within itself. Sterne's novel reveals how Christianity universalizes its definition of virtue at the same time that it frees belief from doctrinal propriety. In conjunction with Sterne's published sermons, *Tristram Shandy* ultimately promotes a worldview similar to today's liberal-secular order—that is, as bifurcated between true religion and bad belief.

Chapter 4 returns to Cugoano's jeremiad to frame a discussion of two abolitionist novels from the turn of the nineteenth century, *Obi* and *The Woman of Colour* (1808). Like *Thoughts and Sentiments on the Evil of Slavery*, these works of fiction route their sharp critiques of proslavery Christianity through Calvinist semiotics of character. Unlike Cugoano, however, the authors of these novels do not espouse Calvinism as a faith system; they receive it in its secularized form, an adaptable epistemology of character that moves outside the constraints of doctrine. In *Obi*, William Earle uses this model to show the continuities between the natural religion espoused by enslavers and the danger posed by Obeah, a syncretic African-Caribbean religion. Both disrupt the relay of sign and signifier upon which colonial medicine and plantation discipline rely. *The Woman of Colour,* published anonymously a year after the abolition of slavery in Britain, abstracts race from secular dialecticism. Olivia Fairfield, the novel's protagonist and a self-professed "mulatto West Indian," divests markers of racial difference of their representational qualities. Asserting the pure materiality of race, and her own reified objecthood, she gestures forward to aesthetic politics that Fred Moten ascribes to a later, trans-media archive of black radicalism. But Olivia also insists that other characters measure her piety and her sexual value against the familiar ideal of inside-outside symmetry, upholding the normative force of semiotic representation. Read together, these texts help contour the wide ambit of secularist ideology, which comprehends polemics against marriage and chattel slavery as well as conservative positions.

My first four chapters, then, elucidate an eighteenth-century formation of the secular by tracking the gradual release of English Calvinism's idea of character from singular doctrinal propriety and then its redistribution within an ostensibly pluralized market. The liberalized form of Protestantism produced through this process stands in ambivalent relation to the project of racialized empire. Some of the writers who espouse this secular faith use it to mount a challenge to the racializing logic undergirding the transatlantic slave trade. They attempt to deracialize empire, but they inevitably ratify the mechanics of differentiation in and through which secularism—during the eighteenth century, as today—divides the world and creates the subjects proper to itself. While my analyses of works like *The Noble Slaves, Tristram Shandy,* and *The Woman of Colour* focus on illustrating the internal machinery of secularism, the book concludes by shifting focus to the margins of this discourse.

The texts under consideration in my final chapter and conclusion ask what forms of belief and dispositions of the self might exist beyond the perimeter of secular self-legitimation. Chapter 5 finds one answer in Gothic Romances that subvert the disciplinary program of secularist ideology: Inchbald's *A Simple Story,* Charlotte Dacre's *Zofloya, or The Moor* (1806) and James Hogg's *Private Memoirs and True Confessions of a Justified Sinner* (1824). These works implicate the novel form in violence perpetrated in the name of true religion, scrutinizing the way it uses Calvinist semiotics to imagine bodies and beliefs in need of domestication. *A Simple Story* and *Zofloya,* especially, demonstrate the potential of the Gothic as a genre of immanent critique that anticipates the mood and method of postsecular scholarship today. The book concludes with a brief reflection on this postsecularist mode, which combines self-interrogation with what I call subjunctive criticism in order to reinflect (if not escape) the discursive grammars of secularism.

1

∿

Character Detection

REVIOUS STUDIES OF THE PURITAN INHERITANCE of the early
English novel emphasize the introspective and individualist logic
of Calvinist theology. Ian Watt attributes the genre's defining focus
on representing "the inward moral being of the individual" to the abiding
cultural relevance of the Puritan requirement of "continual scrutiny of
[one's] inner man."[1] He regards novels' attention to the "day-by-day mental and moral life" of their heroes as the "vestigial remnants of Calvinist
introspective discipline."[2] Leopold Damrosch shares Watt's conviction
that a Calvinist-inflected psychology of "inwardness" shapes the emergence of the novel as a genre, which depicts "the private experience of the
individual faced not so much with society as with the ultimate order of the
universe."[3] As they situate the history of the novel within another critical metanarrative, that of the rise of individualism, such accounts identify Bunyan and the Reformed Protestant tradition for which he stands
with "profound spiritual isolation."[4] This approach, as Michael Davies has
pointed out, "elides, if not erases entirely, the significance of community
from Bunyan's writings."[5] Scholars such as Davies who recover the "social
and communitarian" spirit that subtends both Bunyan's pastoral career
and Congregationalist practices in general focus on intraecclesiastical
texts, and especially on conversion narratives that were circulated as evidence of election.[6]

This chapter bridges these two bodies of criticism by demonstrating
the striking sociality of Bunyan's fiction. I begin by showing that *The
Pilgrim's Progress*, like the genre of the conversion narrative, reflects a

culture of accreditation. Conversion narratives, including those circulated within Bunyan's own congregation at Bedford, document the individual believer's struggle to satisfy the principal criterion for admission into an ecclesiastical polity: to tell a story of personal experience that maps onto the paradigm of election.[7] In *The Pilgrim's Progress*, Bunyan approaches religious accreditation from the opposite perspective, that of "standers by." The inwardly focused subject central to spiritual autobiographies— and to the familiar account of the "rise" of the novel as a genre—gives way to a community of believers engaged in careful, collaborative authentication of claims to saving faith. Bunyan thus turns the celebrated Calvinist introspective gaze toward an external world of characters whose credit at once demands and resists final assessment. In doing so, he illustrates the high stakes of character discernment undertaken in this context. Bunyan's inscribed adherents reckon with predestinarian theology's contradictory but entangled conceptions of election as predetermined and aspirational. Denied certain knowledge of his own spiritual state, the Calvinist believer strives to become what he projects through outward sanctification—much as Mr. Honest hopes to grow into the character advertised by his name. In both *Grace Abounding* (1666) and *The Pilgrim's Progress*, this spiritual project comes under threat in the form of contaminating "conversation," the danger that saints might somehow sabotage their election by admitting false professors into their company (*P*, 66). The immediacy of this threat within Bunyan's writings distinguishes them from the Congregationalist conversion narrative, a genre underwritten by confidence that the marks of grace are subject to "discovery" and interpretation.

The problematics of character in *The Pilgrim's Progress* unsettle two critical commonplaces, one about literary history and one about intellectual history. Bunyan's characters suggest the need to revise our understanding of the way Calvinist theology influenced the novel as a form. Existing scholarship tends to displace characterological concerns onto notions of providence. To the extent that character matters in such accounts, it matters as a reflection of the introspective, individualist bent of Calvinist—or, in the argot of twentieth-century criticism, "Puritan"—theology.[8] I emphasize Calvinism's outward orientation, arguing that what this religious tradition passes down to the early novel is not a model for narrating interiority but a set of ways of reading character. Those interpretive meth-ods, moreover, destabilize dyadic arrangements of critical reason and tra-ditional knowledge, orthodoxy and critique, that still pervade religious and intellectual histories. Bunyan suggests that we resolve the problem of character discernment by coordinating rational individual agency and providential interposition, natural and revealed religion. His real and fic-tional readers balance scrutiny of outward signs with deference to social networks of reputation and especially to a narrative authority that approx-imates God.

In the second half of the chapter, I turn to *The Holy War* to illustrate how Bunyan racializes the threat of the false professor. Calvinism's prob-lematics of character already function, there, as an idiom for cultural dif-ference and a rationalization for the biopoliticized exclusions of empire. Published between the two installments of *The Pilgrim's Progress, The Holy War* reveals a compatibility of Calvinism's exclusionary logic and semiotic practices, on the one hand, and visions of racialized European domina-tion, on the other. The generalized xenophobia in *The Pilgrim's Progress* (evident in, for example, stereotypes of the faithlessness of Ottoman merchants) here narrows into a kind of race-thinking. Bunyan not only employs a crusade allegory, invoking medieval clashes between Chris-tian and Islamic states to describe the zero-sum conflict between good and evil, but also identifies diabolical nature with racial blackness. In *The Holy War,* the followers of Satan are black, and the failures of previously reliably empirical signs of religious characters are the result of "strange" and "unlawful" sexual mixtures of Diabolonians and natives of Mansoul.[9] Although, of course, less enduringly popular than *The Pilgrim's Progress,* this work is indispensable for what it tells us about the Calvinist inheri-tance of the early novel. Without undermining the theological specificity or intensity of Bunyan's faith, *The Holy War* anticipates the movement of the characters of Calvinism, with their push-pull of flatness and inscru-tability, inside and outside, from the sectarian contexts of Restoration dissenting culture to the imperial contexts of later fictions.

To illustrate the flexibility of the Calvinist idea of character when it functions as a hermeneutics of race, the chapter concludes with an analy-sis of an eighteenth-century black Calvinist writer's response to *The Holy*

War. Although it is presented to him as a source of religious consolation, James Albert Ukasaw Gronniosaw finds Bunyan's book disturbing. I argue that this is because *The Holy War* confirms his preexisting fear that the color of his skin indexes the state of his soul. Yet Gronniosaw's autobiography also evidences the capacity of Calvinist ways of reading character to promote mutual intelligibility between members of the elect, white and black alike, and therefore to create inclusive religious community. Reading Bunyan and Gronniosaw together clarifies that the racializing logic of *The Holy War*'s characters does not inhere to Calvinism. The affinity between Calvinist soteriology, its exclusionary doctrine of salvation, and racial hierarchies *can* harden into the disciplinary structures of empire, but that is only one outcome of its application to racial difference.

As I move through these readings, I pay particular attention to the way the need to determine the spiritual states of other professed believers bears on the representational status of Bunyan's literary characters. At various points in "The Author's Apology for His Book," Bunyan calls *The Pilgrim's Progress* an "allegory," a "parable," and a "fable," using the terms interchangeably to denote fictions that rely on "Metaphors/ To set forth Truth" (5–9). This method requires readers to bridge literal and figurative planes of meaning. Bunyan envisions a reader who actively "seeks to find out" the veiled correspondence between the image called for and the meaning set forth—but he affirms that the "precious stones" of truth are accessible and "Worth digging for" (7–8). Taken at face value, Bunyan's method accords with J. Paul Hunter's vision of the "emblematic" Puritan imagination.[10] As the work proceeds, though, this mode of reading strains under the difficult task of deciding whether fellow professors are in good faith. Rather than a straightforward course in Christian hermeneutics, *The Pilgrim's Progress* serves as a cautionary tale about the limits of available protocols for discovering grace in other people.[11] Bunyan aligns his method of characterization with a Calvinist model of spiritual character by constructing characters that are two-dimensional and nonetheless difficult to read.

Form and content are aligned in *The Holy War,* too, though this text uses both to reassert referential correspondences that come under scrutiny in Bunyan's other writings. *The Holy War* documents the dangers of the misapprehension or the absence of exterior signs of interior religious conditions, but the text presents those failures as ultimately avoidable. Here, Bunyan shows unflagging confidence in protocols of character detection—to use a term that befits the diegetic context of state surveillance and control—that bring outside and inside back into alignment. The simplified, coherent allegorical structure of *The Holy War* reflects this confidence in semiotic activity, and it rewards the style of reading that Bunyan describes in his prefatory comments on *The Pilgrim's Progress*. Navigating between the text and Bunyan's marginal glosses, readers find the literal and the figurative, image called for and truth set forth, arranged in stable, one-to-one relationships. The balance between reason and revelation shifts toward the former faculty, demonstrating the inherent flexibility of the model of character that later writers would inherit from Calvinism. The individual reader, the congregation, the state—as he toggles between these scales, Bunyan addresses the problem of knowing other people's salvific states (and social viability) with a more or less muscular piety, more or less emphasis on the role that humans and God play in the detection of errant subjects.

"Puritan" Introspection, Externalized:
The Pilgrim's Progress

There are two kinds of assurance at play in predestinarian arguments. The first is well documented: the doctrine of double predestination acts as assurance that election is both indefectible and entirely dependent on the freely granted grace of God rather than on the strivings of an imperfect creature. Faced with his natural depravity and inevitable moral failings, the believer takes comfort in the doctrine as a guarantee that God will fulfill his promise by serving the elect and preventing a second fall. But the doctrine also places a demand upon the believer to cultivate assurance of his own status vis-à-vis predestination. Dewey Wallace and Joel R. Beeke demonstrate that, persistent disavowal of works notwithstanding, the doctrine of double predestination does not obviate the believer's responsibility to interpret the facts of his experience for signs of salvation.[12]

Proponents of Reformed theology vehemently rejected Catholicism's vision of a universal order charged with sacramental significance, but they also held that the individual's actions concealed markers of his predetermined fate. Critics and historians have made much of the consequent impulse to self-scrutiny, especially in Bunyan's imaginative works.[13]

For Bunyan, the work of spiritual self-reflection entails negotiating a lived biblical typology, an interpretive key unavailable to the readers of other persons. In *Grace Abounding*, for example, Bunyan's program of self-scrutiny depends on a typological system whereby characters from biblical texts act as "metaphorical foreshadowings" of the reader's internal struggles with sin ("convictions," in his vernacular) and external circumstances ("judgments").[14] Unlike the version of literary character exemplified by Talkative, this typology flattens out the temporal scale by positing an identification between biblical characters from different epochs (Adam, David, Moses, or Christ) and their extratextual counterpart: the Calvinist believer engaged in the search for evidence of their election. Spurred on by the lingering sense of his irredeemable sin—he fears that he has sold his "birthright" by agreeing implicitly to trade Christ's saving love for sublunary goods—Bunyan searches sacred history for characters whose sins carry equal weight but who nevertheless find redemption. "I began to compare my sin with others," he writes, "to see if I could find that any of those that are saved had done as I had done" (42). Bunyan weighs his transgression against those perpetrated by David and Peter, but decides that their crimes, though "hainous," fall short of his "selling of my Saviour" (43). He realizes "that I came nearer to Judas, than either to David or Peter" (42). Though Bunyan fails to match his experience to an exemplar of the redeemed sinner, he does find an analogue in Judas, the New Testament's very archetype of apostasy. Reading the Bible in this way requires an active engagement. Correspondences between character and reader are not necessarily self-evident, and they are constructed carefully according to Bunyan's preferred logic of substitution, a logic later upheld through his successful attempts to compare himself to the apostle Paul.

In *Grace Abounding*, Bunyan performs reading practices that resemble those he describes in his "Apology" to *The Pilgrim's Progress*. Like the "Dark Figures" of that text, biblical types such as David, Peter, and Judas "doth call forth one thing, to set forth another" (P, 8–9). Specifically, they call forth the genealogy of sacred history to set forth both the external circumstances and the spiritual struggle of the individual believer. The typological reading practices enacted in *Grace Abounding* promise a solid ground for assurance of one's own character, in the Calvinist sense of spiritual status. They extend the existing sacred narrative, enfolding the historical scope of the Bible within the personal history of the Christian believer and indulging the fantasy of a continuous and recursive epoch. The "characters" of this expansive narrative, creations of the Bible and creatures of the present moment, become so many reflections of one another, and reading them ultimately becomes an act of recognizing and inserting oneself into a set of stable correspondences.

Although it functions primarily as a record of introspective piety, *Grace Abounding* also gestures toward the social and ecclesiological concerns of *The Pilgrim's Progress.* More than their contents, the contexts of these narratives highlight the need to test prospective coreligionists. The church records from Bunyan's own congregation at Bedford evoke confidence in a collaborative, layered admissions protocol: appointed members interviewed the applicant and then either invited them to deliver a public relation of their conversion experience at the next meeting, deferred their application, or denied them admission. Visitations allowed the church to police its existing membership: "Two brethren should be made choice of every monethly meeting, to go abroad to visit our brethren and sisters, and to certify us how they doe in body and soule."[15] Such entries depict a religious community optimistic about its capacity to "certify" the salvific states of its members and achieve "full satisfaction" of the "truth of the worke of grace in their heartes."[16]

Like the spiritual testimonies for which it served as a model, *Grace Abounding* articulates a religious identity in the terms provided by Calvinist doctrine, and it does so in the service of church formation.[17] Even here, though, Bunyan betrays his sensitivity to the problem of discerning religious character that comes to preoccupy his allegories. His own initiation into the church highlights the difficulty of distinguishing true saints from those who merely profess the Christian calling. Bunyan's outward godliness—the "great and famous alteration of my life and manners"—secures his place in Bedford Church. It does not, however, index a genuine conversion: "Yet I knew not Christ, nor Grace, nor Faith, nor Hope" (13). By regarding his adherence to mere morality as an outward manifestation of his election, Bunyan's interlocutors at Bedford confuse a possible effect for its cause.

Bunyan goes on to write that cultivating a reputation for godliness does not satisfy the conditions of the Covenant of Grace. He suggests, moreover, that living life according to the letter of the law in order to achieve a pious character represents a particularly threatening form of religious hypocrisy. Bunyan fleshes out this notion of hypocrisy in *The Doctrine of Law and Grace Unfolded* (1659), a treatise on the respective roles of faith and works in salvation. He uses a sequence of scriptural examples to show how closely a reprobate may resemble a saint in deed as well as in word. The damned may practice piety, secure admission into the visible church—they may even preach and perform miracles. Yet they remain damned. The distinction between salvific categories hinges on the spiritual motivation behind a given action: the pious life serves as a marker of grace only where it stems from "saving faith" rather than from a "legal spirit."[18]

Thus far I have tried to show that, in Bunyan's scriptural exegesis as well as in his spiritual autobiography, cultivating the personal assurance of salvation means recognizing the difference between the inner workings of grace and the false start of an ineffectual call. The recursive quality of the narrative paradigm of election, which Bunyan dramatizes through Christian's famously "anti-progressive" pilgrimage, makes it difficult to parse the backslidings of a true believer and the signs of irredeemable depravity.[19] When one of Christian's companions, Hopeful, compares the latter condition to the biblical image of the dog that eats its own vomit, he casts a thin veil over the complex psychology of damnation. Recourse to sin suggests a parallel with the reflexive response of a sickened animal, but the movements of the human agent's "free mind" demand more careful accounting (P, 117). *The Pilgrim's Progress* avers the lesson in spiritual self-scrutiny delivered by *Grace Abounding*. Guilt, fear, and shame must be set in the proper constellation for awakened conscience to produce the faith necessary to salvation. Both the elect and the damned exhibit these mental states, though in different proportions and with antithetical consequences, making the cultivation of self-assurance difficult, uncertain work. In the following section, I argue that *The Pilgrim's Progress* extends the interpretive task incumbent upon the Calvinist believer to an evaluation of other people's claims to membership in the community of true saints. The difference between the two terms of Calvinism's dyadic arrangement of character, the elect and the reprobate, proves nearly impossible to see from without.

Knowing Talkative

Bunyan's turn from spiritual autobiography to allegorical fiction represents the shift from introspection to character detection demanded by Congregationalist ecclesiology. The consequent change of objects—from self to other—puts pressure on the logic and intelligibility of his two-dimensional characters. Bunyan's perspectival shift yields an alternative model of character that simultaneously gestures toward the rigors of specific reading practices and calls the efficacy of those practices into question. Scenes of character detection in part 1 of *The Pilgrim's Progress* demonstrate that the knowledge of predestined states rests on the potentially shaky evidence of external markers.

Journeying toward the Celestial City, Christian and Faithful encounter a personification of religious hypocrisy called Talkative. The ensuing interview foregrounds the dangers of admitting claimants into the "company of Saints" without first investigating their characters. Christian's final word on the version of hypocrisy practiced by Talkative includes a sober warning about the consequences of accepting fraudulent claims to affiliation: "They are these Talkative Fools, whose Religion is only in word, and are debauched and vain in their Conversation, that (being so much admitted into the Fellowship of the Godly) do stumble the World, blemish Christianity, and grieve the Sincere" (*P*, 68). Bunyan plays on several senses of the word "conversation" in this passage; throughout his writings, the term frequently carries the sense of social intercourse—"the action of living or having one's being in a place or among people" or "mode or course of life"—in addition to the more familiar denotation.[20] The multiple connotations of the term highlight the contaminating influence of false pilgrims like Talkative, who by his speech and the proximity it seems to license threatens to lead sincere professors like Christian and Faithful out of the Way. The possibilities of the gathered church, chief among them its promise to transform the quest for personal assurance into a collaborative spiritual enterprise, must be balanced against the pervasive danger of hypocrisy.[21]

As an embodiment of that danger, Talkative stands opposed to characters like Turn-away, whose fate is forecast by his name as well as by his place of origin ("The Town of Apostacy") and whose status as a reprobate is inscribed on his person. Hopeful spies a scrap of paper affixed to Turn-away's back. It reads: "Wanton Professor, and damnable Apostate" (P, 97). Turn-away is quite literally reading material, and his fully legible character renders his place in Bunyan's allegorical schema self-evident. Talkative preserves the apparent correspondence between outside (name) and inside (nature). Bunyan's scant physical description ("He was a tall Man, and something more comely at a distance than at hand") accords with Talkative's eventual classification as the kind of religious hypocrite who pays homage to correct doctrinal positions without living a life according to his profession to saving faith (63). Yet the veracity of his profession—and so of his character qua spiritual condition—is not immediately evident. Registering him as a threat requires more than recognition of his correspondence with an ethical-religious type. In disabusing Faithful of his mistaken impression, Christian leans on empirical evidence and Talkative's reputation:

> Deceived! you may be sure of it. Remember the Proverb, They say and do not: but the Kingdom of God is not in word, but in power. He Talketh of Prayer, of Repentance; of Faith, and of the New-birth: but he knows but only to talk of them. I have been in his Family, and have observed him both at home and abroad; and I know what I say of him is the truth. . . . There is there, neither Prayer, nor sign of Repentance for sin: Yea, the bruit in his kind serves God far better than he. He is the very stain, reproach, and shame of Religion to all that know him; it can hardly have a good word in all that end of Town where he dwells, through him. Thus say the common People that know him, A Saint abroad, and a Devil at home. . . . Men that have any

dealings with him, say 'tis better to deal with a Turk then with him, for fairer dealing they shall have at their hands. (62–63)

Christian's knowledge of Talkative's public and private past actions stems from both firsthand observation (aided by an unexplained intimacy of access to Talkative's home, servants, and relations) and the corroborating testimony of "common people that know him" or "have dealings with him themselves." Christian relies as much upon Talkative's reputation, his "character" in the sense of circulating, "detailed reports of a person's qualities," as he does upon the evidence of personal experience.[22]

He may do so safely for two reasons, as he goes on to explain. First, these "reports" are grounded in the established credit of "good men," known quantities rather than "enemies to Religion," so they may be distinguished from the "slander" spewed by "bad men" (P, 63). Secondly, he may rely on "my own knowledge" to prove Talkative guilty of the sins of which he stands accused. Though he invokes his own experience and perspicacity as a failsafe, Christian demonstrates confidence in the reports of Talkative's reputation because they are underwritten by a prior and stable sense of the good character of Christian's sources. The accuracy of Christian's judgment, which does hold up in this episode, hinges on the prerequisite and off-stage process by which he sorts potential witnesses into sweeping categories of "good men" and "enemies to Religion" and then credits or discredits their accounts accordingly. Bunyan suggests that if the witnesses to Talkative's hypocrisy had not been vetted already, then this scene of character evaluation would necessarily proliferate into a series of further acts of assessment. Faithful appears to get the message, acknowledging the weight of external opinion when he points out to Talkative the "great wickedness" of projecting a false character in the face of the contradictory evidence of reputation, of saying, "I am thus, and thus, when my Conversation and all my Neighbors tell me, I lye" (P, 67). Christian does not read Talkative as one might a straightforward emblem typical of coherent allegorical systems.[23] Rather, he insists upon the essentially empirical approach of collecting and analyzing evidence to establish the religious content of Talkative's character.

Faithful's attempt to answer the question raised by the Talkative episode—"How doth the saving grace of God discover it self, when it is in the heart of man"—reinforces Bunyan's emphasis on interpreting external evidence. It also reveals the probabilistic quality of knowledge produced by that interpretation (P, 64). Faithful argues that grace discovers itself to "him that hath it" through the sequence of awakening and conversion familiar to readers of *Grace Abounding* and other conversion narratives influenced by Reformed Protestant theology. He acknowledges, as Bunyan frequently does in his spiritual autobiography, the difficulty of recognizing those processes at work within one's own soul. Faithful then makes the same perspectival shift I have attributed to Bunyan's work overall, outlining a protocol for identifying grace in other professed pilgrims. "To others," Faithful explains, "it is thus discovered": "1. By an experimental confession of his Faith in Christ. 2. By a life answerable to that confession, to wit, a life of holiness; heart-holiness, family holiness (if he hath a Family) and by Conversation-holiness in the World: which in the general reacheth him, inwardly to abhor his Sin, and himself for that in secret, to suppress it in his Family, and to promote holiness in the World" (P, 66).

The observer must, on Faithful's account, reason from effect to cause—precisely the interpretive step Bunyan cautions his readers against in *Grace Abounding*. Even here, Faithful acknowledges the crucial role played by the inaccessible inward motions of the professor by stressing the impulse "inwardly to abhor his sins," which manifests in efforts to promote "holiness" and to preserve both his loved ones and the "world" at large from the deadly allure of sin. Outward righteousness and proselytizing represent signs of a "heart-holiness" located within. For Bunyan's "standers by," these are the best, because the only available, indices of grace.

In this instance, Faithful's criteria suffice to discredit Talkative's claim to membership in the invisible church and therefore to bar him from the community of the elect. His protocol nevertheless fails to settle the question raised by Bunyan's treatments of religious hypocrisy. How does the reprobate discover himself to the world when his life closely resembles the paradigm of election? Even under the best of circumstances, standers by are susceptible to error, and strategies of character detection that rely on external evidence yield only probable knowledge. Such strategies may expose a disjuncture of "confession" and social "conversation," as they do in Talkative's case. They cannot, however, determine with any certainty whether "conversation-holiness" reflects genuine "heart-holiness" or belies the heart of a reprobate. The question goes without a final answer until the day of judgment, when, as Christian reminds his companion, God collects the "fruit" of his "Harvest" and casts the damned aside (P, 63–64). To imitate God in his capacity as harvester, attempting to separate the spiritual wheat and chaff, is to fulfill an imperative of Congregationalist ecclesiology. But doing so also courts error and exposes the limitations of human faculties of perception and discernment.

Because the "truth" of his character is not self-enclosed, Talkative does not function allegorically. For Angus Fletcher, a logic of "doubleness" structures allegory; its characters have concrete narrative functions and symbolic functions within a "total cosmic order."[24] Like those described in Bunyan's preface, readers of allegory reconcile this duality by "read[ing] into literature."[25] The shared vocabulary of excavation or penetration and the rigidity of the categories imposed by the doctrine of double predestination suggests a natural affinity with the allegorical mode. Yet *The Pilgrim's Progress* does not bear out their compatibility. Fletcher contends that the characters of allegory are fixed to specific ideas; by contrast, Bunyan's false professors exhibit fluid characters. True, each of these characters reduces to one of two sweeping genera. Their oscillating frames of spirit and the impenetrability of their fundamental salvific conditions nevertheless thwart efforts to attach them to their correspondent ideas. Access to his character depends on both secondhand accounts of his life outside the concrete narrative of part 1 and on Christian's prior decisions about the character of those who provide such accounts, evidence accumulated in the margins of Bunyan's text and then synthesized and interpreted within the episode. Faithful learns the hard way that Talkative's defining lack of grace does not "discover it self," after all, nor does it submit to active interpretive engagement in a vacuum.

His instability calls to mind eighteenth-century anxieties, documented by Stephen Knapp, about the capacity of formerly inert personifications to move within their narratives.[26] Especially in responses to *Paradise Lost,* writers from the period worry about the transformation of allegorical personifications from ornamental or emblematic figures into characters in the more familiar sense of inscribed agents. Talkative proves monstrous more because he resists efforts to affix meaning to him than because he acts within the narrative, but he does take on some of the force and dimensionality of literary personae through the inscrutability of his spiritual condition. Such clues as Talkative affords are gathered over time and pieced together into a coherent report of his hypocrisy. As Christian asserts to the devil Apollyon, religious character manifests gradually, and it is ultimately confirmed only by the supreme arbiter: Christ's "forbearing at present to deliver them [i.e., pilgrims] is on purpose to try their love, whether they will cleave to him, to the End" (P, 47). Christian's defense of Christ's belatedness includes an acknowledgment that election maps out onto a temporal rather than a spatial axis. The task of evaluating character in Calvinist terms means speculating as to how the claimant will fare at the "Harvest," at the "End," rather than penetrating a deceptive surface to uncover a static inward truth.

Superintended Reading

Part 2 of *The Pilgrim's Progress,* as Damrosch has observed, exhibits an overt "social emphasis."[27] Christiana's tale examines the Protestant believer cast as a "member of a sect or community." I would add that Bunyan's sequel also functions as an extended metaphor for proselytizing, preaching, and martyrdom—for the social duties that fall to those who, like Bunyan himself, answered Christ's "particular calling" to minister to other claimants to the invisible church (GA, 76). Part 2, therefore, dramatizes the foundation of the fellowship of saints and the interpretive activity of its members as they negotiate a world littered with enigmatic characters. Despite his stated intention to use his sequel to teach readers "Twixt Idle ones and Pilgrims to discern," Bunyan dwells on the difficulty of adjudicating between sincere and inauthentic claimants. He promises to inculcate a method of reading suited to the task. Almost in the same breath, however, he acknowledges the possibility of misinterpreting available evidence of religious character. Just as counterfeit pilgrims may pass for saints, so certain types of sincere pilgrims "may look . . . as if their God had them forsook" and therefore invite mistaken classification as reprobates (135–36). The evidentiary model of reading that Christian applies to the encounter with Talkative works in part 1—he correctly classes Talkative as a hypocrite, according to various external clues—but the abundant scenes of character reading and emblematic interpretation staged in Bunyan's sequel cast doubt on the efficacy of that approach. Part 2 betrays Bunyan's skepticism about an evidential paradigm that shifts away from the "truth" promised by his two-dimensional method toward the tenuous assurance achieved via probabilistic reasoning.

Christiana's visit to the House of the Interpreter demonstrates that even straightforwardly emblematic representation proves troublesome in the context of evaluating the spiritual content of character. As if to make good on Bunyan's prefatory promise to teach his readers how to distinguish between authentic and fraudulent claims to saving faith, the Interpreter presents Christiana and her company with an allegorical set piece:

> Then, as they were coming in from abroad, they espied a little Robbin with a great Spider in his mouth. So the Interpreter said, look here. So they looked, and Mercie wondered; but Christiana said, what a disparagement is it to such a little pretty Bird as the Robbin-red-breast is, he being also a Bird above man, that loveth to maintain a kind of Sociableness with man? I had thought that they lived upon crums of Bread, or upon other such harmless matter. I like him worse then I did.
>
> The Interpreter then replied, This Robbin is an Emblem very apt to set forth some Professors by; for to sight they are as this Robbin, pretty of Note, Colour and Carriage, they seem also to have a very great Love for Professors that are sincere; and above all other to desire to sosciate with, and to be in their Company, as if they could live upon the good Mans Crums. They Pretend also that therefore it is, that they frequent the House of the Godly, and the appointments of the Lord: but when they are by themselves, as the Robbin, they catch and gobble up Spiders, they can change their Diet, drink Iniquity, and swallow down Sin like Water. (*P*, 159)

The Interpreter likens the robin, and its false promise of harmless sociability, to the "kind" of insincere professor who obscures their spiritual status through a deft negotiation of the public vs. private distinction. Bunyan's robin only "seems" domesticated, its natural diet of creeping things hidden from the view of the humans with whom it seeks to achieve "Sociableness" (159). The version of the false professor "set forth" by this emblem, like the reprobate of Bunyan's *Doctrine of Law and Grace*, looks the part of the true saint and makes an outward show of fellowship that disguises his appetite for sin. His mention of the robin's preferred fare recalls an earlier spectacle that likened pilgrims (tainted, as they are, with both original sin and particular transgressions) to hideous "spiders" dwelling in "the best Room in the House" (158). Invoked just a page later, the image of the robin snatching and "gobbl[ing] up" spiders carries at least some sense of the threat that Christian makes explicit when he chastises Faithful for his credulity. The kind of "Professor" figured by the robin devours sin in secret and, in feigning continuity with the mission of the visible church, consumes its sincere members.

That Christiana expresses surprise at the Robbin's defiance of the character she assigns to its species reflects her—and, by extension, all believers'—susceptibility to pretended sanctification. Unlike Talkative, whose life at home and abroad flags his disqualifying impiety to the student of reputation, such professors hide their true natures in public. Bunyan thus raises questions about the viability of past, public actions as evidence of the spiritual statuses of professors. Beyond exposing the limits of such evidence, Christiana's encounter with the "Robbin" and the "Spider" foregrounds the pilgrims' reliance on recipients of God's "particular calling," ministering agents like Evangelist and the Interpreter, to fill in the gaps left by their own interpretive efforts (*GA*, 76). Mercy simply "wondered," suspended in a state of awed confusion. For her part, Christiana remains preoccupied with the literal plane of meaning; she fails to disclose the "truth" behind the "dark matter" of the Interpreter's emblem (*P*, 157–58). That meaning is delivered rather than left to the believer's apprehension.

The equivalent episode in part 1 sets Christian and the Interpreter in the same relation. Balanced against his requests for direct explication—"What means this?" he importunes three times in as many pages—Christian's claim to "know the meaning" of his host's final vision fails to demonstrate his readiness to assume the intellectual burden incumbent upon the interpreting subject of Calvinist tradition (*P*, 26–29). Neither

Christiana nor her husband before her learns to expound independently on the significance of the Interpreter's visions. By unpacking the moral of each emblem, enjoining Christian to "keep all things so in thy mind, that they may be as a Goad in thy sides," the Interpreter inculcates habits of mind based on remembrance and application rather than rigorous interpretive engagement (32). Christian must treat each episode of his journey as a further iteration of a familiar object lesson. In doing so he performs the appropriate affective responses to demonstrations of God's exacting wrath and Christ's infinite benevolence: "fear" and "hope" (32). The pilgrims' visits to the House of the Interpreter resonate with books 11 and 12 of John Milton's *Paradise Lost* (1667–74), which depict Adam's failure to interpret the scenes of Christian history unfolding before him. Like the Archangel Michael, Bunyan's Interpreter must explain the spectacles, supplementing Christian and Christiana's benighted faculties with divinely imparted wisdom.

Bunyan's sequel places readers in a similarly dependent position. While the reader of part 1 is treated to the certainty of allegory even when his characters are not—we recognize Talkative by the consonance of his appearance and essence—the reader of part 2 loses that perspectival advantage. In the former case, reading other persons and reading the text are incommensurate activities, but in the sequel the distinction between them erodes, and with it the certainty of allegorical reading. Without the Interpreter's explanation, the meaning of the emblem of the Robbin is no more transparent to Bunyan's readers than to his characters. At House Beautiful, to cite one further example, Mathew's call-and-response with Prudence confirms that Bunyan regards natural phenomena as so many metaphors for the vertically structured, mediated relationship between God and his creatures:

> *Mathew.* What should we learn by seeing the Flame of our Fire go upwards? and by seeing the Beams, and sweet Influences of the Sun strike downwards?
>
> *Prudence.* By the going up of the Fire, we are taught to ascend to Heaven, by fervent and hot desires. And by the Sun his sending his Heat, Beams, and sweet Influences downwards, we are taught, that the Saviour of the World, tho' high, reaches down with his Grace and Love to us below. (*P*, 181)

Mathew proceeds from the belief that the created world holds symbolic significance, that there is something we ought to learn by observing the "upwards" flickering of a flame or the downward cast of the sun's rays. The grammar of his tutor's response—"we are taught"—evokes the passivity of both Mathew and Bunyan's readers. It is only through Prudence's direct instruction that we, alongside Christiana's eldest son, come to understand the figurative significance of these phenomena and, thus, the spiritual lessons disclosed by creation.

Contrary to the familiar account of the didactic dimension of his allegorical fiction, Bunyan stops short of training readers. Just as Christiana and her troupe of pilgrims rely on inscribed agents of revelation, so the reader relies on Bunyan for exposition of and reflection on episodes and emblems with otherwise oblique morals. Rather than teaching interpretive techniques, he stresses the limits of human faculties and advocates deference toward both revealed knowledge and his own narrative authority. Reconsidered in this light, the awed expressions of Christiana and Mercy when confronted with the emblem of the robin look less like failures of reading than appropriate responses to the conditions of experience in a sublunary realm where probability has usurped the place of truth.

Instances of divinely abetted interpretation and direct instruction in both parts of *The Pilgrim's Progress* underscore the plight of the stander-by in her confrontation with religious hypocrisy, as well as introducing Bunyan's proposed solution. Bunyan hints at a question that haunts *Grace Abounding* as well as his didactic writings: What does it mean to be cast into Faithful's position before Christian's intervention? In the absence of reliable reports and firsthand observations of an object's words and deeds—or, at times, despite of the availability of those clues—pilgrims must turn to the evidence of revealed knowledge. Bunyan argues for the necessity of mental habits and reading practices that facilitate the discovery of grace (or its absence) in other people. But he also acknowledges throughout these scenes of failed and superintended reading that the "lonely interpreter" associated with Calvinist spiritual practices is not so lonely in the end.[28] She has recourse to the final authority on questions of character and credibility—to God and his agents of revelation. *The*

Pilgrim's Progress locates the grounds of assurance at the intersection of human discretion and appeals to providence.

Reason, Grace, and History

At stake in my reading of *The Pilgrim's Progress* is a clearer sense of the role of English Calvinist theology in both literary history and the history of ideas. Michael McKeon asks, "What happens when we try to read *The Pilgrim's Progress* as though it were a novel?"[29] The query leads McKeon to a deliberate "misreading" of Bunyan's work that extricates the literal plot from its figurative dimensions.[30] To him, *The Pilgrim's Progress* looks most like a novel where its diegetic world courts autonomy, standing up to the obtrusiveness of allegorical meaning. I contend that the distinctively novelistic quality of *The Pilgrim's Progress* plays out at the level of characterization rather than the conflict between microcosm and allegory, as McKeon proposes. Novelistic character inherits from Bunyan's "allegory" and the English Calvinist tradition more broadly a preoccupation with the productive incongruence of surface and essence. The subsequent chapters of this book illustrate my claim about the role that this understanding of character plays in the novel's origin story. In this space, I look farther ahead, and take up the unexpected affinity between Bunyan's epistemology of character and postenlightenment knowledges.

Writing in the late 1970s, Carlo Ginzburg and Paul Ricoeur both identified semiotic epistemology with the advent of critique. Ricoeur famously labels this mode the "hermeneutics of suspicion" and traces its origins to Freud, Marx, and Nietzsche.[31] As Rita Felski recapitulates it, this interpretive model resembles the readerly labor Bunyan assigns in "The Author's Apology" for *The Pilgrim's Progress,* down to the spatial and photic metaphors used by its proponents. "Truth lies beneath, behind, or to the side of" language, and the critic, like Bunyan's ideal reader of Christian similitudes, must "bring to daylight what has languished in deep shadow."[32] Similar to Calvinist character reading, the hermeneutics of suspicion requires careful "scrutiny of signs" whose "unreliability" entrenches suspicion and leads to "ever more interpretation."[33] Ginzburg also places the emergence of an epistemology based on clues, symptoms, and signs in nineteenth-century Europe. He adopts a wider disciplinary purview, proposing that the symptomatic reading practices of humanistic inquiry, their constitutive "evidential paradigm," originate in medical science.[34] Ginzburg nevertheless shares Ricoeur's convictions that critique is essentially semiotic, that it produces conjectural knowledge rather than truth, and that it contrasts the traditional interpretive model afforded by religion. Ginzburg contends that "the body, language, and human history" became subject to "objective examination" only after European societies achieved "new social and epistemological autonomy" from religion.[35]

More recently, Felski has repurposed Ricoeur's concept as a challenge to critical exceptionalism, arguing that the hermeneutics of suspicion emerges not from the spontaneous genius of three German philosophers but from a broader cultural sensibility routinized through instruments of state control. Like Ricoeur and Ginzburg, however, Felski casts critique as "secular" in the sense of extra- or anti-religious. It represents a break from traditional, religious knowledge production in which the "reader luxuriates in the fullness of language rather than lamenting its poverty; the text's latent meaning 'dwells' in its first meaning, rather than exposing, subverting, or canceling it out."[36] Where the interpreters of sacred texts were characterized above all by faith in the revelatory potential of language and texts, the suspicious reader presumes deception, disguise, or misdirection. Suspicious reading reflects, in Felski's memorable rephrasing, "a spirit of ferocious and blistering disenchantment—a desire to puncture illusions, topple idols, and destroy divinities."[37]

Yet, in Bunyan's writings, religious reading *is* suspicious reading. Not only *The Pilgrim's Progress* but also his less well-known allegories depict and enact vigilant, penetrative interpretation—sometimes drawing direct comparisons between religious character detection and "medical semiotics" that snag Ginzburg's through-line from premodern to modern epistemes.[38] *The Life and Death of Mr. Badman* (1680), for example, uses "signes" and "symptoms" interchangeably to name manifestations of spiritual pathology.[39] It's true that Bunyan describes his suspicious hermeneutics with specific reference to revelation, as mediated by sacred text and pastoral authority. Even in that detail, though, he anticipates modern critique as Felski (and Ginzburg and Ricoeur before her) conceptualizes it. For all its iconoclastic ferocity and indeterminacy, critique by this definition evokes confidence in the clear-sighted expertise of the critic whose mood and methods elevate them above the interpretive slough. The parallel assurance of the critic in this paradigm and the vectors of revelatory authority in Bunyan's allegories confirm that the semiotic sensibility of critique obtains to sectarian religious as well as secularist discourse.

I have tried to suggest how Bunyan's heuristics destabilize binary arrangements of critical reason and religious faith. This is not the same thing as arguing that his writings qualify as either secularist, or, as Lori Branch has recently suggested, "post-secular" avant la lettre.[40] Branch describes the faith inculcated through *The Pilgrim's Progress* as though it flattens historical temporality. Bunyan is "a sufferer at the hands of modern rationality," she writes, a thinker who made concessions to norms of an episteme still in embryo.[41] Branch describes him as "a martyr of a sort, that is, for modernity, whose great appeal and comfort lie in his showing how, in the deathly shade of the tree of the knowledge of good and evil and its binary, deterministic framing of the world, one may hope—for freedom from egotism, for love, for life."[42] Readers gain by this figurative martyrdom a resilient and liberatory faith, religion within and beyond secular modernity. Such a faith might free us from the search for objective truth—contributing, in the process, to what Branch, following the theologian John Caputo, calls "post-secular reason"—as well as from the absolutist schema of Christian morality.[43] On my reading, *The Pilgrim's Progress* instills a faith in rather than a faith beyond Calvinist theology's "binary, deterministic framing of the world." Readers of the allegory derive "comfort" from the stability of this epistemological architecture, which withstands empirical failure because it is buttressed by God's omniscience. Bunyan preserves the revealed knowledge of character as a guarantor of meaning. Together with the doctrinal coherence it enables, this preservation marks his writings as presecular.

The Pilgrim's Progress and *Mr. Badman* exemplify the resilience and complexity of Calvinist orthodoxy, and not the transformation of religion through its encounter with imperatives that we tend to conceive of as distinctively modern. They show that one such imperative, to rationalize

Protestant belief, informs even the strictest applications of Calvinist theology. In Bunyan's imagining, Calvinism accommodates reason and grace without undergoing secularization. The object of analysis in my next section, *The Holy War*, confirms the historical lesson of Bunyan's other writings by representing an encounter between Calvinism's suspicious hermeneutics and another, more overtly political and modern imperative: colonial expansion. Here, a paradigm based on penetrative scrutiny and haunted by the possibility that truths of character are potentially inscrutable even where they are profoundly stable becomes a lens through which to view corporeal difference and the threat it poses to both the soul and the state. *The Holy War* transposes the types of the saved and the damned onto ethnoracial difference and represents semiotic activity as the means to identify and discipline unviable forms of life.

"Diabolonian by Nature": Racializing Religious Character

Bunyan's books are associated formally, material, and culturally with the project of empire. Sylvia Brown surveys these connections, helpfully synthesizing three critical perspectives on the nature of the relationship between Bunyan and British imperialism.[44] The first, exemplified by Tamsin Spargo and Isabel Hofmeyr, shows how the global circulation of Bunyan's writings, and especially of *The Pilgrim's Progress*, consolidated his authority as a canonical writer.[45] For John Pahl, the reverse is also true: *The Pilgrim's Progress* cements colonial authority through the fact of its popularity with Evangelical and Nonconformist missionaries and through its form.[46] Pahl conceives of allegory as an inherently colonial literary logic—it abstracts experiential and material meaning from place, making it habitable for the "real" meaning of Christian transcendence— but Brown herself highlights the openness of Bunyan's form. She writes, "As English Nonconformity's most influential global text, *The Pilgrim's Progress* has, over the last two centuries, proved a remarkably capacious and flexible container for a range of imperial as well as antiimperializing strategies directed at, and sometimes coming from within, colonial populations, both indigenous and settler."[47] *The Holy War*, as we shall see, is no less involved with the rise of imperialist ideology. It proves less pliable than *The Pilgrim's Progress*, however, and specifically less amenable to repurposing as a critique of empire. This is because *The Holy War* invokes crusades to represent the internal, individual struggle between good and evil. Bunyan sees the war within the Christian subject as analogous to wars between Christianity and other faiths in imperial history.

Composed between the publication of *The Pilgrim's Progress* and its sequel, *The Holy War* is committed to stabilizing meaning through the interplay of the body and margin of the text. The result is a work that is less formally interesting, less novel-like in its ironclad referential correspondences, but nevertheless instructive. *The Holy War* represents Calvinistic spiritual struggle as a protracted contest between the armies of Diabolus (Satan) and Shaddai (God) for sovereignty over Mansoul, a city in the Kingdom of Universe. The narrative begins with Mansoul under the loose control of Shaddai, its population innocent but vulnerable to Diabolus's influence. The latter potentate seizes control of the city without violence, seducing Mansoulians into changing their allegiance from a remote to a proximate sovereign. Shaddai deputes Boanerges, a fire-and-brimstone preacher, and, later, Prince Emmanuel, who represents the Son, to reclaim the city. The duration of the work focuses on Mansoulian efforts to repulse Diabolonian forces that continually lay siege to the city and to purge the Diabolonians who remain within its walls, furtive but menacing, after Emmanuel's preliminary victory. In *The Holy War,* the soul is a citadel beset not only by external evil but also by internal enemies, sinful thoughts and impulses depicted as the naturalized progeny of a now-expelled occupying force.

That such characters are represented as not only foreign but also racialized subcategories of the damned indicates *The Holy War*'s participation in an emergent novelistic discourse, which made Calvinist soteriology into a language of corporeal difference. *The Pilgrim's Progress* offers hints of this direction, implicating reprobation with cultural and racial otherness through its representation of religious hypocrisy. In part 1, Christian explains the danger of engaging hypocrites like Talkative in economic exchange as well as spiritual fellowship: "'Tis better to deal with a Turk then [*sic*] with him, for fairer dealing they shall have at their hands" (63). Employing the "Turk" as a point of reference for Talkative's bad credit,

Bunyan uses assumptions about the deceptiveness of an imperial rival to illustrate the material consequences of hypocrisy among coreligionists. Thus, he creates a stable but skeletal comparative frame, in which the inherently faulty religiosity of cultural others and the insincere Protestantism of British "runagates" are analogous (HW, 165). In addition to stereotyping Ottoman traders, The Pilgrim's Progress creates a figurative correspondence between reprobate character and epidermal race that Bunyan explores further in The Holy War. Srinivas Aravamudan cites part 2 of The Pilgrim's Progress among the early modern texts that use whitewashing as a trope of impossibility.[48] The shepherds of the Delectable Mountains lead Christiana's troupe to "a place where they saw one Fool, and one Want-Wit, washing an Ethiopian with intention to make him white, but the more they washed him, the blacker he was. They then asked the Shepherds what that should mean. So they told them, saying, Thus shall it be with the vile Person; all means used to get such an one a good Name, shall in conclusion tend but to make him more abominable. . . . So it shall be with all hypocrites" (P, 224). The shepherds at once assert the essentiality of religio-ethical character and fulfill the believer/reader's need to have the meaning of emblems explained to them, reiterating and resolving the works' defining epistemic tension. Through its figurative logic, the vignette also impresses reprobate character onto flesh. While he makes no direct claim about the nature of black people, Bunyan's figure brings evil to the body's surface by making an "Ethiopian," or African, the vehicle for a moral archetype, "the vile person."

The Holy War makes more extensive use of this framework, implying tertiary referents for Diabolus and Shaddai. Explicitly, the characters refer to Satan and God. The phrase "Holy War," the depiction of Mansoul as the site of continually renewed conflict between imperial antagonists, the distinctively premodern technologies, strategies, and codes of martial conduct that Bunyan describes with peculiar faithfulness all invite further comparisons to historical crusades and, thus, to struggles between Euro-Christian and Islamic sovereigns over possession of Jerusalem.[49] More consistently than The Pilgrim's Progress, The Holy War affirms the spiritual significance of corporeal difference as it attempts to brace its allegorical structure.

Bunyan opens *The Holy War* where *The Pilgrim's Progress* leaves off—
with an acknowledgment of the author's responsibility to elucidate
meanings that are not self-evident. In his "Note to the Reader," Bunyan
promises guidance:

> But I have too long held thee in the porch,
> And kept thee from the sunshine with a torch.
> Well, now go forward, step within the door,
> And there behold five hundred times much more
> Of all sorts of such inward rarities
> As please the mind will, and feed the eyes
> With those, which if a Christian, though wilt see
> Not small, but things of greatest moment be.
>   Nor do thou go to work without my key,
> (In mysteries men soon do lose their way;)
> And also turn it right, if though wouldst know
> My riddle, and wouldst with my heifer plough.
> It lies there in the window. Fare thee well,
> My next may be to ring thy passing-bell. (5–6)

A series of semiautonomous metaphors unfolds over this passage,
explaining the relationship between the author, the reader, and the text.
The governing metaphor of the first paragraph, like the images of min-
ing and uncovering in "The Author's Apology" for *The Pilgrim's Progress,*
creates an inside-outside dichotomy. Here the discovery of "inward rari-
ties" appears to be an easier task: we have only to "step within the door, /
And there behold" innumerable religious truths on display. While the
second paragraph suggests that the text requires more of readers than
simply walking inside Bunyan's allegorical structure, it nevertheless
promises greater ease than does "The Author's Apology." The prefatory
homage to the individual agency of readers of *The Pilgrim's Progress,* as
I've argued, belies the experience of reading a text that depends on frequent marginal annotations and almost compulsive scriptural citation to
make its larger, spiritual meanings effable. *The Holy War*'s "Note to the
Reader" shows greater self-awareness of the parallel between the author
and the Interpreter. By describing his marginal explanations as a "key"

to interpretive "mysteries," Bunyan extends the figure of book-as-edifice from the previous paragraph. Allegory remains a structure we inhabit, but its interpretive key "lies there in the window," on the periphery of the material text itself. This image flattens out the surface/depth metaphor that predominates in *The Pilgrim's Progress*. We are invited to imagine our progress through the text as movement on a one-dimensional plane, a journey back-and-forth from center to "margent." The final comparison, between the reader's "work" and the labor of ploughing, confirms the alleviated burden of interpretation in *The Holy War*. What the text asks of readers is to harness the energy of living machinery. Bunyan's marginal glosses are animated as a beast of burden; we direct the application of their force, but the strenuousness of the task falls on the heifer, not the ploughman. Cumulatively, the language in Bunyan's "Note" presents allegory as a habitable world and allegorical reading as the work of cultivating with borrowed tools and the harnessed strength of another being.

Almost immediately, *The Holy War* uses this system of reference to identify damnation with blackness. The narrator describes travelling through the Kingdom of Universe, a continent in which "the people are not all of one complexion, nor yet one language, mode, or way of religion; but differ as much as ('tis said) do the planets themselves. Some are right and some are wrong, even as it happeneth to be in lesser regions" (7). Geographical, linguistic, and religious demarcations are also moral ones: some of the "modes" of life practiced by the inhabitants of Universe are right, and "some are wrong." Among the measures of variability on the continent, which rises to an astronomical scale in the narrator's telling, is "complexion." James F. Forrest, editor of the most recent scholarly edition of *The Holy War*, glosses the term as "character, temperament," but the *Oxford English Dictionary* includes a more comprehensive definition in circulation before and after the period in which Bunyan wrote: "The natural colour, texture, and appearance of the skin, especially of the face; originally as showing the temperament or bodily constitution."[50] Bunyan's subsequent introduction of Diabolus strengthens the case that complexion denotes not only variety of temperament, as in Forrest's note, but also its physical expression.[51] Marginal explanations work to racialize the salvific taxon of the damned:

Well, upon a time there was one Diabolus,
a mighty giant, made an assault upon this famous Town of Mansoul,
to take it, and make it his own habita-tion.
    This giant was King of the Blacks or Negroes. (9)

In the margins, alongside the first and fourth lines of verse narration, Bunyan glosses Diabolus as "The Devil" and "Blacks or Negroes" as "Sinners, or the fallen angels." Within the microcosm of Bunyan's fiction, the black people(s) of Universe are subjects of a wicked master. In the allegory, they serve as vehicles for two kinds of reprobate creatures. The "or" in Bunyan's racial categorization expresses synonymy, but the comma between "Sinners" and "fallen angels" holds open the possibility that racial blackness refers simultaneously to human and seraphic orders of the fallen. This contiguity of racial and spiritual blackness anticipates the efforts of later writers to superimpose Calvinism's exclusionary soteriology onto visions of racialized global hierarchy.

A further connection between Bunyan's allegory of spiritual combat and the eighteenth-century imperial imaginary emerges later in *The Holy War*. However welcome and salubrious their management proves to be, Emmanuel and his captains are a colonizing force. After defeating Diabolus, Emmanuel sets about "new-model[ing]" Mansoul, reorganizing its political and ecclesiastical structure under a governor, Mr. Gods-peace, "who was not a native of [Mansoul], but came with the Prince Emmanuel from the Court" (170). To secure the city from threats of incursion and insurrection, Prince Emmanuel institutes a program of biopoliticized violence. He grants Mansoul's elders, its civil and ecclesiastic officers, and "all the inhabitants of the town of Mansoul, full power and commission to seek out, to take, and to cause to be put to death by the cross, all, and all manner of Diabolonians, when and wherever you shall find them to lurk within, or to range without the walls of the town" (165). The "chief" Diabolonians Emmanuel lists—personifications like Lord Fornication, Mr. Witchcraft, and Mr. Heresy—are easily distinguished from native Mansoulians according to physical appearance. "They may certainly be known" by studying "their physiognomy, and such other characteristical notes of them" (164). Bunyan gives no indication in the body or the margin that "other characterstical notes" refer, like physiognomy, to embodied qualities. Nor does he make a second reference to the terms "Blacks or Negroes." Emmanuel's statement nevertheless extends the racializing logic of Bunyan's initial description of Diabolonians by assigning salvific meaning to somatic signs.

Directly equating blackness and damnation, *The Holy War* affirms the symbolic association posited by the so-called "curse of Ham," the archetypal site in Christianity for aligning racial difference with moral categories. Bunyan's allegory, however, exhibits a more elaborate internal logic. Genesis, which describes the curse entailed on Ham's progeny for gazing at "the nakedness of his father," Noah, was cited for centuries as a justification for racial slavery.[52] Because the text includes no mention of skin color, such applications depend less on biblical exegesis than a dubious, racist mythology. Bunyan, too, relates heritable sin to skin color, but he deploys the complex semiotics of Calvinism to establish that relation. With his introduction of a second type of Diabolonian, Bunyan recreates the problem of false coreligionists from *The Pilgrim's Progress*. Emmanuel ends his call to purge the Diabolonians from Mansoul with a warning:

> Now as I have set out before your eyes the vagrants and runagates by name, so I will tell you that among yourselves some of them will creep in to beguile you, even such as would seem, and that in appearance are, very rife and hot for religion. And they, if you watch not, will do you a mischief, such an one as at present you cannot think of.
>
> These will show themselves to you in another hue than those under description before. Wherefore, Mansoul, watch and be sober, and suffer not thyself to be betrayed. (*HW*, 166–67)

His confidence in the legibility of Diabolonians persists—"these will show themselves to you," like the others—but Emmanuel acknowledges that these particular characters present an as-yet-incomprehensible form of harm, and that their detection requires heightened watchfulness. This is because they dissever the correspondence between "hue" and diabolic nature posited by the earlier, marginal gloss and developed through Emmanuel's instruction to practice physiognomic reading. Bunyan's subsequent explanation for how, precisely, they short-circuit the semiotic relay that structures Calvinist character lends spiritual intensity to fears of miscegenation.

Mr. Carnal Security exemplifies the subversive threat posed by "domestic Diabolonians" (HW, 194). It is through his influence that the townspeople lower their gaze to sublunary goods and thereby forfeit Emmanuel's protection. Carnal Security acts as a "false prophet," disseminating the "doctrine" of worldly ease amongst town elites (178, 171). He succeeds in this because he passes for a Mansoulian himself. But Carnal Security is, in fact, the product of a mixed union: "Wherefore, there being then in Mansoul those strange kinds of mixtures, 'twas hard for them in some cases to find out who were natives, who not; for Mr. Carnal Security sprang from my Lord Willbewill, by mother's side, though he had for his father a Diabolonian by nature" (171). The specific language in this passage is misleading. Despite his emphasis on the blurred lines between "native" and non-native Mansoulians, Bunyan appears to be describing something closer to ethnic than natal distinction. Carnal Security belongs to the demographic category of Diabolonians who "had there [in Mansoul], by reason of unlawful mixtures, their birth and breeding and bringing up" (183). Participation in this kind isn't contingent on geographical or cultural place, nor is it inscribed on the flesh; it is determined by heredity and thus depends on the Diabolonian's errant "nature" persisting, unalloyed, through processes of sexual mixture and cultural assimilation. On his mother's side, Carnal Security is the grandson of an eminent regenerate, Lord Willbewill. Because his father, Mr. Self-conceit, was a Diabolonian, however, Carnal Security "also was a Diabolonian by nature." The narrator repeats this point by way of explanation when the townspeople eventually burn down Carnal Security's house with him inside it (178).

Unlike the army Diabolus leads into combat against Mansoul at the beginning of The Holy War, domestic Diabolonians like Carnal Security are not explicitly racialized. Either Bunyan loses the allegorical thread between racial blackness and spiritual depravity, or their interrelation is implicit in his lament of the epistemic consequences of exogamy. I incline toward the latter explanation because it supplies logical content for the otherwise vague causal claim presented alongside Carnal Security's backstory. Bunyan asserts that the knowledge of ethnicity is elusive during this period in the city's history "wherefore," or as a result of, the contemporary practice of intermarriage. How, specifically, does this practice make it "hard . . . to find out" who is a "true-born" Mansoulian and who is a "foreigner" (255, 68)? The more or less explicitly racializing descriptions of Diabolonians in previous episodes—the marginal gloss at the beginning of the narrative and Emmanuel's reference to physiognomy—suggest miscegenation as a likely mechanism. Read this way, *The Holy War* conceptualizes racial difference as a tenuous religious language. Interracial marriage, on this understanding, weakens the semiotic link between body and soul, without undermining the stability of Calvinism's fundamental salvific types. Thus, while its outward expressions are effaced, Diabolonian nature endures generational change.

Expansive sections of *The Holy War* are dedicated to the perceptual modes required to fulfill Emmanuel's commission where "no great difference" at first appears "betwixt Mansoulians and Diabolonians" (205). In the early days of Emmanuel's occupation, a familiar evidential model emerges. As in *The Pilgrim's Progress*, errant religious character may be established through witness testimony. The former text applies forensic vocabulary figuratively, but *The Holy War* slips into forensic realism as "burgesses and aldermen" appointed by Diabolus stand before a "Court of Judicature" (135). Alderman Atheism, Alderman Hard-heart, Alderman False-peace; burgesses Mr. No-truth, Mr. Pitiless, Mr. Haughty: all are convicted on the basis of testimony, specifically genealogical accounts of their Diabolonian character. The court sentences Atheism to death after three Mansoulians, Mr. Know-all, Mr. Tell-true, and Mr. Hate-lies, confirm his patrilineal descent. Know-all states, "He is a Diabolonian, the son of a Diabolonian: I knew his grandfather, and his father" (137). Next to the bar, Tell-true offers corroborating testimony: "I know him to be a Diabolonian, the son of a Diabolonian, and an horrible man to deny a deity. His Father's name was Never-be-good, and he had more children than this Atheism" (137). Implicitly, the court proceedings aver the object lesson of the encounter with Talkative in *The Pilgrim's Progress*. Here, too, confidence in the knowledge of character depends on the already-established credibility of witnesses. Much as Christian and Faithful depend on the authority of their neighbors' reports of Talkative's bad character, juror and reader alike may in this case trust to the comprehensiveness of Know-all's testimony and to the veracity of Tell-truth's. In this respect, the trials of the aldermen work according to a similar logic to the one prevalent in *The Pilgrim's Progress*. But there is an added stress, here, on heredity. If it's not quite sufficient evidence to convict him on the charge of promulgating the notion that "there is no God, and so no heed to be taken to religion," Atheism's identity as a Diabolonian appears in the testimony as a matter of equal importance to the specific crimes ("brisk talk" and blaspheme) of which he stands accused (*HW*, 136). As in Calvinist metaphysics more generally, predestined character and particular behavior stand in mutually reinforcing relation. The latter makes the former cognizable.

Shaddai's law, as revealed by Emmanuel, sanctions extrajudicial prosecution, as well. In that context, surveillance replaces testimony as the relevant evidential strategy. With an army of Doubters arrayed against the city gates and Diabolonian rebels weakening its institutions from within, Lord Willbewill hears rumors that Jolly and Griggish, sons of his former servant, have been "tickling and toying" with his daughters (*HW*, 222). Although Willbewill knows that their father was a Diabolonian, and that "by the law of Mansoul all Diabolonians were to die," he imposes on himself a burden of proof: "Now his lordship, being unwilling unadvisedly to put any man to death, did not suddenly fall upon them, but set watch and spies to see if the thing was true; of which he was soon informed, for his two servants, whose names were Find-out and Tell-all, catched them together in uncivil manner more than once or twice, and went and told their lord" (223–24). Despite the escalating stakes and intensifying language—the term "spies" replaces "standers-by," and confirmation of evil character results in public crucifixion rather than ostracization—Willbewill's surveillance of Jolly and Griggish evinces the same suspicious mood and evidentiary method of character detection observed in *The Pilgrim's Progress*. Reports of bad works travel through the vertical channel of feudal organization in *The Holy War*, rather than circulating informally within a Congregationalist social network like the one that connects Christian, Faithful, and Talkative. But such intelligence serves the same purpose: to confirm through the scrutiny of outward evidence other peoples' salvific states. Willbewill's servants "catched" Jolly and Griggish in the act and, by communicating what they've seen to their lord, convert suspicion into the empirical evidence required to justify their execution as enemies of the state.[53]

The efficacy of surveillance and legal procedure notwithstanding, there is a clear imperative in *The Holy War* to usher in an episteme in which the difference between the Mansoulian and Diabolonian races is self evident. Emmanuel's initial victory portends a clear, binary frame previously limited to pitched warfare between ensign-waving bands. The prince declares, "That which I am now about to do is to make you known to the world to be mine, and to distinguish you also in your own eyes, from all false traitors that may creep among you" (166). Emmanuel indeed acts "now," disbursing "white and gleaming robes" as "livery" for his servants (166). Yet the promised effect of distinguishing between his true followers and "false traitors" does not follow immediately. In fact, the episodes of confusion and crisis discussed above occur after Emmanuel's gesture.

A scriptural citation in the margins suggests that Emmanuel, like the angel of Revelation, speaks in "the spirit of prophecy."[54] In the margin next to his speech, Bunyan cites the verse: "And to her was granted that she should be arrayed in fine linen, clean and white: for the fine linen is the righteousness of saints."[55] Explicated through Calvinist soteriology, these lines confirm the representative function of good works. The wife of the lamb of God (the antecedent of "her" in verse 8) is "arrayed" in pristine linen; in the same way, the elect, or saints, whom she figures will be clothed in acts of "righteousness." Adherence to moral law is the outward sign of their salvific status. Rewriting this eschatological vision, Bunyan emphasizes epistemological consequences. What interests him is the guarantee of intelligibility that attends the second coming; Bunyan adds the remarks about saints being "known to the world" and known to themselves through the reliable signification of white robes. Those garments externalize saving faith, answering the question of assurance more definitively than *Grace Abounding*, *The Pilgrim's Progress*, or *The Doctrine of Law and Grace Unfolded*. In Revelation, the image of the bride arrayed in white comes between the fall of Babylon and the defeat of the armies of the beast. There is a similar chronological relationship, and implicit causal one, in Bunyan's version. Emmanuel distributes his livery directly after the order, discussed above, to purge the city of Diabolonians. White linen, here, symbolizes reward for labors not yet performed, and specifically the program of violent differentiation that Emmanuel assigns to the officers and citizens of Mansoul. Personal assurance and social intelligibility, signified by the robes, will follow from their identification and execution of "false traitors who creep among" them. With this threat removed, whiteness may be restored to its privileged position at the nexus of aesthetic and spiritual purity. Until then, readers and Mansoulians soon discover, sinners mix with saints, some Diabolonians even donning counterfeit robes to disguise themselves as the espoused faithful. As an emblem of righteousness, white linen is part of a larger system of signification. Diabolonians disrupt that system by disjoining spiritual value from its grounding meaning.

They do this, specifically, through racial exogamy. Children who inherit the innate sinfulness but not the corresponding, embodied "characteristic notes" alienate the two meanings of "complexion," moral disposition and skin color. The Whore of Babylon yet lives at this juncture of the story Bunyan is retelling, taking the form of sexual-social contamination. To replace her with a radiantly innocent bride is to establish new epistemic conditions, in which "hue" as well as garment match the condition of the soul. The charge to restore the correspondence, between racial blackness and spiritual depravity, created by Bunyan's textual apparatus and reinforced by Emmanuel's endorsement of physiognomy takes on millenarian urgency. Bunyan consistently renders the symbolic recoupling as biopolitical violence; it entails surveilling and, often without judicial process, destroying an errant form of life. Diabolonians are not fit objects of readers' compassion, of course, because they belong to an absolute category of evil. Emmanuel justly warns against the dangers of permitting them to live in Mansoul, and the town suffers from their leaders' failure to heed their restored prince.

The external referent for the reprobate characters in *The Holy War* is an abstract danger, the same danger represented by Talkative in *The Pilgrim's Progress,* and not the spiritual insufficiency of any historical ethnoracial demographic. It is nevertheless significant that Bunyan chooses racial difference as the idiom for describing Calvinism's binary characterology. His choice demonstrates that, in late seventeenth-century England, and specifically within the culture of Protestant dissent, racial blackness was available as a metaphor for damnation. Is the semiotic coupling of external and interior blackness within this character regime inevitable? In the final section of this chapter, I turn to one of Bunyan's eighteenth-century readers, the black Calvinist Gronniosaw, to make the point that Calvinism serves more than one argument about the salvific status of people of African descent.

Gronniosaw Reads *The Holy War*

When we examine Gronniosaw's account of reading *The Holy War* in light of both the preceding analysis of Bunyan's text and Gronniosaw's reflections, elsewhere in his *Narrative,* on the religious meaning of race, what we find is evidence of Calvinism's multivalence. Gronniosaw's reaction confirms that the vehicle/tenor relationship in Bunyan's governing metaphor for damnation proves reversible. If the fictional "Blacks or Negroes" of Universe could set forth the abstract spiritual value of reprobation, the same abstract idea could be affixed to actual people of color. Yet, as Gronniosaw's *Narrative* shows, the character of Calvinism also facilitates the mutual intelligibility of the elect within multiracial communities of faith.

The Holy War appears in Gronniosaw's autobiography as an obstacle along the path to assurance of salvation, if not the source than an intensifier of the author's racial-spiritual self-loathing. Before his enslavement, before he even encounters white Europeans, Gronniosaw intuits the basic structure of Christian monotheism. Contrary to the pagan, animist beliefs of his Bornu society, Gronniosaw senses "that there was some GREAT MAN of power which resided above the sun, moon, and stars, the objects of our worship."[56] He is delighted to have this intuitive knowledge confirmed and elaborated upon when, as an enslaved person, he encounters the teachings of Christianity in colonial America. This joy becomes fear as Gronniosaw learns the expansiveness and severity of God's judgment from his second enslaver, Theodorus Jacobus Frelinghuysen, a Reformed Dutch clergyman living in the Colony of New Jersey.[57] Gronniosaw is "excessively perplexed" to discover that damnation comprehends Christians and heathens, that "GOD would judge the whole world; ETHIOPIA, ASIA, and AFRICA, and every where" (N, 14). He becomes deeply anxious about the state of his own soul as a result, and it is during this period that Eva Turhune Frelinghuysen, who was married to Theodorus, presents Gronniosaw with a copy of *The Holy War.* Gronniosaw relates,

> I continued in a most unhappy state for many days. My good mistress insisted on knowing what was the matter. When I made known my situation she gave me John Bunyan on the holy war, to read; I found his experience similar to my own, which gave me reason to suppose he must be a bad man; as I was convinc'd of my own corrupt nature, and the misery of my own heart and as he acknowledg'd that he was likewise in the same condition, I experienc'd no relief at all in reading his work, but rather the reverse. (N, 15)

Reading *The Holy War* exacerbates rather than assuages Gronniosaw's anxiety about his salvific status. His stated explanation for this effect is identification with Bunyan. Gronnoisaw recognizes that Bunyan's work allegorizes individual spiritual struggle, and he attributes the "experience" and "condition" that it represents in this way to the author himself. Not yet realizing that this condition corresponds to that of the Calvinist subject awakening to sin and initiating the process of regeneration, Gronniosaw responds with aversion to his perceived similarities with Bunyan. A pair of episodes from earlier in his *Narrative* introduce the possibility of another identification at work here, as well: identification between Gronniosaw and Bunyan's black characters.

By the time he encounters *The Holy War,* Gronniosaw has already come to attribute spiritual value to the sign of blackness. Watching his first enslaver read the Bible aboard the slave ship transporting them to Barbados, Gronniosaw imagines that "I saw the book talk to my master," but, to his great disappointment, he finds the sacred text silent when he holds his own ear to it: "When I found it would not speak, this thought immediately presented itself to me, that every body and every thing dispis'd me because I was black" (N, 10). The exclusion that Gronniosaw attributes to his epidermal race is not exclusively religious—he understands the book's refusal to speak to him as an example of universal contempt—but his perception of it nevertheless arises in a religious context, the moment in which (he believes) he is denied accessed to revelation.

In the next paragraph, the young Gronniosaw makes a more direct connection between blackness and damnation by racializing the devil. An older enslaved person admonishes Gronnoisaw, who has "called upon God to damn" the maid who dirtied silverware that he has just scoured: "This old black man told me I must not say so. I ask'd him why? He replied there was a wicked man call'd the Devil, that liv'd in hell, and would take all that said these words, and put them in the fire and burn them" (*N*, 11). Gronnoisaw's immediate reaction, fear, extends to sympathetic worry when, soon after, his mistress curses the same servant. He tells Eva Frelinghuysen that "there is a black man call'd the Devil that lives in hell, and he will put you in the fire and burn you, and I shall be very sorry for that" (11). Gronniosaw, not his admonisher, makes the Devil a "black man." It stands to reason that Gronniosaw, having already equated blackness with infernal character, would be discomfited by the African identity of Diabolus's subjects in Bunyan's text. That may be the reason Gronniosaw does not return to *The Holy War* even after gaining a measure of confidence in his election and redefining his relationship to other religious writings in the Nonconformist tradition, like Richard Baxter's *A Call to the Unconverted to Turn and Live* (1658), that had once intensified his anxiety. Bunyan's text could only have revived his youthful fear that blackness marks irremediable sinfulness.

Although it may have been fed by his encounter with the most famous author in the English Calvinist tradition, Gronniosaw's racial self-loathing is not a direct consequence of *his* Calvinist outlook. In fact, after achieving "full assurance that my sins were forgiven me" through solitary reflection and scriptural study, Gronniosaw finds social validation of his election when he moves through Calvinist circuits of legibility familiar from *The Pilgrim's Progress* (*N*, 18). He travels to Amsterdam to deliver his conversion narrative to an audience of Dutch clergy. "The Calvinist Ministers," he recounts, "desired to hear my Experience from myself, which proposal I was very well pleas'd with. So that I stood before 38 Ministers every Thursday for seven weeks together, and they were all very well satisfied, and persuaded I was what I pretended to be" (28). The Dutch ministers' vetting proceeds with the same goal as the collective accreditation process of Bunyan's Bedford congregation, to evaluate the truth of a profession of saving faith, and with similar confidence in social protocols that make religious character intelligible. Gronniosaw frames the point at issue in ontological terms, a matter of his really *being* what he says he is—saved—and, in that way, evokes the static classifications of Calvinist taxonomy.

The preface to Gronniosaw's *Narrative* likewise attempts to persuade readers of Gronniosaw's election, in this case by invoking layered testimony like the evidence that damns Talkative in the eyes of Christian and Faithful in the first part of *The Pilgrim's Progress*. Written by a clergyman cousin of Selina Hastings, Countess of Huntingdon, the prominent Methodist and patron of elite black writers like Phillis Wheatley Peters, John Marrant, and Olaudah Equiano, the preface makes a direct claim about Gronniosaw's religious character. Huntingdon's cousin, William Shirley, asserts that Gronniosaw "belong'd to the Redeemer of lost Sinners; he was the Purchase of his Cross; and therefore the Lord undertook to bring him by a Way he knew not, out of Darkness and into Marvellous Light" (*N*, 5). Blending the idiom of redemption with economic language, Shirley recasts Gronniosaw's enslavement as the "way" of his salvation. Like other redeemed sinners, Gronniosaw "belongs" to Christ as the "purchase" of his sacrifice. Shirley supports his claim with an appeal to Gronniosaw's reputation: "His Character can be well attested not only at Kidderminster, the place of his Residence but likewise by many creditable Persons in London and other Places" (6). Knowledge of Gronniosaw's "character" circulates within English communities, including in his home neighborhood of Kidderminster, Birmingham, and the center of London, as attestations of "creditable Persons." Shirley does not present us with examples of these reports, nor does he instruct readers to ask around; instead, he asks them to adopt his own faith in the veracity of unknown, unnamed witnesses. Shirley, the white Calvinist-Methodist clergyman with powerful connections, is the arbiter. Readers of the preface, therefore, find themselves in much the same position as Faithful in *The Pilgrim's Progress*. Like him, they are reliant on the credibility of second- and thirdhand testimony, making direct judgments not about the object of discernment but about "standers-by."

While both the preface and Gronniosaw's account of his interrogation in Amsterdam describe Calvinist protocols for evaluating religious character, neither passage broaches the topic of Gronniosaw's race. His white coreligionists implicitly deny the correspondence between blackness and sinfulness that *The Holy War* insists on. Gronniosaw himself gives only a hint that his racial identity is a factor in his mature spiritual self-assessment, the thought processes by which he develops and then maintains assurance of his redemption. The clue is nested in a metaphor that he uses to describe the endurance of his confidence despite experiencing a series of economic hardships after his marriage to a white Methodist laborer named Betty. He declares, "I have been wonderfully supported in every affliction.—My GOD never left me. I perceive light through the thickest darkness" (*N*, 32). Gronniosaw's penetrative metaphor is reminiscent of Bunyan's description of the ideal reader's relationship to figures, of the necessary and fruitful task of reading *through* opaque surfaces to discover interior truths. Gronniosaw refers most directly to his unfailing perception of God's presence shining through the figurative clouds of suffering. Might his statement also give us a clue as to the religious hermeneutics he applies to overcome his youthful anxiety about the equation of external blackness with internal evil?

In any case, Gronniosaw does overcome or, at least, circumvent the conflation of racial and spiritual blackness on his journey toward self-assurance and religious belonging. The path he follows is contained by Calvinism's system of character. The ontological definitiveness of Gronniosaw's self-understanding—"I *was* what I pretended to *be*"—befits the rigid typology created by the Doctrine of Double Predestination, while the processes by which he becomes legible as such to an international community of adherents matches the protocols of Bunyan's congregations, real and imagined. Even Gronniosaw's prioritization of social accreditation over the potential weight of somatic signs mirrors the inadequacy of individual semiotic activity documented in *The Pilgrim's Progress*. Unlike Cugoano's *Thoughts and Sentiments on the Evil of Slavery*, the *Narrative* refuses to reinterpret markers of racial difference through direct argument, instead denying their heft implicitly, by omitting them as factors of religious character detection. Together with Bunyan, both black Calvinist authors show the flexibility of Calvinist two-dimensionality. Although premised on the congruence of surfaces and essences, this model supports different—even contradictory—forms of race-thinking by enabling writers to toggle between individual and collective agency, and between different forms of superficial evidence. It is this idea of character that the novelists considered in chapter 2, Behn and Aubin, abstract from its doctrinal setting and adapt as a framework through which to make sense of the forms of property and forms life that travel through channels of imperial exchange.

2

꙼

Empire of Types

I N HIS PROVOCATIVE, sweeping exploration of the intersections of literary character and personhood, John Frow contrasts characterization in the modern novel, not to typologies per se but to "religious typology."[1] We do not think of Bunyan's allegory as novelistic, he proposes, because of the rigidity of its Christian theory of character. *The Pilgrim's Progress* and modern novels similarly present "schemata which generalize and simplify human being," Frow argues, by "distinguishing between inner and outer, identifying mental states and models of motivation, and extrapolating from acts to an underlying and *more or less fixed* moral character."[2] In contrast to Bunyan's "highly formalized" religious characterology and other "folk psychologies" (e.g., the doctrines of humoral pathology and the ruling passion), novelistic "typological abstraction works as an informal and secular operator of extrapolation through layers of 'sociological' generality. Age, gender, occupation, and social class are the characteristic markers that we read from the persons of the novel."[3] Frow does not define religious typology except through contrast to the novel's more "sociological" and "secular" approach of "extrapolation," a difference that he expresses in part through spatial metaphor. We "read from" characters in novels by "extrapolating through" strata of generality, proceeding along orders of abstraction until we reach fundamental "sociological" categories like age, vocation, and class. Christian typologies, we infer, create correspondences on a comparatively untextured plane of fictionality. The phrase "highly formalized" thus conveys flatness as well as well as stability.

My aim in this chapter is to examine more closely the relationship between religious and novelistic typologies, specifically by tracking the influence of Calvinism's character system beyond the precincts of Bunyan's culture of Protestant dissent. Frow's description of the logic of type rings true, for the most part, when applied to both Calvinist doctrine and its elaboration in Bunyan's fiction. As we saw in the previous chapter, *The Pilgrim's Progress* and *The Holy War* relate external characteristics—actions, reputation, physical traits—to "underlying" classes of person. It is likewise true that these types or genera are static, fixed in this case by the dualism of the Calvinist doctrine of salvation. Yet Bunyan is no less interested in sociological layering than later, nominally "secular" writers. His characters and readers are meant not only to reason from particular figures to the basic categories of the saved and the damned but also to reason through social categories of intermediate degrees of abstraction: the various moral natures organized under the heading of reprobation (like Talkative's) as well as civic roles (the legal and political officials of Mansoul) and ethnoracial demographics (the Diabolonians). Bunyan thematizes the process of typological abstraction through encounters like the one between the pilgrims and the false professor Talkative, emphasizing its insufficiency as well as its urgency. The protocols by which we identify motivations and spiritual states and then sort them into classes of person conduce to probabilistic knowledge, which means that vessels of indirect revelation—ministers and narrators—must intervene to bolster individual and communal efforts to read character correctly.

Although they write from outside the Calvinist tradition, Aphra Behn and Penelope Aubin adapt its understandings of character and character-reading through their representations of New and Old World imperialism. Behn's *Oroonoko,* often noted for its generic hybridity and ideological dissonance, also exacerbates the inherent instability of Calvinism's two-dimensional, typological model of character. Behn calls into question the reliability of outward evidence—verbal pledges, body language, physiognomy—as well as the integrity of types. The categories of interest to her are racial, social, political, and generic rather than religious, but they are constelled (however provisionally or confusingly) by the title character's assertions, evaluations, and disavowals of faith. Behn's novel is not, therefore, "secular" according to the sense implied by Frow's distinction between religious and novelistic character systems; *Oroonoko* does not inscribe an actual social order that is fully separate from Christian morality. In fact, Behn's methods of characterization demonstrate the gravitational pull of religion for a writer concerned with the contradictions of the project of empire. Although she focuses on the context of colonial exchange and circulation rather than church formation, Behn asks essentially the same question that Bunyan does in the Talkative passages of *The Pilgrim's Progress:* How does personal character ground claims to, or claims backed by, religious belief?

For Behn as for Bunyan, this query puts pressure on systems of literary reference premised on semiotics. Oroonoko discovers that demonstrable character, evidence made accessible by reputation networks and physiognomic reading, does not reliably index interior truths like motive or moral disposition. Twentieth- and twenty-first-century scholarship on *Oroonoko* attests that modern readers experience a different sort of symbolic confusion when they encounter Behn's "royal slave." Instead of the alienation of sign from value, extrinsic evidence and intrinsic character, the scholarly record reflects a multiplication of referents. Oroonoko's face becomes a site of interpretative accumulation in which ethnoracial, generic, and religious types accrue and collide. Irresolvable conflicts between types— English sovereign, African-diasporan rebel, romance hero, Christ proxy— play out on the preternaturally legible surfaces of Oroonoko's body, and through those conflicts a larger, ideological incongruity appears. Christianity and colonial capitalism are incompatible explanatory frames.

The two typologies in Aubin's *The Noble Slaves* are more overtly religious and, ostensibly, more rigid. One structures the world according to clash-of-civilizations dualism between Christianity and Islam; the second gives the narrative an iterative structure. Aubin depicts a coterie of white, aristocratic Europeans brought together through Ottoman slavery in Algeria, Morocco, Tunisia, and Numidia. As they relate their personal histories, exchanging the roles of auditor and narrator, these "noble slaves" reveal shared character functions, their interchangeability within a repeatable moral fable of Christian captivity and sexual persecution. Aubin in this way unites different European nations and Christian denominations under a broad umbrella of typical virtue, and she presents that virtue as antithetical to the appetitive, cruel violence of Muslim enslavers.

Despite her binary framing, however, Aubin does not present "Moors," "Turks," and Algerian pirates as essentially different from the European Christians they enslave. The categories of difference that structure this imaginary are not racial: Muslim characters' susceptibility to conversion combines with the fungibility of cultural signs that define their type to suggest that Euro-Christian and Islamic peoples are not absolutely and fundamentally differentiated. Aubin's particular view of Christian superiority demands fluidity, a tacit rejection of "religious race" that is premised on Christianity's expansiveness—its capacity, perhaps not universal but recurrent, to subsume theological alternatives.[4] The same assimilation is not available to black characters in *The Noble Slaves*. Race does operate in this text, just not to police the division between Christian virtue and Islamic vice. Aubin holds culture and corporeality apart when it comes to the antagonism between Europeans and Ottomans, yet she more subtly asserts essentialized, embodied difference—epidermal race—in the case of "Blackamoor Slave[s]" like Domingo and Attabala.[5] Aubin largely ignores African slavery in the Islamic world, focusing instead on the captivity of white Christians, but she does write black characters. They attend their Christian masters in Barbary, inhabiting an unnamed space between the religious types whose opposition structures Aubin's geopolitical view. Physical markers of their difference are intractable, and their exclusion from Christian polity, though less violent than the conflict between white Christians and Muslims, is more permanent. While the position of Aubin's black characters sometimes furnishes a practical advantage—the novel regards Attabala's house on the literal and figurative fringe of Algierian society as insulated from Ottoman aggression, a place where white Europeans can gather in relative safety—it also reflects the complex interweaving of antiblackness and Christian chauvinism within a dawning secular age. Aubin represents Christianity as a global religion that promotes affiliation across national and sectarian borders and imperial rivalries but not across the black/white divide. Christianity, the one true religion, transcends religious race but enforces epidermal race, excluding people of African descent.

Oroonoko's Faith

Interpretations of *Oroonoko* have helped to reshape the teaching canon and propel feminist-Marxist and postcolonialist perspectives from the margins to the center of eighteenth-century and novel studies. Laura Brown, Srinivas Aravamudan, Laura Doyle, and Ramesh Mallipeddi, to name only a few of Behn's contemporary readers, have much to teach us about this text and the volatile backdrop of its composition and publication in 1688.[6] Despite the widespread, acute interest in Behn's writings and in this text particularly—an interest, Aravamudan not unreasonably observes, that "borders on the obsessional"—their religious dimensions remain understudied.[7] Perhaps this is a reflection of the field, which has only lately begun to reckon with the persistence of religion not merely alongside but at the core of enlightenment thought, or perhaps it is because Behn's fictions betray no clear theological commitments. Her Catholic sympathies trouble her Anglican Protestant affiliation, and they seem as likely to be shrewd declarations of allegiance to the Catholic Stuart kings Charles II and James II as they are to be sincere. Yet this evasion of theological specificity, I argue in the following section, reflects the capaciousness rather than, say, the artificiality or impoverishment of Behn's religious thought.

More specifically, I hope to show the importance and the fluid content of faith in *Oroonoko*'s treatment of cultural and racial difference. The "royal slave" himself adheres to a European code of honor that, in McKeon's phrasing, "enjoins implicit faith in the words of others," faith in parole.[8] And he derides the English colonists in Suriname for their faithlessness, their tendency to go back on their word despite backing their promises with professions of Christian piety. Yet the narrator complains that, despite Oroonoko's mental acuity and the easy fluency he exhibits with European history, literature, and institutions, "no one could make him understand what faith was."[9] One of his last acts of defiance is to issue his own rejection of faith. Vastly outnumbered, bereft, physically diminished almost past recognition, Oroonoko declares, "you will find no more Caesars to be whipped, no more find a faith in me" (*O,* 74). He acts against type by adopting a posture of wary skepticism toward the white colonists' promises. The appellation "Caesar," as several scholars have observed, connects the African prince to the Stuart royal line and to the concept of divine-right sovereignty more generally. Behn frequently refers to Charles II as "Caesar" in her occasional poetry, and in her day the term carried the figurative denotation of "an absolute monarch."[10] As he sloughs off the name, Oroonoko assigns it new meaning. "Caesars" take their persecutors at their word and submit to the indignity of the lash. His act of deidentification signals a toiled awareness of the primary way that he (and, the pluralization suggests, other enslaved Africans) has been "caressed" or placated: through empty homages to his exceptionalism, his status as a king among the other black people enslaved on the plantations of Suriname.[11] Violence is required to secure this extrication of self from assigned character. After making the declaration, Oroonoko disembowels himself and kills an English assailant with consecutive strokes of his knife. But his rejection of the title also suggests the *in*extricability of character and religion. For the "faith" that Oroonoko has by this time lost, the credulity he now recognizes as dangerous in English lands, originates in religious devotion.

Faith in/as Parole

What is the nature of the faith we once *did* find in Oroonoko? Focusing on his exchange with the English slave trader who first captures him and his entourage, scholars tend to describe Oroonoko's faithfulness as adherence to honor, a "social and secular moral principle."[12] During the voyage from the Gold Coast to South America, the captain promises to return Oroonoko and his followers to Africa in a bid to end their hunger strike. Oroonoko "believed in an instant what this man said," but the slave trader expresses ironic distrust of the prince on the basis of their "difference of faith" (*O,* 39). He is reluctant to release Oroonoko from fetters because he "could not resolve to trust a heathen he said, upon his parole, a man that had no sense or notion of the God that he worshipped" (39). Oroonoko responds by execrating Christian oathing practice and the doctrine of rewards and punishments upon which the practice is founded. "Let him know," Oroonoko instructs the slave trader's emissaries,

I swear by my honour, which to violate, would not only render me contempt-ible and despised by all brave and honest men, and so give myself perpetual pain, but it would be eternally offending and diseasing all mankind, harm-ing, betraying, circumventing and outraging all men; but punishments here-after are suffered by oneself, and the world takes no cognizances whether this god have revenged them or not, it is done so secretely and deferred so long; while the man of no honour suffers every moment the scorn and con-tempt of the honester world, and dies every day ignominiously in his fame, which is more valuable than life. (39)

Fear of social disgrace carries more coercive force than a religious oath, even taking the latter at face value, because the repercussions for a "man of no honour" are immediate, severe, and public. To swear by God is to trade on a fantasy of speculation and futurity, and to accept that pledge is to invest in another person's belief in and fear of an omnipotent deity who metes out consequences in the hereafter. As Oroonoko points out, the slave trader's compact is with God and not him. If the captain should break his promise, there would be no way to redress the wrong. Oroonoko prefers a model of reciprocal word-giving that invests character qua repu-tation with intrinsic "value" and perfidy with stakes in "the world" rather than the afterlife.

Although this passage tends to attract straightforwardly secularist readings—as Oroonoko's and, by extension, Behn's privileging of a social and moral perspective over Christian theology—what it in fact proposes is a transparent alignment of action and belief.[13] In an exception to the rule of Behn scholarship, which tends to emphasize her works' sexual libertinism, protofeminism, or humanitarian sentiment at the expense of an accounting of their theological investments, Sarah Ellenzweig fore-grounds Oroonoko's critique of Christianity. Ellenzweig discusses this speech, briefly, as an example of Behn's literary freethinking, which she defines as "a skeptical religious posture that saw Scripture and the truths of Christian teaching" as fictions while upholding the institution of Angli-can Protestantism as a civic good.[14] For Ellenzweig, *Oroonoko* affirms the tenet that "the cure for today's theological ills" (i.e., for the detachment of religion from a practical system of action) was "to remember that religion's end was not the rightness of a particular doctrine but rather the practice of virtue and good conduct."[15]

In his rebuttal to the slave trader and in more general social commentary, Oroonoko does criticize societies that uphold the "bare name of religion" without "the virtue or morality" that is, for him, religion's end (*O*, 17). His critique of Christianity is of a piece, in this regard, with the project of English literary freethinking, which was concerned with organized religion's "sacrificing real virtue and moral probity for empty doctrine."[16] But the practical piety that Ellenzweig ascribes to freethinkers ultimately corresponds to an archly cynical view of religion that Oroonoko does not share. Although it is premised on the complementarity of the social-secular principle of honor and Christianity, freethinking depends on assent to politically expedient "heuristic fictions."[17] As Ellenzweig reads it, *Oroonoko* contributes to a reinvestment of religion as winking suspension of disbelief for the good of civil order. Yet Oroonoko's faith is genuine rather than tactical, and it references a specific theological tradition that Behn relocates to West Africa. While honor is "the first principle in Nature," Oroonoko's commitment to it derives from a Calvinistic understanding of religious character and community and an intensity of feeling that she presents as a non-Christian, non-European devotionality.

This is, to be sure, a surprising argument to make about Behn, who tends to be regarded as Catholic in the rare cases when she is taken seriously as a religious thinker. The claim, that Behn houses a form of Calvinism in the fictive West African religion of a hero who in some ways resembles the Catholic Charles II, nevertheless makes sense if we approach the author not as Catholic or Anglican but as a *secular* thinker. *Oroonoko* is secular in the precise sense that it liberates faith from theological specificity. The novella wrests Calvinism from its doctrinal contexts and, indeed, from the value of doctrinal propriety. We shall see in chapter 3 how this liberalizing gesture intensifies at midcentury, and how the resulting idea of religious pluralism can naturalize the ideology of empire. In the present section, though, I ask how—by what means, and to what extent—secularized religious morality can be accommodated to racial slavery.

When he criticizes Christian oath-giving, Oroonoko repurposes Cal-vinist soteriology and its ideal epistemology of character. Bunyan's *Grace Abounding* and *The Pilgrim's Progress* portray the reprobate's sin as both fixed and distributed across the community in the form of spiritual con-tagion. Oroonoko cites similar consequences as a guarantor of honesty. If he violates his word, he will "give myself perpetual pain" and "eternally" affront "all men." Social death and eternal punishment, individual and species-level effects link his concept of honor to Bunyan's Calvinist char-acterology. Dualism operates here, as in the Doctrine of Double Predes-tination; one is either "brave and honest" or not, an honorable person or a "man of no honour." Perhaps the most striking resemblance consists in Oroonoko's sanguine attitude toward reputation. The dishonorable per-son permanently injures their "fame," the value assigned them within a social network like the one on which Christian depends for evidence of Talkative's salvific status. In both cases, character circulates as reports of past, public actions, and this collective knowledge informs individual decisions of whether to credit a promise. Oroonoko conceives of the knowledge of character as finite, measurable, and transmissible within the sphere of social accountability. When he affirms his "belief in the invi-olability of promises," as Aravamudan describes his conviction, Oroonoko professes a form of faith rather than a social-secular alternative to reli-gion.[18] He avers the efficacy of collective accreditation of character on the model that develops, as we have seen in the previous chapter, at the inter-section of Calvinist theology and Congregationalist ecclesiology.

The ill fit between this model and the social relations that govern English Suriname redounds more to the discredit of the colonial enterprise than of Oroonoko's belief. Behn offers implicit criticism of an economy that promotes deception, disregards social hierarchy (closing the natural, vertical distance between the African king and common Africans), and rewards deception of the sort practiced by the English slave trader and the perfidious lieutenant governor, William Byam. Moreover, Oroonoko proves to be less "gullible" or "quixotic" in the face of such deceit than previous scholarship has suggested.[19] He learns the hard way that "there was no faith in white men or the gods that they adore," and responds with increasing wariness to the settlers' assurances (*O*, 66). Oroonoko's experience of betrayal converts him to "skepticism," as McKeon suggests, but his doubt is entrenched in religion rather than opposed to it.[20] When cast headlong into circumstances structurally parallel to those of Bunyan's pilgrims, Oroonoko, too, relies on a model of evaluating claims to credibility through active interpretive engagement.

Oroonoko turns to semiotic reading after having learned that neither the fear of God nor the possibility of a tarnished reputation ensures faithfulness among the English. He decides to trust the planter who buys him upon his arrival, John Trefry, because "he saw a kind of sincerity and aweful truth in the face of Trefry; he saw an honesty in his eyes, and found him wise and witty enough to understand honour, for it was one of his maxims: a man of wit could not be a knave or villain" (*O*, 42). In some ways, Oroonoko's enslaver demonstrates the honorable character advertised by his physiognomy. Trefry uses his political influence and legal knowledge to protect Oroonoko from Byam's jurisdiction after the prince attempts suicide, and Byam only succeeds in capturing and executing Oroonoko because he lures Trefy away from Parham plantation. Oroonoko's choice to believe Trefry nevertheless turns out to be a mistake. Neither the virtues manifest in the planter's face nor Oroonoko's maxim comprehend Trefry's character, or his relation to Oroonoko as an enslaved person. The typological logic that inheres to both sources of knowledge—Trefry's face should communicate what kind of person he is; Oroonoko's maxim should preclude the intermingling of the types of the Wit and the Knave—does not stand up to experience.

Trefry is not a "villain," it's true—especially compared to Byam—but neither are his actions toward Oroonoko entirely honorable. If his intention to secure Oroonoko's release and transportation back to Africa are "sincere," he appears not to take any step toward fulfilling them, instead adding his voice to the chorus of those plying Oroonoko's restive spirit with empty pledges: "They fed him day to day with promises" (*O*, 48). Oroonoko's interactions with Trefry present a different kind of problem than his encounter with the captain of the slave ship. There, he confronts both the outright deceptiveness licensed by religion's abstraction from morality. Here, Oroonoko confronts the limitations of typology to contain the ambivalent moral character of colonialism. Alongside uncomplicatedly villainous characters, this project yields ambivalent figures, like Trefry and the narrator, who can see and celebrate Oroonoko's innate nobility and perhaps even imagine his liberation, but who perpetually defer the unification of promise and performance. The narrative provides no evidence, one way or the other, about such characters' motivations. They sit somewhere between sincerity and dissembling, forever astride intention and action, and only take on clarity once Oroonoko becomes an obvious threat to plantocracy.

Continually disappointed by such interlocutors, Oroonoko quite reasonably adopts a posture of wary "defence" (*O*, 66). It is at this point that Oroonoko, in his own telling, loses faith. He replaces it with an attitude of suspicion and a contractual understanding of social intercourse. Pressed by Trefry to surrender to Byam's forces, Oroonoko names his conditions and demands that the agreement "be ratified by their hands in writing, because he had perceived that was the common way of contract between man and man amongst the whites" (67). Oroonoko attempts to adjust to the system of the colonists, abandoning his faith in verbal pledges and assuming that setting the agreement in writing will make it binding. If he makes an error, it is in not moving far enough to the side of incredulity when he is forcefully transported to a New World governed by a new character regime. And if he is slow to lose faith in parole, it is because of the intensity of feeling he attaches to the act of believing other people.

"Inspired with Eloquence"

Whereas the Christian theology of the English colonists encourages hypocrisy by disjoining the name from the nature of religion, Oroonoko's belief promotes mutual intelligibility. Oroonoko's first meeting with Imoinda in Coromantien explains the durability of his faith in the words of others. It is a faith that develops from his experience of a force above reason and that erases the distinction between social principle and religious devotion. Behn's narrator remarks, "I have often heard him say that he admired by what strange inspiration he came to talk things so soft, and so passionate, who never knew love, nor was used to the conversation of women; but (to use his own words) he said, most happily, some new and till then unknown power instructed his heart and tongue in the language of love, and at the same time, in favor of him, inspired Imoinda with a sense of his passion. She was touched with what he said, and returned it all in such answers as went to his very heart, with a pleasure unknown before" (*O*, 17). Although he does not name the gods, Oroonoko attributes his unwonted fluency in the language of romantic love to an "unknown power," and he describes the lovers' reciprocal declarations as the result of "strange," shared inspiration. This power works within Oroonoko to produce otherwise unaccountable persuasiveness, and it works on Imoinda to produce a "sense of his passion." The term "sense" links Imoinda's comprehension to her phenomenal experience of Oroonoko's love, an emotional relay between self and other metaphorized as "touch." By quoting Oroonoko's "own words" with respect to the supernatural mechanism behind his eloquence but omitting the specific language of his declaration, the narrator foregrounds belief over rhetoric. Her selective citation indicates that what is important is not the content of Oroonoko's speech but the source of its eloquence, the strange inspiration that transforms rhetorical effect into affect, projecting love into the space between him and Imoinda.

While the couple's first interview depicts the feeling of being understood as an almost intersubjective religious experience, their stolen-away consummation is charged with the pleasure of belief. Oroonoko's grandfather, the king, has marked Imoinda as his new favorite and called her to his seraglio. Oroonoko, by this time secretly married to Imoinda, recruits a superannuated beauty to join his plot to infiltrate the grandfather's harem. His lieutenant, Aboan, seduces the woman, Onahal, with exaggerated professions of love. The novella lessens the immorality of Oroonoko's choice to dupe Onahal by declaring that Aboan is only "half-feigning" when he courts her. In any case, the ends appear to justify the means, as Onahal succeeds in bringing Oroonoko and Imoinda together for a sexual encounter freighted with religious meaning. The narrator says:

> It is not to be imagined the satisfaction of these two young lovers, nor the vows she made him that she remained a spotless maid till that night; and that what she did with his grandfather had robbed him of no part of her virgin honour, the gods in mercy and justice having reserved that for her

plighted lord, to whom of right it belonged. And it is impossible to express the transports he suffered, while he listened to a discourse so charming from her loved lips, and clasped that body in his arms for whom he had so long languished. (*O*, 29)

Oroonoko's ecstasy, so acute as to be "suffered"—endured more than enjoyed—derives not from the moment of "ravishing," which Behn encapsulates one paragraph earlier, but from listening to Imoinda's vows. Her pledge of inviolate "virgin honor" is backed by belief in divine justice. When Oroonoko assents, with pleasure so intense that it crosses the border to pain, he assents not only to Imoinda's account of her sexual-social condition but also to her idea of providential order. He believes her in part because he shares her belief in gods who interpose directly in human affairs out of "mercy and justice," in this case by enforcing Oroonoko's proprietary sexual claim over Imoinda. Later, the penitent old king takes the providentialist view, too: "He believed now that his love had been unjust, and that he could not expect the gods, or captain of the clouds (as they call the unknown power) should suffer a better consequence from so ill a case" (31). The passage supports heteropatriarchal fantasy: the old king's sexual impotency mitigates threats of incest and ruination, ensuring that Imoinda remains a viable object of desire for Oroonoko, according to the European expectation of chastity. But there is an undercurrent of autocritique running through these lines, as well.

Together, the couple's first interview and the delayed consummation of their marriage sketch out a religion antithetical to the Christianity of Oroonoko's enslavers. In this system, divinities intervene to ensure mutual intelligibility and render vow-giving as a pleasurable, secure act rather than the toilsome and ultimately unreliable empirical procedure that Oroonoko eventually adopts among the English. Of course, Behn's representation of West African religion carries no comparative value; the narrator makes no claims to expertise and shows little interest in Coramantien religious institutions, even admitting that she "forgot to ask" about the details of the marriage ceremony (*O*, 19). Laura J. Rosenthal observes that "the social, political, and educational institutions of Coramantien, as Behn describes them, are more like those of Restoration

England than those of the Gold Coast of seventeenth-century Africa."[21] Along those lines, I propose that the Coromantien episodes of *Oroonoko* encode Restoration religion, though not the normative Anglican Protestantism of the English state nor the barely disguised Catholicism of its maligned sovereign, James II. Behn displaces the theory of character from the tradition of Protestant dissent onto a virtuous pagan society, exaggerating and exoticizing its belief.

She does so not in defense of Calvinist theology, exactly, but to a valorize the sociality its underlying idea of character enables. I want to be careful not to give the impression that I see Behn as a crypto-Calvinist who deliberately uses the stylistic and narrative conventions of the Oriental tale to mask her participation in a disallowed theological tradition, nor would I dispute biographical arguments as to Behn's Catholic leanings. My point here is that the faith espoused by her hero is unsystematized, a technics of character that has been freed from doctrinal orthodoxy and religious controversy. The character of Calvinism is therefore available to the (probably) Catholic Behn just as it would be to Anglican writers Aubin and Fielding in the early and mid-eighteenth century: without reference to religious controversy or pastoral difference, neither anchored to nor contradicting any theology in particular. Behn draws on a liberalized form of Calvinism, initiating the secularization process that shapes the early history of novelistic character. The specific way that she reconstructs the semiotics of character underlines Christianity's estrangement from itself. Oroonoko's unassimilability to the norms of English Suriname, despite his mental acuity and his European education, damns the context instead of the character. His fate literalizes the conflict between a "faith" in which belief in the gods affirms trust in other people and one that severs doctrine from morality. Good faith is absent from England's South American dominions, and Behn confers it instead to a geographically and racially distinct culture.

Typing Oroonoko

Through Oroonoko's evaluations of other people, whether failed or successful, Behn articulates her religious autocritique. She reveals the disjunctive Christianity practiced by English participants in colonial enterprise—the captain of the Gold Coast slave ship, the English settlers in Suriname—in part by contrasting it to an African belief system in which correspondences between the name and the substance of religion, and between the value and meaning of personal character, are airtight. This system, I have argued, subtly reconstructs the theory of character that obtains to Calvinist, congregationalist Protestantism, abstracting it from its sectarian setting and ascribing it to an atavistic society to make it at once more remote (because culturally foreign) and familiar (because accessible without reference to Nonconformist dogma).

The scope of the novel's criticism of empire only expands where Oroonoko functions as an object of interpretation rather than an interpreting subject. Oroonoko embodies virtue so perfectly that his elevated social standing is preternaturally legible to both his English counterparts and fellow enslaved Africans. To readers, too, he appears as a ready text—too ready, it turns out, to submit to our efforts to assign straightforward meaning. Behn loads her title character with various, often clashing, referents, inviting typological interpretations that do not, in the end, cohere into a system of reference. A clear message emerges from this mélange of referents, however: that Christianity, reduced to its essential fable, fails to comprehend imperial ambition.

Critics have long responded to Oroonoko's typological resonances by tracing them to specific literary and historical referents. George Guffey and Laura Brown have explored the character as a representation of the Stuart kings.[22] Like Charles I, Oroonoko is ultimately betrayed by his followers, and like that king he bears his execution with stoic resolve. The name by which the narrator most frequently refers to Oroonoko is "Cæser," an appellation that Behn frequently assigns to Charles II in her occasional poetry. In the sense that he possesses an inherent virtue and nobility that legitimize his claim to the admiration and obedience of his subjects, even when deprived of his political base, Oroonoko resembles James II as Tories imagined him in the late 1680s, when that monarch's religious orientation stoked the flames of opposition to his economic policies.[23] Laura Doyle extends this line of argument, teasing out the relationship between Oroonoko's documentarian representation of colonialism and its "allegory of English revolutions."[24] Both meanings are "encoded" within Oroonoko's body, making the royal slave emblematic of "African-Atlantic slave captivity" as well as the lamentable (from Behn's royalist perspective) erosion of Stuart legitimacy in England.[25] In a reading evocative of Frow's theory of novelistic typology, Mallipeddi argues that *Oroonoko* alternately represents its title character as a "typical romance hero" and an exceptional African, creating tension between generalization and individuation.[26] Whereas Mallipeddi seeks to resolve this tension by viewing Oroonoko through the prism of commodity fetishism, Aravamudan contends that the multiplicity of referents is the point.[27] "As a literary character," he writes, Oroonoko "is a cipher echoing lost persons, subject effects or statistical numbers, called up—rhetorically—to represent the Triangle trade, the birth of plantation capitalism, and the African diaspora."[28]

My own interpretation builds on previous scholars' observation of the tension between the two terms in Behn's subtitle—"royal" and "slave"—while also foregrounding another typological referent for Oroonoko, a principal character from sacred history. Oroonoko's shifting relation to the character of Christ confirms what the novel hints through the contrast between his faith and the avowedly Christian colonists' faithlessness. That is, his inconsistent reference to Christ suggests that Christianity and empire are incommensurate discourses, however attractive the former may appear as an explanatory or justificatory logic for the latter. Rather than conducing to interpretive open-endedness, as Aravamudan argues, Oroonoko's overdetermined typification carries a fixed ideological meaning. Behn's narrator cannot make Oroonoko comprehensible except in relation to the foundational Christian moral fable, yet she cannot reconcile his Christomimetic function with his position in the plantation-capitalist economy, and particularly with his status as a self-liberating African. These characters belong to different narratives. The categorical distinction between colonialist narrative and Christian moral fable appears through the interplay between these types (one sacred, one racial), with the effect of undermining the narrator's endorsements of English colonialism in the abstract.

Oroonoko seems the example par excellence of a legible character on the Calvinist model. He exhibits the perfect consonance between interior and exterior: the surfaces of his body convey his nature. During her initial sketch, the narrator observes that both Oroonoko's "soul and body" are "admirably adorned," and that "the perfections of his mind" do not "fall short of those of his person" (*O,* 15). He is remarkable for his innate and transparent gentility, in the senses of nobility of birth and magnanimity: "He was adorned with a native beauty so transcending all those of his gloomy race, that he struck an awe and reverence even in those who knew not his quality" (13). Yet Oroonoko ultimately fails to embody the model of character he espouses during his confrontation with the English slave-ship captain. Upon finally seeing Oroonoko in person, the narrator stresses that circulating reports fall short of giving a full account: "This great and just character of Oroonoko gave me an extreme curiosity to see him," she writes,

> But though I had heard so much of him, I was as greatly surprised when I saw him as if I had heard nothing of him; so beyond all report I found him. . . . He was pretty tall, but of a shape the most exact that can be fancied. The most famous statuary could not form the figure of a man more admirably turned from head to foot. His face was not that brown, rusty black which most of that nation are, but a perfect ebony, or polished jet. His eyes were the most aweful that could be seen and very piercing, the white of 'em being like snow, as were his teeth. His nose was rising and Roman, instead of African and flat. His mouth, the finest shaped that could be seen, far from those great turned lips, which are so natural to the rest of the Negroes. . . . Bating his colour, there could be nothing in nature more beautiful, agreeable, and handsome. . . . Whoever had heard him speak would have been convinced of their errors that all fine wit is confined to white men, especially those of Christendom, and would have confessed that Oroonoko was as capable even of reigning well and governing wisely, had as great a soul, as political maxims, and was as sensible of power, as any prince civilized in the most refined schools of humanity and learning, or the most illustrious courts. (15)

What the narrator "heard" cannot prepare her for what she "sees," and what she sees in turn outpaces her expository powers. Her awed depiction of Oroonoko's personal qualifications dwells on the inexpressible singularity of her subject. He threatens to exceed the standards of analogical representation; his form is the "most exact," his nose of the "finest shape," his skin is a "perfect ebony," and the discipline of statuary cannot furnish a better example of the masculine form.

Behn's treatment of Oroonoko's exceptionality in this passage would seem to illustrate the representational conflict that, for Frow, distinguishes typologies in the European novel from those of religious and folk psychologies. Frow identifies the novel form with unresolvable "tension between reading character as a contingent particularity and reading it as the representation of a larger class of persons. Much of the energy of the novel has gone into refusing allegorical or symbolic reference; yet to the extent that character is a structural moment of the semantic patterning of the novel, that refusal is almost impossible to achieve."[29] Yet the more significant fault line, here and throughout *Oroonoko,* obtains between different general orders—generic and social kinds—rather than between particularization and generalization. The narrator turns to available categories for sorting persons (white and black, European and African, royal and slave), but none adequately captures the effect of the object of her gaze. Advertised in the very title as a character type, Oroonoko actually exhibits an overloading of types. As Behn surveys his body, referents accumulate without coalescing into a comprehensible whole. Superlative descriptors ("most," "best" known or even imaginable) accrue at the same rate, and in response to, the proliferation of types on Oroonoko's countenance. This multiplication prevents him from signifying in the manner of Bunyan's emblems—by setting forth, for instance, Stuart kingship, racial blackness, or the archetypal virtue of heroic romance. An overarching claim of this book is that the novel forms through writers' experimentations with the resources of two-dimensional literary systems of reference. Behn's famous early entry in the catalog of novelistic fiction indicates that such trials produce excesses as well as "refusals" of "allegorical and symbolic reference."

The excessive referentiality of Oroonoko's character is temporarily suspended when he begins to resist his enslavement with violence. After leading a failed revolt and murdering the pregnant Imoinda, thus disrupting the chattel model by preventing their child from being born into slavery, and ineffectually trying to take his own life, Oroonoko becomes jarringly flat. He now presents with static, emblematical value: "If before we thought him so beautiful a sight, he was now so altered that his face was like a death's head blacked over, nothing but teeth and eye-holes" (*O*, 75). Doyle argues that the initial description of Oroonoko's face articulates a transition from an older model of race, based on a demarcation between common and noble classes of people, to the model demanded by Atlantic slavery, which is predicated on differences of skin color.[30] The emaciated form before the narrator in this passage presents no such nuance. A black "death's head," Oroonoko's face relates two clear ideas: epidermal race, and the inevitability of death. His blackness, however overlayed or ennobled by previous description, now conveys the unambiguous meaning of a memento mori.

Even at this point in the narrative, however, when Oroonoko presents a direct and explicit threat to colonial order, Behn's characterization slips back into representational excess. Dying for his disruption of the plantation economy, Oroonoko appears Christlike. For Aravamudan, "Oroonoko's final moments are clearly Christomimetic, where the victim's refusal to reproach"—he "gave up the Ghost without a Groan or a Reproach," Behn writes (*O*, 76)—"is a figure of speech that signifies his own irreproachability, making him into a sacrificial object."[31] Oroonoko is, thus, "assimilated into a similar model of martyrdom" to the one inhabited by the Stuarts, who in Royalist accounts also resemble Christ.[32] His assimilation isn't perfect, however, as *Oroonoko*'s perverse reprisal of the Lord's Supper illustrates. In between the failure of his rebellion and his execution, when Byam's forces discover him in the jungle alongside Imoinda's decaying corpse, Oroonoko taunts his pursuers: "*Look ye, ye faithless crew,* said he, *it is not life I seek, nor am I afraid of dying,* and, at that word, cut a piece of flesh from his own throat, and threw it at them" (74; emphasis original). His grisly gesture parallels communion, at once evoking Christ and demonstrating Oroonoko's distance from that figure. St. Paul tells the Corinthians that Jesus "took bread" the same night as his betrayal: "And when he had given thanks, he *brake* it, and said, Take, eat: this is my body, which is broken for you: this do in remembrance of me."[33] Jesus's act of breaking bread symbolizes his imminent suffering on the cross; Oroonoko's self-mutilation, beyond corroborating his boasted fearlessness, presages his own death and disincorporation.

Two pages later, once Oroonoko finally dies on the whipping post, Byam's officers "cut Cæsar in quarters, and sent them to several of the chief plantations" as a deterrent against further uprisings (*O*, 76). Behn rewrites the Lord's Supper, intensifying the metonymic logic of the eucharist, expanding the scope of betrayal, and emptying the scene and the execution it foreshadows of their recuperative potential. Oroonoko offers communion, a piece of his actual body rather than an object that represents it symbolically, to a "faithless crew," a group of followers in the sense of pursuers rather than acolytes. The gesture distills his defiant character rather than the self-effacing character of Christ, and the death it preemptively figures confers no redemption—least of all to the enslaved Africans whom Oroonoko now contemns as fit instruments of white Christian exploitation. An intratextual allusion in this passage further undermines Oroonoko's Christomimetic function. Oroonoko's self-mutilation recalls the venerable indigenous warriors who vie for preeminence through displays of stoic "dismemberings" (59). The war captains appear to the narrator as infernal creatures, "hobgoblins, or fiends, rather than men." Her description tinges their "brutal" method of demonstrating valor with a demonic or infernal quality. Oroonoko's act resembles this supposedly hellish practice, countervailing the extratextual allusion to Corinthians. His actions in defiance of colonial rule, including the killing of Imoinda and their child, allude at once to the Christian ideal of redemptive self-sacrifice and a needlessly violent, anti-Christian display of martial courage.

Rather than mediating between two types, the king and the slave, Oroonoko gathers typological referents that gesture simultaneously to the incompatible genres of Christian myth, colonial romance, and slave narrative.[34] Through this excess of signification, Behn passes onto readers a version of the problematics of character that Oroonoko confronts after his Atlantic crossing. A sequence unfolds on both the thematic and formal planes of the novella: a problem is identified, its solution promised, and then that solution exposed as fantasy. Despite Oroonoko's initial confidence, claims to trustworthiness cannot be grounded in "good" character any more than it can be grounded in professions of faith. The collapse of typological representation under its own weight follows a similar pattern.

Behn entertains the possibility that the discursive worlds of her novella comprise coherent systems of meaning. But that coherence hinges on the protagonist's status as a proxy for Stuart kingship or Jesus Christ, and Oroonoko's racial otherness intermittently disrupts that symbolic relationship. The hyperviolent conclusion of Oroonoko's tale, especially, forecloses each of the various frames introduced by the novel. That Behn unsettles the picture in the last pages of her work suggests that she borrows a central lesson from the Calvinist Protestant literary tradition. Like Bunyan, Behn suggests that the end of the story is what matters. However consumers of narrative strive to line up expectations with evidence—asking, what sort of story is this, or what sort of man is he?—those expectations are often disrupted at the last moment. Just as a Calvinist believer discovers their true salvific status on the Day of Judgment after passing life as a saint, Behn reveals the disorder of her representational model with the final strokes of her pen. If she remains committed to narrative ways of knowing (to the project of representing experience through fiction as well as to the task of evaluating character according to external evidence), Behn is equally invested in revealing the inadequacy of her typological reflex.

In this respect, and despite their sharply divergent attitudes toward doctrinal systems, *Oroonoko* recalls *The Pilgrim's Progress*. Bunyan's allegory initiates the work of renarrativization that Behn carries forward, with each writer struggling to identify the form or forms for representing experience when the sacramental order no longer holds. The need to locate grace in the word and words of other people shapes both writers' work. Unlike Bunyan, whose implicit critique of the Bible's authority (his doubt, expressed through exegetical compulsion, that it tells us all that we need to know) is balanced against his confidence that the believer has final recourse to God. In colonial Suriname, Oroonoko cannot look up to God as an arbiter of character. Oroonoko's own relation to Christian typology, which swings between replication and parody, makes this point most vividly. His strained Christomimesis similarly bespeaks the incomprehensibility of the Atlantic slave narrative in the terms of Christian myth, indicting the anti-Christian character of plantation capitalism more than it argues for the insufficiency of Christianity as an explanatory frame.

Against Type: Christianity, Islam, Slavery

Aubin's *The Noble Slaves* appears, at first glance, as a foil to *Oroonoko*, erecting rigid taxonomies of readers and characters. The preface of *The Noble Slaves* conjures types of bad readers, a chorus of malign dispositions against which to define the novel's aim of coordinating entertainment with religious edification: "Methinks now I see the Atheist grin, the modish Wit laugh out, and the old Letcher and the young Debauchee sneer, and throw by the book; and all join to decry it" (xi). Aubin wears their denunciation as a badge of honor; her book's projective unfashionableness indicates its moral superiority to contemporary fictions and the sorts of people who read them. In this section, I present reasons to question this adversarial posturing. When viewed through the prism of religious typology, Aubin's work looks more like popular early and midcentury novels than their reactionary antithesis. I would also stress that Aubin organizes readers and genres in much the same way that she structures her vision of the early eighteenth-century Mediterranean. In the preface she lays out a simple character scheme, setting "we Christians" against "the Infidels, or Mahometans" (58). Adam R. Beach writes that Aubin's prefatory comments introduce a "dogged anti-absolutist and anti-Islamic agenda," departing from the enlightenment discourse of "Islamic republicanism," which described Islam in more favorable, deistic terms.[35] Aubin makes generalizations about "Mahometans" in the body of the text as well, often treating ethnicities gathered under the aegis of the Ottoman Empire as continuous or interchangeable. In one of several scenes of erotic appraisal of Christian women, for instance, Muley Arab, "son of the Emperor of Fez and Morocco," illustrates the moral nature of the "Moorish Nobility, and indeed the whole Nation," who are "much inclin'd to Love, very amorous and gallant" (*NS*, 107). The remarks illustrate Aubin's tendency to conflate the national and ethnic classifications affiliated by their shared faith, Islam, in the service of creating a comprehensive religious type. "Moorish" rather than "Moroccan" modifies "Nation," making Muley Arab an exemplary "Moor," a term initially applied to Muslim inhabitants of Maghreb and by this time to people from the Arabian Peninsula, North Africa, and Western Asia.

Intercultural relations in the novel, while ostensibly conflictual and often violent, evidence that Aubin's religious characterology is less "simplistic" than either Beach or her own front matter suggests.[36] The two organizing types in *The Noble Slaves*, virtuous European Christian and vicious Muslim, are separated by a porous boundary. Daniel O'Quinn has recently explored the representational disturbances, which he labels "vexed mediations," produced when eighteenth-century European diplomats and artists attempted to represent the Ottoman Empire in print or visual media.[37] O'Quinn argues that "representational discord" results from challenges inherent in capturing their subject, as well as from mediation through "European practices and expectations."[38] Discord in *The Noble Slaves*, which represents less a historical state or system of faith than a religious archetype, has a different cause. It arises from the superficiality and susceptibility of the character of Islam, its tendency to be subsumed or inhabited—even put on like a costume—by Christians.

What's more, *The Noble Slaves* imagines a third, racialized subject position askew of the dyadic conflict presented in the "Preface." "Blackamoor Slaves," people of sub-Saharan African descent like Domingo and Attabala, profess Christianity, and they are treated with less overt hostility than are "Moorish" Muslims (*NS*, 6). The entrenched division between black and Ottoman characters distinguishes Aubin's race-thinking from early eighteenth-century trends. Felicity Nussbaum observes the conflation of blackness and Islam in the Earl of Shaftesbury's formulation of the dangerous fantasy that circulates with the first serials of *The Arabian Nights* in 1711. Shaftesbury fears that "England's daughters would imitate Desdemona in succumbing to the enchantment and tales of seduction wrought by Othello," associating "the African man [Othello] and Eastern woman [*The Arabian Night*'s Sheherazade]" through the "sexual threat of blackness and interracial union."[39] Against this tendency, which Nussbaum tracks through several French and English translations of *The Arabian Nights*, Aubin preserves the distinction between "Oriental" and black subjects. The former category may be admitted to Christianity alongside white Europeans in Aubin's vision of global Christian polity, whereas, in the cases of Domingo and Attabala, racial difference supersedes religious affiliation.

Conjugal Conversion and "Religious Disguise"

The organization of *The Noble Slaves* mirrors the novel's fronted logic of type. Eve Taylor Bannet explores Aubin's use of the structure of romance, which introduces multiple characters who go on to narrate their own histories.[40] While Bannet argues that this narrative structure broadens the representation of women's experiences of the psychosexual trauma of slavery, Aparna Gollapudi sees not variety but reiteration. Aubin's fiction, according to Gollapurdi, tends to follow an "ur-plot" that in turn hinges on the character type of "the chaste heroine."[41] This type is "afflicted with various mishaps such as kidnappings by robbers, shipwrecks resulting in being stranded on desert islands, confinement by lustful Oriental potentates or ruthless pirates, great deprivation, and constant assaults on her virtue. Through these calamities the heroine remains firmly virtuous and retains faith in the wisdom of God's Providence. In the end she is, of course, delivered from her troubles."[42] As Gollapudi suggests, the eminent consistency of Aubin's chaste heroine, rather than varieties of experience of sexual slavery, comes into view when we center Aubin's use of the form of romance. But the formulaic quality of her narrative(s) belies the surprising pliability of one of its key variables, the "lustful Oriental potentate." *The Noble Slaves* acknowledges the possibility that the latter figure will bend to the rigidity of the chaste heroine and cross the barrier separating Christendom from the Ottoman world.

The interpolated story of Tanganor, the only Ottoman character to narrate his own history, exemplifies this religio-cultural fluidity. A distinguished Persian soldier in the service of the Emperor, Tanganor falls in love with one of Aubin's chaste heroines, Maria, an enslaved Spanish lady. Maria rejects Tanganor's sexual advances on the basis of the difference of their faiths, stating the case plainly: "You . . . are an odious Mahometan, and I am a Christian" (*NS*, 28). But, when he treats her well, almost "as if I had been her Slave," Maria agrees to marry Tanganor on the condition that he "turn Christian" (29). Gollapudi compares their relationship to a passage in Aubin's *Count de Vinevil*, published one year earlier, to show how consistently Aubin imagined sex as a strategy of "the imperial missionary agenda."[43] In it, a priest exculpates Violetta for yielding to her master, a Turk, because "it might have been a Means of his Conversion."[44] The missionary enterprise licenses both marriage and sex across culture, while "Maria is constructed by Aubin as a warrior in the ideological crusade against the heathen, ignorant, immoral East."[45] Like Violetta, she wields her desirability as a weapon and practices the "feminine counterpart of conquest, conversion."[46] But Tanganor's easy conversion to Christianity softens the militancy of this construction. Intercultural marriage no doubt serves Christian supremacy, contrasting Tanganor's susceptibility to Maria's implacable virtue, but it also indicates that Muslims may be reformed and admitted to the category of the Christian.

While Tanganor's conversion attests to the malleability of Islamic character under Christian sexual influence, cross-dressing by several of Aubin's Europeans shows its superficiality. On the run from the forces of Muley Arab, Emilia and Teresa encounter a European Christian living as a hermit in the foothills of the Atlas Mountains. The hermit explains that he has survived by adopting a "religious Disguise": "I pass for a religious Man, a Hermit, the people reverence me as I pass. . . . I am call'd *Ismael*, the Holy Hermit" (*NS*, 141). "Ismael" lives undetected in the borderland of Numidia, "passing" for an Islamic ascetic by donning the dress associated with that character. Emilia and Teresa adopt the same disguise, and with the same effect. As the ladies depart, "the poor Villagers having conceiv'd a high Opinion of their Sanctity, accompany'd them on the Road a great way, praying the good Dervises [*sic*] welfare, as they call'd them" (165). Emilia and Teresa inhabit the character of dervishes, a Sufi Muslim order renowned for austerity, simply by appropriating their "Habit," or manner of dress.

Their clothes, which Aubin does not describe particularly, signify independently of somatic markers like skin color. When Tanganor disguises himself as an enslaved sub-Saharan African in order to elude the emperor's surveillance, he "black'd my Face and Hands and changed my Dress" (*NS*, 30). Neither the hermit nor the ladies perform in blackface, however, which suggests that dress alone suffices to determine the villager's collective "opinion" of their shared, sanctified character. This, despite Teresa and Emilia's superlative whiteness. "They are the fairest Creatures my eyes ever saw," a subordinate reports to Muley Arab (104). Their disguises are consistent with those assumed by their husbands, Don Lopez and Count de Hautville, as the men navigate cosmopolitan Algiers. Don Lopez and Count de Hautville "drest themselves in the habit of Grecian Merchants, which Habits *Attabala* bought for them at the City, and both speaking Greak [*sic*], they doubted not to pass for such if question'd. Thus meta-morphosed, they went daily out" (75). The men transform themselves by adopting ethnic dress, with language serving as an additional layer of dis-guise. Emilia and Teresa don't speak Ottoman Turkish, as far as we know, but they, too, manage the fungible external signs of dress, overriding any physical indices of their true identities as European Christians and hint-ing that, in *The Noble Slaves,* religion is a cultural and not a racial cate-gory of difference. Clothes are what effectively separate members of an Islamic religious order from Catholic ladies of Spanish and French origin. That their disguises impose on a shipwrecked European nobleman—he mistakes Emilia for a male "Turk" (167)—suggests that Aubin means to emphasize the flatness of Islamic character, its composition by change-able outward signs, rather than the credulity of the Numidian villagers who reverence the hermit and the ladies.

Emilia and Teresa's disguise shows Aubin's religious typology to be flex-ible—without undermining her Christian-dominionist ideology. Emilia enforces the Christianity-Islam divide early in the novel, explicitly framing her violent resistance of the Ottoman Governor of Algiers as religiously motivated. "I'll sacrifice you to preserve my Vertue," she declares. "Die Infi-del, and tell your blasphemous Prophet, when you come to Hell, a Christian spilt your Blood" (*NS,* 48). More than Maria, Emilia sounds like a crusader, and she backs up her speech by stabbing the Governor with his own dag-ger.[47] The success of Emilia's cross-dressing, though, confirms that at least one of the terms of opposition that the preface introduces and that Emilia upholds with violence is culturally constructed rather than absolute. "We Christians" may assume the character of "Infidel or Mahometan"—even one of its most notoriously devout forms—by manipulating the signifiers of dress. This movement across the two structuring characters of the novel mirrors the movement within it, illustrated by Don Lopez and Count de Hautville's "metamorphosis" from one of the ethnonational designations (Spanish or French Catholic) housed within the broad classificatory term of Euro-Christian for another (Greek).

Yet Aubin's religious types ultimately carry unequal representational weight. "Christian" refers to a substantive and, often, strikingly active moral character anchored in providentialism, reiterated by the romantic structure of *The Noble Slaves* (through the consistency of, and between, paragons like Emila and Maria), and mapped across national and sectarian divisions within Christendom. "Mahometan" loosely confederates the ethnic identities "Turk," "Moor," "Arabian," and "Persian" under Islam. To what kind of character do *its* cultural markers refer? The habit of the Sufi ascetic accurately signifies "sanctity," but it is the sanctity of true-believing Christians who have appropriated that manner of dress as their disguise. In the preface, Aubin defines the ethical content of "Mahometan" character. "Turks and Moors have ever been famous," she remarks, for the "cruelties of slavery," and in their territories "the Monarch gives a loose to his Passions, and thinks it no Crime to keep as many Women for his Use, as his lustful appetite excites him to like; and his Favourites, Ministers of State, and Governors, who always follow their Master's example, imitate his way of living" (*NS*, x). Tanganor directly contradicts much of this description. While motivated by "Passions," Tanganor subordinates them to Maria's will and eventually defies his sovereign's example and orders, abandoning Islam for Christianity and the seraglio for monogamous coupledom.

Aubin also writes Muslim characters who operate outside of this top-down moral-religious typology before or without converting to Christianity. Tomaso and his wife, Seraja, rescue the Venetian slave Antonio by purchasing him from a particularly cruel master, a Jewish merchant of Algiers. In contrast to the Jewish merchant and his Portuguese wife, "the good Tomaso" and Seraja behave toward Antonio "as if I had been their own Child"—and while Seraja converts to Christianity after her husband passes, Tomaso himself dies both a Muslim and a "good Man" (*NS*, 125). Too few, by far, to countervail the novel's overwhelmingly anti-Islamic sentiment, these counterexamples nevertheless complicate the representation of Islam in *The Noble Slaves* and undermine the text's dualism. Aubin's characterization of Tanganor, Tomaso, and Seraja, together with her depiction of cultural cross-dressing, divide the sign and signified or, borrowing the language of *Oroonoko's* narrator, the name and the moral substance, of religion. Rather than indicate a homogenous religious and moral type, "Mahometan" comprehends different moral dispositions. And, as we've observed, this character may be shed for that of convert or strategically performed by Christians.

Semiotics of religious character in *The Noble Slaves* extend Christianity's global reach. Elizabeth S. Kim has argued for Aubin's Christian ecumenism, which erases or overrules denominational difference.[48] Indeed, *The Noble Slaves* promotes a nonsectarian, pan-European Christianity. While many of Aubin's readers were, like her, Anglican Protestants, her chaste heroines and valorous lords hail from Spain, Venice, and France, and their ranks include Roman Catholics and Huguenots.[49] Kim proposes that Aubin's ecumenical instinct serves her bifurcated imaginary, with Christianity consolidating in the face of the existential threat of Islamic aggression. But Christian belonging extends further still, beyond Europe. "We Christians," the group addressed by Aubin's preface, is defined partly through identification with the exemplary virtue of European noblewomen and partly through juxtaposition to the Islamic type. Because this latter category is culturally constructed, however, it proves assimilable by the Christian collective. The concomitant plasticity of Christianness strengthens Christian hegemony, positing that its greatest imperial rival may be contained within its own, ever-expanding perimeter, and specifically through the missionary sexuality of its female paragons.

"Not Fit to Enter Her Bed": Domingo's Absolute Alterity

Instances of conversion and cross-dressing in *The Noble Slaves* indicate that Aubin's main typology is religious, not racial. This is not to say that Aubin's work is unconcerned with race, however. Geraldine Heng hypothesizes that race comprises varied, historically particular ways of articulating fundamental and absolute difference, including, among other examples, "religious race" and the conventional synonymy of race and skin color.[50] At times, these forms overlap or entangle—we might think, for example, of Bunyan's *The Holy War*, which inscribes errant theology on the physiognomy of Diabolonians. In the following section, I consider Aubin's black characters, whose representation indicates that religious and racial difference remain discrete in *The Noble Slaves*. While the former religious difference is constructed and inhabitable, the latter is inscribed on the flesh. Interspersed with chaste heroines and the Ottoman potentates who persecute them are characters whose skin color embodies their essential otherness. Aubin's black characters do not enjoy the transcultural possibilities of sexual desire, as Tanganor does, nor do they partake of the character of Christianity despite professing that faith. These characters stand astride the governing binary logic of the novel, revealing the complex negotiations required to mount a religious critique of Islamic sexual slavery in the Ottoman world without acknowledging British dependence on the Atlantic slave trade and chattel slavery throughout its domains.

Aubin represents the Pacific world with geographical and cultural imprecision, but the picture becomes clearer when her narrative turns to the character of enslaved black people.[51] Domingo, enslaved by the Spanish governor of Mexico and identified as a "Blackmore," rescues the governor's daughter, Teresa, from a shipwreck off the colony's Western coast (*NS*, 3). Domingo's initial characterization shows inattention to the specificity of ethnoracial designations. Stranded on a "desolate Island," Teresa and Domingo encounter an "old *Indian* Man" and his family. Domingo exhibits striking facility in communicating with their hosts: "The *Black* who was skill'd in them, by Signs inform'd him of their Distress. The *Indian* who proved a *Japanese,* cast on Shore there, with his Wife and three Children, in the *Chinese* Language invited them to his Home: The *Moor* understood him, and informing his Lady, they went" (4). Aubin provides no explanation for Domingo's linguistic legerdemain, his fluency with nonverbal signs and comprehension of the "Chinese language," instead implying inborn, mutual comprehensibility between Europe's others—be they castaways from Japan or enslaved Africans—and, with that natural sociability, cultural continuity across national and ethnic divisions. Aubin also reverts to the umbrella ethnic term for Ottoman subjects, "moor," to describe Domingo. She uses the term twice in this paragraph to identify him, along with "the Black," briefly suggesting that the earlier designation "Blackmore Slave" may reiterate Ottoman identity, the way that "Turk," "Arabian," and

"Persian" do elsewhere in the novel. When Domingo expresses a fatal desire for Teresa, however, Aubin's terms stabilize.

Epidermal race, unlike the difference of faith that obtains between Maria and Tanganor, acts as a barrier to erotic connection. One morning, as they walk unguided to a remote part of their island, Teresa and Domingo come upon a dense wood. The ensuing scene deploys elements of the myth of original sin within an assertion of absolute difference between "the Black" and the Spanish lady he loves.

> There *Domingo* espy'd a Tree with Fruit he had never seen before, not unlike a European Pear; he boldly ventured to gather, and taste it, tho Teresa warn'd him to forbear tasting it till they had shewn it to the Indian: He eat two of them, putting more in his Pocket; and in a few Minutes after found himself sick, and began to vomit. They hasten'd to return home; but before they could reach half way, he fell down, and embracing his Lady's Knees, cry'd, "Farewel my dear Mistress; may God, to the Knowledge of whom your dear Father brought me, keep you, and deliver you hence; comfort you when I am gone, and have Mercy upon the Soul of your poor Slave. Remember me, charming *Teresa;* my Soul ador'd you, but Christianity restrain'd me from asking what my amorous Soul languished to possess. I brought you to the Wood with Thoughts my Soul now sinks at. I was born free as you, and thought I might with Honour ask your Love, since Heaven had singled me out to save your Life, and live your only Companion and Defender; but God has thought fit to disappoint me. May no other rob you of that Treasure which I no longer can protect." (*NS*, 6–7)

As an allusion to Genesis, Domingo's consumption of the poisonous fruit invites comparisons between him and the biblical Eve. Both characters sin through presumption, Eve aspiring to godhead and Domingo to reciprocal love with his mistress. Domingo narrates the fatal shift in perspective that leads him to transgress the social distance between them. His Christian faith, inculcated by Teresa's father, the governor, initially "restrain'd" him from declaring his passion. Another, errant line of thought releases him: Domingo comes to see his asking—only in the abstract, as he's prevented from proceeding from "thought" to speech— as consistent with his religious instruction. His explicit reasoning is that their circumstances serve as a providential warrant for giving voice to his desire, God having "singled" him out for Teresa's "companion and defender" in an otherwise isolated existence. He, thus, misapplies the concept of particular providence, the only specific theological content that Aubin assigns to Christianity.[52]

Domingo's intention reflects a further, half-articulated misapprehension—that exchanging the colonial context of Mexico for an island approximation of the state of nature levels him with Teresa. He says only that "I was born as free as you," but the implication is that the shipwreck has restored him to this natural condition of liberty. Although Domingo acknowledges God's role in thwarting his desire—"God has thought fit to disappoint me"—and, thus, hints at a perception of divine justice operating through his death, it is Teresa's reaction that clarifies why heaven has intervened. Teresa "was shock'd, she was even ready to follow him [into death]; the Generosity and Love he had shewn, the desolate Condition she was left in, distracted her; yet she could not but applaud the Goodness of God, who had so wonderfully prevented her Ruin; for tho he had a Soul fair as his Face was black, yet *Domingo,* her Father's Slave, was not fit to enter her Bed" (*NS,* 7). God smites Domingo to prevent Teresa's "ruin," the ubiquitous term for women's sexual fallenness. Here, ruin consists of sex with an unsuitable partner. (The question of Teresa's consent is moot; Domingo's "asking" for her love is tantamount to his "entering her bed," as though his gratification were inevitable, regardless of her answer. Even to hear the question posed would ruin Teresa.) Domingo is "not fit" as an erotic partner because of his class position, which carries over from the hierarchy of Spain's Central American colony to their island wild. He remains "her Father's Slave" even outside of the social and economic structures that give this relation meaning. In this way, Domingo contrasts sharply with the novel's titular type, the "noble slave." Providence delivers white Europeans—French, Spanish, and Italian nobles—who epitomize this designation from sexual slavery (for women) or indefinite incarceration (for men).

Although casually rather than causally related to his black skin, Domingo's intractable "slave" character functions racially—that is, as a category of essential difference. The kind of absolute alterity that defines race becomes legible in Aubin's novel as potential for conversion. That potential, in turn, manifests as eligibility for intermarriage. The contrast between Domingo and Tanganor is instructive here. When viewed from within the Christianity that Aubin espouses, Tanganor and other nominally Muslim characters appear in an important respect to be *elected*, destined for Christianity by their virtue. The same moral content of character that distinguishes such characters as eligible for intermarriage marks them out as latent Christians. Domingo, meanwhile, is "unfit" for erotic relations, a condition as fixed and irremediable as his social position as an enslaved person. Moreover, Aubin ties his exclusion from conjugal conversion—from her "elect" Others—to his racial blackness, albeit indirectly.

The compound-complex sentence that explains why Teresa celebrates Domingo's death suspends blackness and slaveness in a kind of nonlogical grammatical proximity. "Tho he had a Soul fair as his Face was black, yet *Domingo,* her Father's Slave, was not fit to enter her Bed," Aubin's narrator remarks by way of vindicating God's "goodness" and Teresa's sexual propriety. Two contrasts operate here, setting off first Domingo's black skin from his white soul and then his purity of spirit from his erotic unviability. The latter measure of difference, enforced by no less than divine authority, bears no evident causal relationship to Domingo's skin color. An appositive phrase does the work of establishing causation: he is not a suitable sexual partner because he is "her Father's Slave." Generally, the stigma of having been enslaved—even for women subjected to Islamic sexual exploitation—tends not to attach to characters in Aubin's writings. Gollapudi surveys Aubin's major works of fiction and observes that "ravished virgins" easily reintegrate into European society alongside other formerly enslaved Christians.[53] Why, then, does Domingo's character qua social positionality remain entrenched despite the change in material conditions that attends the shipwreck, his sincere profession of Christianity, and his unblemished soul? The reference to skin color in the opening clause of the sentence functions not only to highlight the purity of Domingo's soul but also to recall the subject position named at the beginning of this episode of the novel: "Blackamoor Slave." This phrase equates epidermal race and social position, fixing Domingo to the status of slave despite his reasoned pretension to a natural right to liberty.

Attabala's House

Aubin insists that enslavement is a permanent condition or fixed character, but she refuses to imagine the material conditions of European slavery. We aren't apprised of the role Domingo plays in the economy of the governor's estate. We know only that he numbers one of the "attendants" on Teresa's pleasure cruise (NS, 3). On the island, he "range[s] about, hoping to discover Something worth his Labour" (5); in a departure from the plantation-capitalist system, Domingo determines the value of his own labor. Attabala, the other enslaved black character in *The Noble Slaves*, likewise stands in ambiguous relation to the institution of slavery. Attabala was the Venetian lady Eleanora's enslaved domestic servant, a "young *Black* whom her Father had purchased when a Child, of a Captain, and given her" (58). By the time we meet him, though, Attabala has been liberated at Eleanora's request. He now moves freely in contrast to the still-incarcerated Eleanora, but he exercises this autonomy exclusively in her service. In the brief section that follows, I analyze, first, the layering of agency and instrumentalization in Aubin's representation of Attabala and, second, the literal and metaphorical space that Attabala inhabits in the novel. Together, Attabala's voluntarily circumscribed agency and his liminal position in Algerian society reveal the strain of Aubin's effort to critique Islamic slavery without addressing the Christian equivalent.

Attabala exercises a surprising degree of self-determination, evident in the way he drives the plot of this section of the novel and helps the titular "noble slaves" liberate themselves and return to Europe. When Eleanora formulates a plan to escape with Don Lopez and Count de Hautville, it is Attabala who brings them "Files to take off their Fetters, and Disguises to put on to prevent all Discovery" (*NS*, 58). It is Attabala who arranges their passage from Algiers to Venice and delegates tasks to servants, including one whom he has "bred up and made a Christian in secret" (151). The narrator does not otherwise mention religion and Attabala together; his association with Christianity fits the broader trend in his characterization. While it's fair to assume that he professes the same faith in which he educates the *"Turkish* boy," Abra, the fact which takes narrative precedence is Attabala's function as a vehicle for strategic conversion of a Muslim character to the Christian side (150). Combined with Domingo's more explicit exclusion from the erotic relation that reveals the potential for conversion, this privileging of Attabala's usefulness shows that only nominal Christian affiliation is available to black characters.

Attabala's house functions metaphorically to reinforce his social position. Technically, he serves as steward of the Algerian governor's seaside estate, but the narrator consistently refers to the place and the people associated with it in ways that denote ownership or authority. It is *"Attabala's* House" (*NS,* 143, 144, 150); a safe haven for *"Attabala's* Guests" (144); attended by *"Attabala's* servant" (148). It is a site of Christian communion in the heart of Ottoman North Africa—two additional couples, Monsieur de Chateau-Roial and Clarinda and Anna and Antonio, join Eleanora, Don Lopez, and Count de Hautville there—creating the conditions for affiliation across parochial borders: "They all resolved to go away together from *Barbary,* the first Opportunity after *Teresa* and *Emilia* were found; for now such an intire Friendship was contracted betwixt these unfortunate Persons, that not one of them would consent to abandon the rest, till all could be happy together. Villainy and base Designs often unite Men for a time, but end generally in their Ruin, and Hatred to one another; but when Religion, and vertuous noble Designs are the basis of Mens Friendships, they are lasting and successful" (*NS,* 126). "Religion," here, collapses denominational divisions (Anna is a Huguenot; the rest of the party are adherents to Roman Catholicism) and provides the foundation of enduring, "successful" friendship between people from Spain, France, and Venice. The consolidation of liberalized Christianity is possible only at Attabala's house, which is remote from Ottoman authority by virtue of its geographical situation and its peculiar association with a legally free black person. Attabala doesn't own the house as private property; it falls into his hands temporarily, at first, because the governor, Selim, does not use it during the winter season, and then indefinitely, when Selim dies at the head of the Ottoman army in Morocco. To the extent that Aubin can imagine black property, it takes the form of precarious, contingent ownership—and it can be appropriated readily by white Europeans. Rather than contradict the pattern of grammatical possession in the way Aubin writes about Attabala and the home, this extralegal form of ownership clarifies the relationship between the agent and the object. "Attabala's House" *belongs* to him as an attribute rather than legal property, a feature of his character: his inexhaustible capacity for service, represented spatially.

Just as Attabala's house insulates Christian fellowship from Ottoman authority, the character of Attabala preserves *The Noble Slaves*'s conceptual demarcation between Christianity and Islam. Aubin depicts Attabala as suspended, perpetually, between slavery and voluntary servitude. He joins Eleanora and her coalition of white European nobles on their Mediterranean crossing, and, once in Venice, he is "much caress'd for his faithful Service to his Lady" (178). What is his legal status now that he has returned to Christian territories, having been freed in Barbary? Does he choose to continue serving Eleanora? The narrator evades these questions, ending Attabala's arc with a reiteration of his function as a fact independent of the issue of volition. Thus does Aubin acknowledge a subject position that would otherwise subvert her structuring typology, which depends on two religious cultures' antithetical relationships to slavery. To Christians, "the notion of slavery is a perfect Stranger," incompatible with their values and inconceivable outside of the horrors of Islamic sexual slavery (ix).

Aubin participates in this estrangement, not only by exoticizing slavery, focusing on Ottoman enslavement of white Europeans, but also through her characterization of the black Christians Domingo and Attabala. She acknowledges their presence, their moral rectitude, and, up to a point, their coreligiosity. At the same time, Aubin asserts their essential difference and introduces considerable ambiguity around their personal agency. And she abstracts Domingo and Attabala from the specific historical violences—the African slave trade and plantation capitalism—that would implicate Western European states named in the novel, and Britain with them, in the horrors of an institution she takes pains to identify with Islamic cruelty. The result is a fictional representation of enslaved black people without slavery.

Behn, Aubin, and Secularization Stories

Points of strain in Behn's and Aubin's religious typologies shed new light on the relationship of their fiction to the secularization stories in literary criticism. We might describe Behn's viewpoint as secular, though not because she presents a desacralized world. *Oroonoko* describes colonial Suriname as a world in which the sacramental order no longer holds, but in that respect the text carries forward the renarrativization initiated by the doctrinally orthodox Bunyan. Nor does *Oroonoko* contribute to the secularizing premise of English literary freethinkers, who, according to Ellenzweig, upheld the Anglican hegemon as a guarantor of order and pointedly not as a belief system. This surprisingly conservative movement rejected Christianity as a divine truth but reinvested in its forms of worship and its social arrangements; proponents imagine Christianity as a justificatory logic, a set of fables and propositions that legitimate social hierarchy and state control.[54] The affective, providentialist orientation of Oroonoko's Calvinistic "faith" militates against the freethinker designation. Behn's novel is *secular,* rather, to the extent that it subordinates theological specificity to the intensity of belief and to the epistemological potential of different religious concepts. *Oroonoko* contributes to the loosening of doctrinal orthodoxy and institutional propriety, which would become more pronounced in the novels of the ensuing decades, including, paradoxically, through the anti-Islamic politics of Aubin's *The Noble Slaves.*

Aubin, too, has been identified with either/or conflict between religion and secularity. Unlike Behn, however, she is usually assigned the reactionary role. John Richetti sees her as a Christian-moral polemicist and, as such, a foil to the male tradition of the early novel. Whereas male novelists deployed the language of providentialism to sanitize the "daemonic secular spirit" of capitalism, Richetti argues, Aubin uses the ostensibly secular genre of travel fiction to make her program of religious and moral reform more appealing to readers: "As a result, the pleasures of travel through the exotic and the marvelous and of observing providential deliverance from the huge disasters attendant upon such rare experience are delivered free of disturbing secular implications: the heroes and heroines of Mrs. Aubin's novels are untainted by the daemonic secular spirit to survive and prosper."[55] Gollapudi takes issue with the way Richetti effaces the specificity of the female fictional traveler, who must answer to different ideological imperatives than the male traveler.[56] By reasoning from the prior conviction that Christian moralism and secularist energy are opposed, Richetti also misses the feature of Aubin's religious thought that aligns her with rather than positions her against the early novel tradition: her thoroughgoing commitment to secularization as liberalization, to an expansive, imperious Christianity constructed in part through the plasticity of her overarching typology.

One of the narratives exchanged at Attabala's house clarifies further how providentialism and ecumenicism reinforce each other in Aubin's theology and also foreshadows the gradual deemphasis on systematicity in fiction by nominally Anglo-Protestant authors. Monsieur de Chateau-Roial, a French Catholic priest who lives outside of orders, relates his own tale of "sacrilege" (NS, 83). He seduces the novice Clarinda from her path to becoming a nun and then, to fund their escape to Protestant territories, pilfers a reliquary. After swapping the valuable gems from relics for counterfeit stones, the couple board a ship to England. Thoughts of that country inspire Monsieur de Chateau-Roial with a tolerationist fantasy:

> I fancy'd my self going to a Country where I should rather be applauded than condemn'd for what I had done, where I should be free in all respects; and tho I never had a thought to change my Religion, yet I fancy'd I should be extreme happy in a place where I should live free from all Constraint: But God, whom I had offended, soon convinced me of my Folly. An Algerine Pirate met us, and after a sharp dispute took the ship, and made us all Prisoners, carrying us into Tunis, where he sold us for Slaves. (85)

His "folly" is in believing that he may "live free of all constraint"—not necessarily because England fails to live up to his romanticized notions of religious liberty (though a long history of anti-Catholicism, if not Aubin herself, would contradict that impression). Monsieur de Chateau-Roial instead errs in imagining himself outside of the bounds of individual conscience, not to be confused with the political good of religious freedom. His "offense" consists in a betrayal of his own religious values; Monsieur de Chateau-Roial "never had a thought to change my Religion," yet he pleases himself with the thought of "applause" for his profanation of objects invested, according to his Catholic faith, with sacramental meaning. The Algerian pirates who capture the ship and sell the couple into slavery in Tunis are vehicles of divine judgment and correction. Monsieur de Chateau-Roial, misled by passion in the moment, interprets his misfortune as a punitive reminder that "in me this was Sacrilege, and a great Crime," even if it would not be so in a Protestant denizen of Holland or England (83).

Through his retrospective, repentant narrative, Aubin indicates that providence enforces self-consistency, adherence to one's self-determined religious character. It is not that she herself believes in the sacramental meaning of the objects in the reliquary, nor that she endorses Catholic prohibitions or practices. Aubin suborns these norms and the doctrines upon which they are founded to a characterological value—authenticity—that extends religious culture beyond sectarian divisions, in this case between Franco-Catholic and Anglo-Protestant. She thus protects the integrity of the several theological systems in play; Monsieur de Chateau-Roial is accountable for violating specifically Catholic prohibitions. This violation is entangled with Aubin's concern over the violation of the legal norms of property ownership, hinting at the coconstitutive relationship between secularism and liberal ideology. The Monsieur believes that his title to the gems might extend from his rejection of Catholic idolatry and reliquary-fetishism, but in acting on this belief he breaks the law. Aubin holds open both the Monsieur's own interpretation that his failure to remain authentic to his confession (Catholicism) provokes providential judgement and the reading that God is really punishing him for theft, for a violation of the legal, liberal norm of ownership. This final example of the loosening of doctrinal orthodoxy in *The Noble Slaves* thus points forward to midcentury novels by Fielding and Sterne, which, as I explore in my next chapter, press doctrinal latitude further and underscore the relationship between secularism and liberalism.

3

Novels and the Nova Effect

T HE FOLLOWING CHAPTER RELATES Fielding and Sterne's methods of characterization to the shape of their religious thought. These authors inhabit a particular moment in the revisionist history of secularization that I am tracking in this book, a moment marked by what we might describe as religion's redistribution within a pluralized marketplace of belief. Both advance the understanding of religion not as a set of doctrines but as a field of possibilities that must be prioritized and rearranged continually, according to the shifting conditions of fallenness. What Talal Asad sees in the liberalization of Islam and John Lardas Modern sees in the harmony of private faith and public reason in the antebellum United States also comes into focus through the instability of fictional characters in novels by Fielding and Sterne.[1] Like Behn's and Aubin's, their writings enact religion's unbinding from singular doctrinal propriety. Sterne and Fielding take this secularist project further, however. Whereas *Oroonoko* and *The Noble Slaves* extricate Calvinism's model of character from its original theological and ecclesiastical milieu and use it as the overarching frame for their exploration of the conditions of racialized empire, showing doctrinal latitude, the works under examination here promote a more pluralistic idea of religion. *Tom Jones, Amelia,* and *Tristram Shandy* reintroduce Calvinist semiotics as one fragilized option among many. The transition between these two chapters, then, marks a distinct intensification of secularist antiorthodoxy. Though it has not, by the eighteenth-century, come to call itself "secularity," the form of liberalized Protestantism these novels espouse closely resembles the liberal-secular order of the present day.

Fielding's religious thought proves responsive to pressures of fallen experience—the imperatives to see through hypocrites or cancel the threat of indeterminacy posed by sexual desire, for example—precisely because he is not in the thrall of any one theology. Taken individually, concepts like Calvinist selfhood and matrimonial character-sharing make for precarious objects of belief. They are contingent, their integrity and their applications regarded by author and character alike with skepticism. Taken together, however, the disparate religious ideas in Fielding's writings comprise a comprehensive and self-reflexive system of meaning. They provide a framework through which to understand the problematics of character as well as a vocabulary of self-interrogation, a means for Fielding to identify and check the deficiencies of his own provisional solutions. For Fielding, this corporate, resilient religiosity is the horizon of mutual fragilization, the phenomenon that Charles Taylor calls the "nova effect."[2] While Fielding's novels are keyed primarily to the personal and social benefits of antiorthodoxy, they also provide glimpses of the way antiorthodoxy can reinforce racial and sexual hierarchies. They hint at something that *Tristram Shandy* makes plain: the disciplinary valence of this midcentury formation of the secular.

Sterne, like Fielding, represents religion's release from singular doctrinal orthodoxy, but he claims its epistemological and moral advantages for "centrist" Anglicanism.[3] Sterne's novel presents a formal corollary of secularist distinction, a theory of literary and personal character defined against the comically presumptuous, dogmatic beliefs of Predestinarian Calvinism. Calvinism serves a dual role in *Tristram Shandy,* acting as a satirical butt and a technology of secular self-legitimation. Through he doesn't name Calvinist characterology, specifically, Tristram's methodological self-reflections parody the two pillars of that system: the ideal of semiotic congruence, and the conviction that character is shaped by deterministic forces beyond the individual's control. Considered by itself, Calvinism is bad belief, a rigid paradigm that underlines Sterne's more flexible compositional practice and the relativist religious epistemology it mirrors. Yet Calvinism can also serve Sterne's project when it is integrated within the open system of character that *Tristram Shandy* promotes and performs. Thus liberalized, the Calvinist model provides the literary language in which to describe the shortcomings of Catholic and Islamic theories of conscience and to recruit the sympathies of readers to the Anglican-Protestant cause. Through form as well as argument, Sterne advocates a form of religious pluralism that carries within it a universalizing conception of virtue, narrowing the acceptable practices of piety to those of a generalized, monolithic Protestantism.

Secular Fielding

In this section, I correlate properties of Fielding's fiction that previous scholarship has obscured: the elasticity of his religious thought and the complexity of his characters. Criticism that engages directly with the role of religion in his novels alternates between poles of, as Richard A. Rosengarten puts it, "valorization" and "denial."[4] Fielding either champions or critiques a Christian view, which refers, narrowly, to the vision of a providentially directed creation. Martin C. Battestin makes the case for positive religious conviction.[5] He argues that Fielding renders into narrative form Latitudinarian emphases on the wisdom and benevolence of providence. Battestin's critics, including C. J. Rawson and J. Paul Hunter, demur from this picture of order, calling attention to ambiguity, irony, and self-contradiction in the novels.[6] For Leopold Damrosch Jr., unresolved tension between imperatives to "mirror the benevolence of divine Providence" and to "describe reality mimetically" index a wider phenomenon "by which fiction finally broke free from myth, establishing its own reality over and against the religious structure which had once provided the sure foundation of all experience."[7] Put another way, Fielding's works prove an aesthetic corollary to the mainline secularization thesis, which presumes the extirpation or marginalization of religion as a precondition for modernity.[8] In fact, whether they describe Fielding as dogmatic or diffident, scholars deploy a key element of the secularization thesis; they define religion as a systematizing perspective to be affirmed or denied absolutely.[9]

While both sides of the debate about Fielding's religiosity rearticulate the secularization thesis, the consensus about his superficial approach to character testifies to the enduring legacy of its undergirding logic of disenchantment. Samuel Johnson famously remarked that "Richardson picked the kernel of life . . . while Fielding was contented with the husk."[10] Beginning with Ian Watt, modern critics have elaborated on Johnson's comparison, ascribing to Fielding an insistence on the legibility of outsides.[11] Battestin reads Fielding's characters emblematically, as "abstractions" that objectify the theme of divine design.[12] Damrosch differentiates them from characters drawn by Bunyan, Defoe, and Samuel Richardson: "Rather than postulating a unique and hidden consciousness at the heart of the self [as his predecessors had done], Fielding sees character as the sum of visible actions and decisions."[13] Deidre Lynch compares Fielding's characters to the figures in William Hogarth's graphic satires, both of which, she argues, exemplify a "typographical culture" invested in the "eloquence of material surfaces" such as the human face or the face of a printed page.[14] Characters in novels like *Tom Jones* are constitutive elements of a "symbolic environment" in which "truths could be self-evident," compensating for the chaos of the protocapitalist market via their ready intelligibility.[15]

Like historians of novelistic character generally, Lynch retells the story of disenchantment. Over the last third of the eighteenth century, on her account, the discursive worlds in fictional texts lose their symbolic charge as writers begin to represent rather than resist the confusion of modern economic life. Fielding's works pre-date a shift in aesthetic values, whereby "characteristic writing," a transmedia genre defined by the ideal of perspicuity, yields to the novel as we recognize it today: focused on representations of richly psychologized interiority.[16] It is true that Lynch brackets the role of religion in literature and the market, and that she refutes the "rise of the individual" metanarrative that animated Watt and his acolytes. The trajectory of her argument nevertheless mirrors that of secularization. Early eighteenth-century character and the premodern, religious past occupy correspondent positions in parallel narratives of progress. Each premises an episteme on the verge of collapse, and each sees the disenchantment of a once cooperatively symbolic world as a generative phenomenon.

Fielding's relation to Calvinist semiotics of character reflect an alternative trajectory of secularization, one based on the redistribution rather than the diminution of religious belief. His writings underscore the potential of mutually fragilized belief to move between epistemological and ethical framings of the problem of inconsistent character and to invest morality with salvific intensity. Local disruptions in *Tom Jones* and *Amelia* nevertheless betray the disciplinary valence of even this formation of the secular, secularism-as-antiorthodoxy. Sophia Western's reticence to serve as the grounding meaning of her lover's characterological value and Amelia Booth's quiet suffering in the same role call attention to the dependence of Fielding's secularist fantasy on asymmetrical gender relations. A model of heteropatriarchy authorized by biblical precedent organizes the otherwise wild proliferation of belief. Fielding's novels thus reveal the flipside of the nova effect, or the tendency of the ethic of pluralism to create new or police existing categories of subalterity—here, that of "wife."

Fielding, George Whitefield, and Calvinist "Diagnostics"

Comparing Fielding's disquisition on hypocrisy, "Essay on the Knowledge of the Characters of Men" (1743), to the published sermons of George Whitefield, progenitor of the Calvinist branch of Methodism, helps us to see the angles of uptake for Calvinism yet available at midcentury. Fielding and Whitefield would seem an unlikely pair; several of Fielding's modern readers classify his religious thought as Latitudinarian, the predominant posture of Church of England writers and clergy by Fielding's time.[17] If he is an example of this strain of Anglicanism, Fielding shows that its name is misleading. For, although he follows leading Latitudinarian Anglicans in downplaying both doctrine and formal worship in favor of a moral-rational practice of piety, Fielding confirms that this practice has a theologically specific orientation: Arminianism. As an Anglican-Arminianist, Fielding disavowed the Calvinist doctrines of justification by faith alone and double predestination on the grounds that they abrogate free will.[18] In his first novel, *Joseph Andrews* (1742), Parson Adams attacks the Calvinist strain of Whitefield's thought in typical Arminian terms.[19] Having granted the accuracy of Whitefield's critique of the clergy, Adams turns to his application of the "detestable Doctrine of Faith":

Can anything be more derogatory to the Honor of God, than for Men to imagine that the All-wise Being will hereafter say to the Good and Virtuous, *Notwithstanding the Purity of thy Life, notwithstanding that constant Rule of Virtue and Goodness in which you Walked upon the Earth, still as thou didst not believe everything in the true Orthodox manner, thy want of Faith shall condemn thee?* Or on the other side, can any Doctrine have a more pernicious influence on Society than a Persuasion, that it will be a good Plea for a Villain at the last Day; *Lord, it is true I never obeyed one of thy Commandments, yet punish me not, for I believe them all?*[20]

Adams casts Whitefield's reassertion of the doctrine of justification by faith as an outright rejection of pious living in favor of empty professions of assent to "orthodox" tenets. The subordination of works to faith transforms religious duty, which ought to consist of honoring public "promises of being good, friendly, and benevolent to each other," into mere words—unverifiable statements of an inwardly held conviction, like those issued by Bunyan's Talkative (65). Through his redoubtable parson, Fielding argues that Whitefield's Calvinism conduces to hypocrisy before God and coreligionist alike.[21] Yet the vexing epistemology of character brings Fielding and Whitefield into surprising proximity.

A Calvinist thinker who, according to Adams, promotes hypocrisy in his followers also dwells on the interpretive practices necessary to preempt its spiritual and social harms, anticipating the aim of Fielding's "Essay on the Knowledge of the Characters of Men." Published in 1739 as *The Doctrine of the Gospel Asserted and Vindicated,* Whitefield's sermons underscore the potential incongruity of the religious content of character and its outward markers. In "Sermon 4: The Necessity and Benefits of Religious Society," Whitefield instructs his audience to preserve the correspondence of those terms. "Let your Practice correspond to your Profession," he enjoins, and show "that you are willing, not barely to *seem,* but to *be* in *Reality, Christians.*"[22] The disjunction between assumed and real character that so fascinates Fielding here threatens Whitefield's vision of ecclesiastical polity.

"Sermon 12: The Marks of the New Birth; or, The Different States of Nature and Grace Described" introduces rubrics for navigating this unstable relationship. It also shows how the inscrutability of salvific states pushes Whitefield past the simple taxonomy prescribed by Calvinist doctrine—an important connection to Fielding's own interest in species or kinds of hypocrite. Instead of the umbrella categories of elect and reprobate, we find in "Sermon 12" a list of "several distinct Classes of Professors" and a set of rules for differentiating them (*D*, 12.16). Whitefield takes the "marks" of election advertised in the sermon's title from Matthew 23. Signs of the operation of grace and, by extension, of election are themselves inward states, but these frames of mind and spirit bear outward proof in specific, correspondent behaviors. Unlike spiritual generation itself, these qualities are self-evident. He who "is joined to the Lord in one Spirit will so order his Thoughts, Words, and Actions aright, that he will evidence to all, that his Conversation is in Heaven" (12.13). Whether they stand in for discrete kinds of professor or stages in the process of spiritual awakening and regeneration—and Whitefield suggests that they do both—the "classes" outlined in this sermon are literally visible to those who know how to interpret evidence of the New Birth. "Grace" is something that we can "see" in other people (12.13). Whitefield's confidence wavers, however, when he arrives at the classes intermediate to the doctrinally mandated, absolute categories of the "abandoned Sinner" and "happy Saint" (12.16). Self-deluders, for example, "those who deceive themselves with false Hopes of Salvation," tend to mislead observers, as well. Their hypocrisy consists of the same inside-outside dichotomy upon which Fielding bases his own definition: these people "appear a little beautiful without, but [they are] inwardly full of Corruptions and Uncleanness" (12.18).

In "Essay on the Knowledge of the Characters of Men," published in the first volume of his *Miscellanies,* Fielding responds to the confusion caused by religious hypocrisy in much the same way that Whitefield does: by turning to the gospel of Matthew and the logic of kind. If real and affected "sanctity" look alike, Fielding asks, "how shall we then distinguish with any Certainty, the true from the fictitious?"[23] The answer he finds in the New Testament parallels the general system of "diagnostics" laid out in the essay: a model of character reading that promises to repair the rift between assumed and real, sign and signified.[24] But Fielding understands character to be classifiable as well as two-dimensional. Reconciling outside to inside represents the first of two steps; the second is to impose order on the moral arena via taxonomy. As in Whitefield's sermon, an abstract distinction ramifies into an array of moral kinds. When he deduces from the evidence of children and "savages" the existence of "some unacquired, original Distinction, in the Nature of the Soul of one Man, from that of Another," Fielding strays quite close to the Calvinist understanding of religious character.[25] He defines "original distinction" as an inborn propensity toward good or evil, rooted in the very "soul." Although Fielding allows that such a propensity might be nurtured or corrected, his proposal that, at a certain level of abstraction, people split into two ethical kinds replicates the dualism of predestinarian theology as it was applied within Whitefield's sermons.

I do not mean to suggest, by illustrating this affinity, that Fielding was a Calvinist according to any strict definition. After all, he never abandoned the commitment to Arminian soteriology evinced by Adams's diatribe in *Joseph Andrews*. Rather, the parallels between Fielding's and Whitefield's thinking about religious hypocrisy indicate that an epistemic model (and the idea of self it presupposes) transcends the parameters of the sectarian discourse from which it emerged, as well as the borders of the religious. In spite of their differences on points of doctrine, Fielding and Whitefield are part of the same genealogy of character, one that coheres around a shared commitment to explore the resources and limitations of Calvinist semiotics. The following readings of *Tom Jones* and *Amelia* show how the novel becomes a privileged site for such experimentation. Calvinism matters in those works not as a totalizing worldview, but as one unstable position among many. The fluidity that results is different than what other scholars refer to as Fielding's Latitudinarianism. Fielding's idea of religion here is not simply moderated—rationalist, practical, lax with respect to an established code—but fragilized. A belief becomes fragile when it cannot stand alone: any potential it carries is compatible with ideas traditionally mobilized against it, and its failures are articulable only via still further religious vocabularies. We might think of this phenomenon as an intensification of Fielding's Latitudinarian posture, something closer to religious pluralism than the historically specific and, by this time, dominant strain of Anglican-Arminianism that stresses moral conduct over doctrine and formal worship. Fielding's novels represent a secular form in the sense that they promote an understanding of religion as pluralized and, thus, reactive to the always encroaching pressures of this world.

Fielding's major works of fiction test Calvinist semiotics against the dangers of a fallen world. Confrontations, especially, with the effects of sexual desire undermine Fielding's confidence that the surface (sign) and depth (signified) of character might be brought into alignment through a particular style of reading. Where the "Essay on the Knowledge of the Characters of Men" uses Calvinist semiotics to contain the threat of hypocrisy, *Tom Jones* and *Amelia* reformulate the terms of the problem and its solution using different religious logics. In his novels, Fielding turns from the spatial and epistemological to the temporal and ethical axes of character. The conclusion of *Tom Jones* develops a distinctively Christian ideal of conjugal love, according to which bride and bridegroom circumvent the challenge of knowing character by sharing it. *Amelia* rejects this possibility as well as Calvinist semiotics. In his final novel, Fielding proposes that by restraining desire within the bounds of coupledom, we might restore the temporality of paradise and, in doing so, obviate the dilemmas of character.

Character Sharing in Tom Jones

Tom Jones, like Fielding's essay, thematizes the potentially vexed relation between outsides and insides. Having related Blifil's successful campaign to turn Squire Allworthy against Jones, the narrator pauses to elaborate the "very useful Lesson" conveyed through the episode:

> It is not enough that your Designs, nay that your Actions, are intrinsically good, you must take Care they shall appear so. If your Inside be never so beautiful, you must preserve a fair Outside also. This must be constantly looked to, or Malice and Envy will take Care to blacken it so, that the Sagacity and Goodness of an *Allworthy* will not be able to see thro' it, and to discern the Beauties within. Let this, my young Readers, be your constant Maxim, That no Man can be good enough to enable him to neglect the Rules of Prudence; nor will Virtue herself look beautiful, unless she be bedecked with the outward Ornaments of Decency and Decorum.[26]

Here, Fielding approaches the interior/exterior problem from the oppo-site angle. Rather than a foul inside deliberately concealed by a fair out-side, the passage asserts the impenetrability of goodness, which is in need of a "bedecked" outside to aid in correct reading. As he casts doubt on the capacity of even the most perspicacious observers to "see thro'" the assumed to the real character, Fielding imports the two-dimensional model from the "Essay on the Knowledge of the Characters of Men." The conflict between Jones and Allworthy demonstrates that inward truths may be sundered from outward signs. Good character may be misrepre-sented, "blackened" falsely and maliciously, as well as feigned. The resolu-tion of this conflict, however, depends upon the integrity of the truth "at the Bottom" of character (621). Both Jones's goodness and Blifil's evil prove knowable. That Allworthy's discovery requires the interposition of provi-dence, manifest, as several scholars have noted, in the "strange Chances" and "odd Accidents" that lead to the novel's denouement, strengthens rather than attenuates Fielding's connection to the Calvinist genealogy of character (600).[27] As we've seen, the devoutly Calvinist Bunyan betrays similar skepticism about the efficacy of interpretation, and he invokes the same failsafe: the revealed wisdom of divine providence.[28]

The discovery of Jones's true character, in the compound sense of class identity, moral quality, and reputation, does not suffice to bring about the novel's comic resolution. For *Tom Jones* to end, in keeping with generic expectations, with marriage, Sophia must be reconciled to her lover's infidelities at Upton and London. In book 18, chapter 12, Jones attempts to persuade Sophia of the sincerity of his repentance and his promise of future constancy. Battestin makes much of their climactic exchange as an illustration of Sophia's emblematic function. It is through this scene in particular, he explains, that Fielding "makes the reader aware that Sophia's beauty is ultimately the physical manifestation of a spiritual per-fection almost divine, that she is for him [that is, the reader] as for Jones, the Idea of Virtue incarnate."[29] Her coherence matches the coherence of divine design. Sophia's virtues and, therefore, her significance within the novel's ethical scheme appear on her physical features, in much the same way that God's presence and plan appear on the face of creation. The following pages offer a different reading—though not by contradicting Battestin's point about the conformity of Sophia's "form" and "essential spiritual nature."[30] Rather, I expand on his interpretation by focusing on the claim that Jones makes on Sophia's legibility, a claim that troubles the understanding of character operative elsewhere in the novel.

Sophia herself is convinced that we cannot stabilize the relationship of outside to inside through interpretive effort. When Jones conflates her power to forgive with God's infinite "mercy," Sophia balks: "Sincere Repentance," she observes, "will obtain the Pardon of a Sinner, but it is from one who is a perfect Judge of that Sincerity. A human Mind may be imposed on; nor is there any infallible Method to prevent it" (T, 634–35). She issues a wholesale rejection of available "methods" for detecting imposition, stressing that God alone can settle the question of authenticity. Sophia distances herself further from the essay's Calvinist model by prioritizing the temporal over the spatial dimensions of character. Sensitive to the weakness of her "human mind," and wary of the leap of faith involved in crediting Jones's promise of future performance, Sophia proposes a trial period of indeterminate length. Such a course would allow Jones to match promise to performance and, thus, to "shew" his fidelity (635). Characterological distinctions no longer map neatly onto an inside/outside binary; deciding whether Jones is a libertine or a "true Penitent" is not a matter of penetrating the surface to disclose an interior truth. Instead, Sophia must either speculate about his future character or, as she prefers it, defer judgment long enough for Jones to live out the veracity of his profession.

As impatient to complete his happiness as Fielding is to effect the narrative's comic resolution, Jones changes tack:

> He replied, "Don't believe me upon my Word; I have a better Security, a Pledge for my Constancy, which it is impossible to see and to doubt." "What is that?" said *Sophia,* a little surprised. "I will show you, my charming Angel," cried *Jones,* seizing her Hand, and carrying her to the Glass. "There, behold it there in that lovely Figure, in that Face, that Shape, those Eyes, that Mind which shines through those Eyes: Can the Man who shall be in Possession of these be inconstant? Impossible! my *Sophia:* They would fix a Dorimant, a Lord Rochester. You could not doubt it, if you could see yourself with any

Eyes but your own." *Sophia* blushed, half smiled: but forcing again her Brow into a Frown, "If I am to judge," said she, "of the future by the past, my Image will no more remain in your Heart when I am out of your Sight, than it will in this Glass when I am out of this Room." (*T*, 635)

Jones grounds an otherwise suspect "pledge" in Sophia's fully legible virtues of person (e.g., her "figure," "face," and "shape") and "mind." The straightforward logic of his response is as follows: Sophia's beauty will make Jones constant, fastening his desire to a single object. She is so beautiful, in fact, that her image would "fix" even the roving gaze of Restoration libertines like the Earl of Rochester or George Etherege's Dorimant. I want to argue that there is another, stranger logic unfolding here. By "possessing" Sophia's person through marriage, Jones intimates, he might also take possession of the spiritual virtues manifest in her physical charms, including the ideal wisdom for which she is named and that she exhibits when she regards his initial promise with skepticism.[31] Jones sees his prospective character in Sophia's face.

He answers Sophia's closing objection—her beauty has not actually fixed his desire to this point, she reminds him—by elaborating on this idea of matrimonial possession. When Sophia observes that his past behavior gives his argument the lie, Jones counters that his inconstancy reflected Sophia's remoteness as the object of his true passion; her distance and his despair had licensed base appetite. Yet "the first Moment of Hope that *Sophia* might be my Wife" renders Jones incapable of infidelity, in large part because it is at this moment that her character, both the "image" in his mind's eye and the abstract moral qualities it communicates, becomes his to claim in expectation (*T*, 635). Sophia need not take Jones at his word, nor strain to interpret his outward behaviors for clues. Once the lovers are married and continually in one another's presence, they will share a transparent character that weds outward and inward perfection. Jones's argument brings together the Christian idea of unification through marriage with the ideal, central to Battestin's interpretation, of a unified inside and outside character. The coupling of distinct individuals becomes intertwined with the promise of coupled physical and moral qualifications.

Fielding's extended meditation on the lovers' reconciliation lays bare the fantasy behind the novel's conventional happy ending. Jones resolves the problem of discerning character by imagining marriage as character sharing, a form of affiliation that obviates the fraught, interpretative work of bridging the gap between subjects. His argument elaborates the conceptualization of conjugal love introduced in Genesis, which figures the bodies of husband and wife as continuous: "And Adam said, This *is* now bone of my bones, and flesh of my flesh: she shall be called Woman, because she was taken out of Man. Therefore shall a man leave his father and mother, and shall cleave unto his wife: and they shall be one flesh."[32] The possibility of intergenerational substitution would no doubt appeal to Jones, whose illegitimate status made him filius nullius, nobody's child, under the law.[33] But it is the biblical chapter's assertion of the continuity of bodies and souls that obtains in his proposal to Sophia.

His fantasy reverses the direction of the relationship (Eve is an extension of Adam's body, whereas Jones imagines himself as an extension of Sophia's), but Jones and Sophia, too, become "one flesh." Jones's argument also perpetuates the gendered hierarchy central to the Christian understanding of marriage. The effect is mutuality, a shared character, but that effect is achieved through Jones's legal and sexual dominion over Sophia's person. What appeal does this model carry for the woman whose character becomes transferable property? Sophia, of course, marries Jones the next day, but the question of why, precisely, she relents is an abiding one. She responds in the moment with ambivalence, suppressing somatic evidence of her pleasure (that blushing half-smile) and reiterating her demand for the hard proofs afforded by time. The ambiguity of her motive hints at something that Fielding's final novel confirms: that, for all its power to fix a good-natured but imperfect husband, Christian marriage cannot resolve the epistemic crisis facing women.

Amelia's "Earthly Paradise"

I have been arguing that *Tom Jones* posits a conjugal desire that overcomes the problem of reading other people by eliding the distance between them. Matrimonial character sharing promotes mutual intelligibility between husband and wife, compensating for the fallibility of available methods of evaluating character. I turn now to *Amelia* to document Fielding's dissatisfaction with this solution. Even if we accept the former text's sanguine vision of marriage—if we think in lockstep with Jones's fantasy—we are left to wonder how its governing logic mitigates the problem of negotiating the "greater stage" of social intercourse. This concern occupies the moral center of *Amelia,* which begins rather than ends with marriage. A new danger emerges from outside the precincts of coupledom. Heterosexual desire produces a variant of hypocrisy that consists not in the obfuscation but the instability of real character. Embodied by Colonel James, this threat revives a question that Fielding deflects at the end of *Tom Jones:* How do we project the knowledge of character into an uncertain future? In *Amelia,* Fielding's answer is to set character and time in a new relation. He does so by imagining retired domesticity as a neobiblical paradise. The novel's eponymous heroine and her husband, Captain William Booth, recover one of the defining conditions of life in the garden: nonlinear, ahistorical time. This solution reflects a dramatic shift in Fielding's attention, from the epistemic to the ethical registers of character.

James is assigned the character of a true friend within both the overarching narrative and Booth's interpolated history. Reflecting on his kindnesses toward Booth's family, the narrator holds James up as an exception to the general rule of human depravity. "So few are to be found of this benign Disposition," he laments, that "scarce one Man in a thousand is capable of tasting the Happiness of others."[34] James exhibits a heightened sympathetic capacity that allows him to derive pleasure from the happiness or relief of its object; this pleasure, in turn, motivates acts of disinterested generosity. Amelia echoes the narrator's panegyric, regaling Mrs. Bennet with a "full Narrative of the Colonel's former Behaviour and Friendship to her Husband, as well Abroad as in *England;* and ended with declaring, that she believed him the most generous Man upon Earth" (*A,* 332). Yet James schemes to seduce Amelia, stepping out of his assigned character. How should we account for his inconsistency?

The narrator points to the transformative power of heterosexual desire, a passion erroneously but "generally called Love." "Of all the Passions," he opines, there is none to whose Posion and Infatuation the best of Minds are so liable. Ambition scarce ever produces any Evil, but when it reigns in cruel and savage Bosoms; and Avarice seldom flourishes at all but in the basest and poorest Soil. Love, on the contrary, sprouts usually up in the richest and noblest Minds; but there unless nicely watched, pruned, cultivated, and carefully kept clear of those vicious Weeds which are too apt to surround it, it branches forth into Wildness and Disorder, produces nothing desirable, but choaks up and kills whatever is good and noble in the Mind where it so abounds. In short, to drop the Allegory, not only Tenderness and Good-nature, but Bravery, Generosity, and every Virtue are often made the instruments of effecting the most atrocious Purposes of this all-subduing Tyrant. (A, 252)

James's desire for Amelia "sprouts" up, unlike ambition or greed, by swift and imperceptible degrees in the best of men. What begins as socially acceptable "admiration" for Amelia becomes an illicit desire that takes hold, the narrator adds, "before [James] had observed it in himself" (253). Such desire does not so much disclose a hidden villainy as corrupt "good-nature" itself. As it flourishes in that substrate, James's passion perverts entrenched virtues into instruments of gratification. Fielding's horticultural "allegory" images James's heart as a patch of land caught between anthropogenic efforts to impose order and the irresistible force of wild, unproductive growth. He proposes that such wildness might be checked by self-command—represented here as cultivation, meticulous pruning—but his metaphor confers a sense of inevitability to the triumph of "Wildness and Disorder." Within James's bosom, desire acquires the organic force as well as the stigma of overgrowth. Once it takes root, this passion is "too apt" to become destructive, to "choak up and kill" the fruits of unwatched virtue. The garden of James's moral character, in the span of an evening spent in the Booths' company and in the space of a paragraph, is overwhelmed with "vicious Weeds."

The instability of James's nature sets him apart from the catalog of hypocrites that Fielding describes in the "Essay on the Knowledge of the Characters of Men," as well as from the pattern established by his "former Behaviour and Friendship" toward the Booths. James's desire retroactively invalidates conclusions drawn from first-hand observations of his actions—the "surest Evidence of a Man's Character" according to

Fielding's essay.[35] When he betrays his friends, James distances himself from the "Hero of [Amelia's] Tale" of selfless friendship, as well as from the logic of plot (A, 343). He neither remains constant nor exhibits character development in the familiar, literary sense. Instead, James's "real character," already established through empirical evidence and rendered in narrative form, ruptures on contact with illicit desire.

This phenomenon defies articulation in Calvinist terms. Although he overstates its individualist ethic, Damrosch rightly points out Calvinism's "two-part conception" of character.[36] Genuine conversion consists of stripping away a false self to disclose the true nature of the soul, the prior and static truth of salvific status. Damrosch contends that "the idea of an interior and mysterious self has little relevance for Fielding, whose neoclassical conception of character assumes that the people we meet in life are in fact types."[37] As the foregoing discussions of Fielding's essay and *Tom Jones* hopefully demonstrate, this idea is both highly relevant to Fielding and compatible with his interest in typification. It is in *Amelia* specifically and not, as Damrosch proposes, his writings generally that Fielding abandons the character of Calvinism. *Tom Jones* ratifies the integrity of the model's bipartite structure, even if the novel also entertains character sharing as a way to bypass the potentially insuperable barrier between its two parts. Colonel James is the true limit case. Unlike Jones or Blifil, James possesses no fixed moral content ripe for discovery and categorization. In her comically inept effort to denigrate Amelia's beauty, the jealous Mrs. James inadvertently captures the monstrous quality of her husband's character. James, and not the object of his adulterous desire, "is a Kind of Something that is neither one Thing or another" (A, 447).

Neither Calvinist semiotics nor the couple form held up as curative in book 18 of *Tom Jones* avails in *Amelia*. Fielding introduces "suspicion" as a recourse when actions give false evidence—whether due to a failed correspondence between surface and essence or because of the mutability of inward selves. The narrator of *Amelia* hails suspicion as a "great Optic Glass helping us to discern plainly almost all that passes in the Minds of others, without some use of which nothing is more purblind than Human Nature" (366). This last line of defense would seem to carry forward Fielding's career-long effort to reevaluate the ways in which one might read the characters of others, with a minor change in emphasis from protocol to posture. I want to stress that Fielding's proposed failsafe actually hints at a more dramatic transformation in his thinking over the course of the novel. Fielding's epistemological concerns become ethical concerns. Suspicion is out of character for people like Amelia. "Openness of Heart" is a concomitant of good nature, Fielding insists, and those who adopt suspiciousness as their default posture toward other people trade a key ingredient of the "true Christian Disposition" for their perspicacity (388). Discovering hypocrisy, then, comes at a tremendous price: the partial loss of humanity, of Christianness. That cost helps account for Fielding's ambivalence toward suspicion, as well as for his frequent injunctions to the reader to forgive Amelia and Captain Booth their lack of circumspection.

Booth unwittingly discovers a more promising and more complex solution earlier in the novel, when he describes to Miss Mathews the "earthly Paradise" that he had forfeited through his financial indiscretions (A, 168). Having left the army, Booth explains, he accepted Dr. Harrison's proposal to rent his parsonage and "turn Farmer" (169). Booth's thwarted efforts to convince Miss Mathews of the joys of this vocation reveal the temporal structure of prelapsarian life:

> "During my first Year's Continuance in this new Scene of Life, nothing, I think, remarkable happened; the History of one Day would, indeed, be the History of the whole Year."
>
> "Well, pray then," said Miss *Mathews*, "do let us hear the History of that Day; I have a strange Curiosity to know how you could kill your Time; and do, if possible, find out the very best Day you can."
>
> "If you command me, Madam," answered *Booth*, "you must yourself be accountable for the Dullness of the Narrative. Nay, I believe, you have imposed a difficult Task on me; for the greatest Happiness is incapable of Description."
>
> "Nay, nay," replied she, "I can guess at your greatest Happiness, but describe as much as you can."
>
> "I rose then, Madam," cry'd *Booth*,—
>
> "O the Moment you waked, undoubtedly," said Miss *Mathews*.—
>
> "Perhaps not so, Madam," said he, "but usually I rose between Five and Six."

"I will have no *usually*," cry'd *Miss Matthews*, "you are confined to a Day, and it is to be the best and happiest in the Year."

"Nay, Madam," cries *Booth*, "then I must tell you the Day in which *Amelia* was brought to Bed, after a painful and dangerous Labour; for that I think was the happiest Day of my Life."

"I protest," said she, "you are become Farmer *Booth*, indeed. What a Happiness have you painted in my Imagination! You put me in Mind of a News-Paper, where my Lady such-a-one is delivered of a Son, to the great Joy of some illustrious Family."

"Why then, I do assure you, *Miss Mathews*," cries *Booth*, "I scarce know a Circumstance that distinguished one Day from another. The whole was one continued Series of Love, Health, and Tranquility. Our Lives resembled a calm Sea." (169–70)

Miss Mathews's allusion to sexual pleasure—"I can guess at your greatest Happiness," she winks—and Booth's repetition of the topos of inexpressibility distract from the specific nature of his joy. Although the fact is not discursively intelligible to him, Booth's happiness consists in an experience of time as undifferentiated, resistant to conventional measures. On Harrison's parsonage, distinctions between quantitative units of time (hour, day, year) lose their force.

This indivisibility staggers Booth's attempts to satisfy Miss Mathew's demand that he choose a superlative day, the "best and happiest," and then enumerate its particular joys. He tries first to describe a typical day in the abstract and then offers to recount the birth of one of his children. In responding, Miss Mathews betrays her own cognitive dissonance about the kind of history that she privileges. She is seduced by its principles of sequence and causation yet repulsed by the results when those principles are imposed onto Booth's experience of the past. Hence her alternation between importunities to particularize—"I will have no *usually*"—and scoffing dismissals of his answers.[38] Through her antagonism, Miss Mathews makes Booth's point for him. In the declamation that punctuates their exchange, he reiterates that conventional history fails to comprehend "one continued series of love, health, and tranquility." The era proves anathema to historical consciousness because the feelings which constitute it must be experienced as a "whole" and at once.

The phrase "earthly Paradise" invites readers to see what Booth himself cannot fully articulate: that the episode comprises not just a brief era in Booth's life, but the first epoch of sacred history. Through the coincidence of personal history and sacred past, both encompassed within the living present, Fielding suggests that salvation is neither mediated through Christ nor deferred to the next life. Instead, it is realized through a form of labor that evokes Milton's account of Eden. The Booths sustain their version of paradise through subsistence farming, carrying out the light cultivation that Milton assigns to Adam and Eve in *Paradise Lost*. Such labor has a figurative equivalent in the pruning that Colonel James fails to perform when his "sudden liking" for Amelia first takes hold. The horticultural trope linking the two episodes—one about the transformative power of lust, one about the conditions of possibility for human flourishing after the Fall—subordinates epistemology to ethics. Paradisal time depends for its integrity on an idealized form of work. Booth casts himself and his dependents out of Eden by forsaking the character of "Farmer Booth," overdrawing on his credit while trying to elevate his social status and then succumbing to his illicit desire for Miss Mathews. Like his friend James, he neglects the garden of his heart.

My interpretation of the Booths' earthly paradise suggests for *Amelia* a more prominent place in Fielding's corpus than scholarship generally allows it. To eighteenth-century and modern readers alike, Fielding's last major work of fiction has registered as a departure from its comic predecessors. Hunter reviews the "charges" commonly leveled against the novel, paying particular attention to its hamfisted moralism.[39] The very feature which, according to Hunter, makes *Amelia* an outlier on my reading in fact confirms its capstone status. For *Amelia* develops the approach to character and characterization introduced within the "Essay on the Knowledge of Character" and *Tom Jones*. What I am calling Fielding's secularism, his willingness to borrow from various traditions of belief without deferring to the doctrinal propriety of any one, inflects the much lamented moral didacticism of his final novel. Through Captain Booth's failings and subsequent rehabilitation, Fielding proposes that we might restore paradise to this world. What Fielding's earlier writings depict as a field of apprehensible objects—apprehensible via Calvinist semiotics or Christian marriage's logic of elision—*Amelia* presents as a theater for action and feeling. At stake in resisting desires alien to coupledom and domestic economy is nothing short of salvation. By making redemption a matter of exercising virtue and its rewards proximate rather than delayed, Fielding invests the human moral arena with the urgency of soteriology.[40]

Attending to the complexity of the characters in Fielding's books clarifies what it meant, in the middle of the eighteenth century to be "secular." The approach reveals, that is, the shifting terrain of religiosity in an era marked by advent of what would later, and with unearned triumphalism, be called secularization. This approach also helps us to resist the disciplinary afterlife of the latter metanarrative. Recent scholarship has established the influence of progressive secularization on the history of the novel as a genre. Alison Conway and Corinne Harol remark that such histories "typically offer a microcosmic version of the secularization thesis."[41] Kevin Seidel observes a more specific pattern of secularizing thought that unites studies by, among others, Ian Watt, John Richetti, and Michael Mckeon. According to each of these accounts, Seidel points out, early novelists "distort" the religious past in order to make it modern: "religion must make room for new social or cultural forces. . . . At the same time these forces carry forward a sense of religion, albeit a transformed or distorted one."[42] The body of twentieth-century scholarship to which these critics refer argues expressly for the inevitable dislodgment of religion by secular forces, variously defined and constellated. It does not, however, give the fullest sense of novel studies' debt to secularizing premises.

For the developmental rationale of secularization shapes even histories of the form that omit "religion" as an analytical term. In describing Fielding's characters as "tell-tale bodies" with no "inside story," Lynch extends a line of argument that, as I have noted, connects eighteenth- to twentieth-century criticism.[43] According to such varied readers as Johnson, Battestin, and Lynch, Fielding externalizes knowledge of character. Whether they signify in the manner of typeface, as in Lynch's study, or emblematically, as in Battestin's, characters like young Blifil and Sophia Western reflect a vision of the created world as imbued with almost sacramental meaning. This model of character marks Fielding's works as prior to a transition from the ideal of legibility to one of indeterminacy—prior, we might say, to the novel's effective disenchantment. An embedded, secularizing logic occludes the tension, operative in Fielding's novels as in earlier contributions to the form, between two-dimensionality and inscrutability. The cases of *Tom Jones* and *Amelia* further suggest that extricating character from disenchantment stories clarifies its paramount cultural function. Britons used character to reimagine the horizons of religion, its potential as a vehicle for interpretation and critique.

Adams, the Anglican curate in *Joseph Andrews*, gives voice to the pluralistic ethos enabled by this imaginative labor. Adams denounces Whitefield and the Calvinist doctrine of justification by faith out of an ecumenical rather than a sectarian instinct. In fact, he extends his definition of salvific virtue past the borders of Christianity. In his unpublished sermons, Adams informs an uninterested bookseller, the Arminian emphasis on works "is inculcated in almost every Page, or I should belye my own Opinion, which hath always been, that a virtuous and good *Turk*, or Heathen, are more acceptable in the sight of their Creator, than a vicious and wicked Christian, though his Faith was as perfectly Orthodox as St. *Paul's* himself" (65). Adams prefers Arminian agency over Calvinistic faith, here identified with Pauline "orthodoxy," because the former extends God's acceptance to the "virtuous and good" of all religious denominations— even as far as professors of Islamic faith. Adams sees himself as liberalizing Protestantism alongside figures like Benjamin Hoadly, the bishop of Winchester whose *Plain Account of the Nature and End of the Sacrament of the Lord's Supper* (1735) attempts to demystify communion. Adams assures the skeptical bookseller that his sermons would, like Hoadly's, survive the "the attacks of some few designing factious Men, who have it at Heart to establish some favourite schemes at the Price of the Liberty of Mankind and the true Essence of Religion" (*JA*, 65). The two values Adam wishes to recover, the "Liberty of Mankind" and the "true Essence of Religion," are mutually dependent. The redefinition of religion as transdenominational virtue, good works in the service of a supreme being and of one another, affords freedom of conscience.

We should be careful, though, not to overstate the liberatory effect of Fielding's antiorthodoxy. The novels' avoidance of direct commentary on race and empire enables a sanguine view of the social effects of Adams's idea of liberalized piety. In the next section of this chapter, through an interpretation of *Tristram Shandy,* I show how this idea congeals into an exclusionary definition of virtue and serves, in that form, as the warrant for Anglo-Protestant superiority on a global scale. Before doing so, I want to close the current section by pointing out that Fielding's fictions suggest how deviations from doctrinal prescript can reinforce structural inequalities, as well. When the narrator of *Tom Jones* worries over the artificial "blackening" of Jones's character, or when Jones himself suggests that Sophia's whiteness is bone deep, Fielding evokes the metaphorical link between epidermal race and religio-ethical content. External blackness should, but in Jones's case does not, signify the internal blackness of sin, just as Sophia's whiteness extends from her porcelain exterior straight to the core of character. In this episode of *Tom Jones,* as in Bunyan's *The Holy War,* a semiotic ideal in which somatic signs and internal values are correspondent serves as the baseline against which to measure both the problem posed by Blifil's hypocrisy (and his smear campaign against Jones) and the exemplarity of Sophia. Even if Fielding refers to blackness in a strictly metaphorical sense, he does so in a way that recalls the figurative logic by which Bunyan racializes religious character.

Furthermore, the solutions that *Tom Jones* and *Amelia* pose for the problematics of character in each case affirm the power of the husband. Sophia's worries about an arrangement in which Jones absorbs her character are not so much allayed as dislodged by social pressure and narrative exigency, and the novel seems untroubled by this resolution. Amelia presents to Booth's wistful recollection of farm life exclusively as an object of the reproductive heterosexual desire that enables the conditions of paradise, giving pleasure (as Miss Matthews infers) and then giving birth. However dynamic the approach to character that leads to it, this understanding of Amelia as a structural feature of lost paradise carries a powerfully conservative energy.

To restore Eden, *Amelia* returns to typology, at least with respect to its principal female character. Fielding rewrites Eve. Although less nakedly patriarchal than its biblical and Miltonic counterparts, his version of the character nevertheless perpetuates the unequal distribution of power and ethical responsibility built into the story of original sin. Impervious where her prototypes are vulnerable, submissive where they are ambitious, Amelia functions as an insulated channel for Booth's heretofore misdirected sexual agency, and not as an agent herself. Amelia suffers for Booth's fall, acutely but with inexhaustible patience, and the novel repeatedly mines her martyrdom for pathos. All she can do to reverse its valence is to adopt an exaggerated posture of sexual subordination, to remain what Sophia also, albeit more begrudgingly, agrees to become: the fixed point of navigation for a wayward lover.

Sterne's Orthodoxy

Tristram Shandy's relationship to the early English novel has long fascinated critics. Watt excludes Sterne's work from the tradition and others, like Thomas Keymer, have followed suit by noting its non- or antinovelistic features.[44] Viktor Schlovsky takes the contrary view; for him, *Tristram Shandy* epitomizes the novel's defining preoccupations with the interiority of characters' minds and the machinery of literary production.[45] Taking stock of the conversation, Julia H. Fawcett observes that the question of *Tristram Shandy*'s genre is really "a question of characterization": Does Sterne follow novelists in depicting "psychologically realistic individuals," or does he revive a satirical practice in which characters are "representative types whose vices are often made visible by certain prominent physical features"?[46] Fawcett's answer is that Sterne does both, borrowing from celebrity autobiography a strategy of characterization that straddles the line between novelistic interiorization and satirical externalization. This method allows Sterne to manage the vulnerability that comes with fame by promising access to the "interior self" but continually relocating readers on the surfaces of the page and the authorial performance.[47] I concur that *Tristram Shandy* is marked by inside-outside play, but I think this feature makes the text representative rather than "idiosyncratic," as Fawcett suggests.[48] Although she proposes a middle way between the two poles of debate in Sterne criticism, introducing a third, mediating genre, Fawcett applies the consensus definition of the novel as a formal-realist medium identifiable by its effort to interiorize character.

Tristram Shandy does not fit this definition, but it does fit squarely within the early novelistic tradition as I have attempted to redescribe it so far. Like *The Pilgrim's Progress, Oroonoko,* and *Tom Jones, Tristram Shandy* explores the possible incongruence of the dimensions of character—and it does so, like those earlier works, in view of defining true religion. For Bunyan, the disjuncture of the signs of character from the two stable meanings prescribed by doctrine—election and reprobation—creates the epistemic conditions for affiliation within a sectarian religious community. These conditions reflect Bunyan's stridently orthodox application of Calvinist theology, and they ultimately bring readers into a proper relation to the divine. Although not, strictly speaking, a Calvinist, Behn draws on the inherent instability of Calvinism's two-dimensional, typological model of character to represent the incompatibility of Christianity and racialized empire. *Oroonoko* marks the errant religion of settler-colonists and slave traders through their violation of the norm of semiotic correspondence, and it depicts the limits of the foundational Christian myth to represent African-diasporan subjectivity through the overloading of types on the body of its hero. The irresolvable tension between inside and outside motivates Fielding's further secularizing gesture, whereby Calvinist "diagnostics" takes its place in an array of religious definitions of character, none of them errant yet none of them sufficient to resolve a problem with high soteriological stakes. What these works share, what defines the form of the novel, is their application of Calvinism's human semiotics to various scenes of character evaluation: religious affiliation, erotic and economic exchange, and cultural encounter. Their applications lead to different, increasingly secularized forms (Bunyan's strict Calvinism, Behn's doctrinal latitude, and Fielding's mutually fragilized belief), but, in each case, the viability and errancy of belief manifest through a play of two-dimensionality.

I make the case in this section that Sterne carries the secularist project of the eighteenth-century novel forward, liberalizing both literary character and religion. Slipperiness of character in *Tristram Shandy* obtains at the level of method as well as individual figure. Sterne's approach to characterization, like Fielding's, is multivalent. Sometimes in apparent earnest and at other times with wry insouciance, Tristram cycles through modes, including the pictorial, the typological, and, famously, the "HOBBY-HORSICAL."[49] Rather than formally enacting the nova effect by putting various religious definitions of selfhood and knowledge production into fluid and mutually reinforcing relation, as it does in *Tom Jones* and *Amelia,* however, the multiplication of character in *Tristram Shandy* shrinks the horizon of belief. Through the proliferation of models of character, Sterne positions the skepticism of mainstream Anglicanism against totalizing, rigid systems of bad faith. Roman Catholicism, Islam, and predestinarianism all come in for criticism. Anglicanism, by contrast, offers a path between systematicity and mysticism. As such, it is the only path toward what truths abide amid the riddles and uncertainties of fallen experience.

In describing Sterne's project this way, I build on the arguments of Melvyn New, who shows how closely Sterne hews to the "established positions" of the English Church, and J. T. Parnell, who argues that Sterne, like Jonathan Swift before him, espouses a mitigated form of skepticism "calculated to deflect readers from the search for *rational* truth and toward acceptance of Anglican orthodoxy."[50] I echo New and Parnell by insisting on Sterne's Anglo-Protestant orthodoxy, with the important differences that I show its formal expression through characterization and locate it within rather than against a formation of secularism. New opposes Sterne's religiosity to "secular progress," referring to the emergent liberal-secular order.[51] Parnell contrasts Sterne's Christian or "fideistic skepticism" to the genuine openness of the "secular skeptics" of the Classical era.[52] By "fideistic skepticism," he means a posture of doubtfulness about the search for rational grounds of truth that is underpinned by "certainty of belief in the Christian deity," and when he refers to "secular skeptics," he invokes the Pyrrhonian tradition exemplified by Sextus Empiricus as well as later writings by Tacitus.[53] For Parnell, Sterne's skepticism is conservative, a "defence [sic] of hard-pressed Christian ideology" under pressure from secular forms of thought that celebrated uncertainty.[54] By contrast, I claim that good belief in *Tristram Shandy* and Sterne's sermons *is* secular because it eschews specific theological arguments in favor of a religious epistemology that (alone) accommodates the failures of rationalism and fanaticism alike. Sterne's "Anglican orthodoxy," thus, consists of paradoxically exclusionary openness—a proprietary claim, on behalf of the Church and its adherents, to epistemic humility that is mirrored by the flux of his techniques of character.

The connection between Sterne's religious epistemology and the discourse of empire is not always explicit. *Tristram Shandy* does not address the material conditions of slavery, as Ramesh Mallipeddi has shown, and in his sermons Sterne lays the violence and cruelty of European colonialism at the feet of Catholic theology.[55] But the latter gesture is a secularist tell, evidence that Sterne is engaged in the project of differentiating true from false belief. Perhaps more significantly, this project extends beyond negative dogmatism—Sterne's vilification of Catholic believers or Muslim qadis—toward positive definition. Sterne joins in the construction of an edifice of liberalized Protestantism that arrogates to itself universalizing principles of toleration and commonsense morality and, with that, the right to power on a global scale. In the service of this recursive form of self-legitimation, Sterne selectively deploys the same technics of character that we have been following from its origins in Bedford Congregation and the citadel of Mansoul to Coramantien and the Ottoman Mediterranean to London and the Allworthy estate. When he wishes to valorize Anglican epistemological humility, Sterne mocks or ironizes fantasies of transparent bodies and nominative determinism—fantasies that oversimplify (in order to dismiss) the Calvinistic ideals of semiotic congruence and orderly taxonomy. But Sterne also appropriates these logics when it serves his argument about the superiority of Anglican notions of conscience over Catholic and Islamic alternatives. Sterne's plastic theory and practice of character—his continuous oscillation between various systems of reference and technologies of representation—enables him to steer readers toward an Anglicanism that defines itself against its theological others.

Gyroscopes, "Hobby-Horses," and Other Technologies

Although multifaceted, Sterne's approach to character is organized through overarching analogy to a single artistic medium—portraiture. It proves a pliant idiom for describing the resources of flatness. Character in the pictorial mode consists of two elements laid out on a level plane of paper or canvas: an outline and a variable number of subtler, particularizing brushstrokes. This model encompasses several genres of characterization. The caricaturist practices economy, using a few bold strokes to emphasize the essential (physical) features of a character. "Such were the outlines of Dr. *Slop*'s figure," Tristram remarks after describing the doctor's squatness, "which,—if you have read *Hogarth*'s analysis of beauty, and if you have not, I wish that you would;—you must know, may as certainly be caricatur'd, and conveyed to the mind by three strokes as three hundred" (*TS*, 93). But this idea of character also serves Tristram's description of a representational strategy aimed at conveying the complexity, even the final indeterminacy, of knowledge production.

While admiring his own digressive skill in volume 1, Tristram explains that nonlinear narrative structure advances the goal of characteristic writing:

> I constantly take care to order affairs so, that my main business does not stand still in my absence. I was just going, for example, to have given you the great outlines of my uncle *Toby*'s most whimsical character,—when my aunt *Dinah* and the coachman came a-cross us, and led us a vagary some millions of miles into the very heart of the planetary system: Notwithstanding all this, you perceive that the drawing of my uncle *Toby*'s character went on gently all the time;—not the great contours of it,—that were impossible,—but some familiar strokes and faint designations of it, were here and there touch'd in, as we went along, so that you are much better acquainted with my uncle *Toby* now than before. (*TS*, 63)

Here, again, characterization entails two compositional acts, contouring and "touching in." What sets this method apart, according to Tristram, is the way its "machinery" reconciles "contrary motions" and contradictory scales. Linear-progressive and digressive movement proceed simultaneously, "one wheel inside another," as Tristram puts it (64). Gyroscopic motion enables Tristram to follow detours into astrology or family history while still fulfilling the duties of the biographer. This machinery is also automated: the "main business" of individuating Toby carries on "in my absence"—that is, apart from authorial attention. "Drawing my uncle Toby's character" is a different process than caricaturing Dr. Slop, and not merely by virtue of the number of brushstrokes each portrait requires. In this case, subtly particularizing traits, or "familiar strokes and faint des-ignations," accumulate before Tristram has delimited the outer boundar-ies, or "great contours," of his uncle's personality. However adventitiously they accrue, the lighter strokes succeed in acquainting us with Toby; we are "much better acquainted" with him now than before Tristram's digression.

Yet the knowledge produced through gyroscopic characterization is both incomplete and uncompleted. Individuating traits that are "here and there touch'd in" through that process don't give us the full picture. We still need to see Toby in outline, and so Tristram turns, in his next chap-ter, to the more direct intervention of his hobby-horsical method. The digressive mode is also marked by unendingness: "The whole machine, in general, has been kept a-going;—and what's more, it shall be kept a-going these forty years, if it pleases the fountain of health to bless me so long with life and good spirits" (TS, 64). The machinery of characterization runs for the duration of the character-writer's life as well as beyond his intentional control. Together these properties contribute to a vision of literary knowledge production consistent with Anglican reaction, a vision contrary to the hubristic promise of rationalism and the Enlightenment centering of the subject.[56] The path to (in this case, characterological) truth is not straight, we do not walk it entirely on our own strength, and we cannot expect to arrive at the destination in this life. Before under-taking an explanation of his primary strategy of characterization, then, Tristram attunes us to its insufficiency.

While the hobby-horsical method does not lead us to the entire truth of character, neither does it lead us astray in the manner of the cultural obses-sion with interiority. How much easier it would have been "to have taken a man's character," Tristram muses, if the philosopher Momus had gotten his way and windows had been installed in the breasts of humans—or, he continues, if our bodies had been "vitrified" by the heat of the climate and rendered see-through like the hypothetical inhabitants of the planet Mercury (TS, 65). As if these comically literalizing descriptions were not enough to express Sterne's contempt for the cultural preoccupation with achieving a cut-away view of the soul, the chapter continues with a sur-vey of technologies of representation and analytical approaches that pur-port, much as Fielding's "Essay" had done, to penetrate the "dark covering of uncrystalized flesh" which, to our great disadvantage, distinguishes humans from other species in the solar system (65). Indulging his most Swiftian instinct, Tristram considers the utility of measuring the winds of fame or studying excrement, then repudiates the notionally mimetic capacity of the pentagraph and camera obscura (66–67). The exaggerated materiality and invasiveness of these attempts to see through character undercuts the value for depth, which, whatever positivist truths it may promise, makes of the character-writer a feces-smearing voyeur and of the soul an insect behind glass, a queen bee caught "engendering" her wriggling "maggots" (65). Tristram prefers the more flattening metaphor of portraiture. "I will draw my uncle Toby's character from his HOBBY-HORSE," he declares at the close of the chapter (67).

The satire of materialism in the previous chapter carries into Tristram's explanation of how, exactly, the "hobby-horse" dictates the character of its rider, but it doesn't quite undermine the explanatory potential of his method. "There is something in it more of the manner of electrified bodies," Tristram writes at the beginning of volume 1, chapter 24,

> and that by means of the heated parts of the rider, which come immediately into contact with the back of the HOBBY-HORSE.—By long journies and much friction, it so happens that the body of the rider is at length fill'd as full of HOBBY-HORSICAL matter as it can hold;—so that if you are able to give but a clear description of the nature of the one, you may form a pretty exact notion of the genius and the character of the other. (TS, 67)

As it pertains to the formation of personal character, the passage reads like bawdy. The process is charged with sexual electricity, "friction" between the horse and the "heated parts of the rider," whose body is "at length fill'd" with the horse's "matter."[57] As a claim about knowing and representing character, however, the last sentence may be taken seriously. Indeed, it connects Tristram's playful methodological reflections with Sterne's unironic theory of character, expressed in one of his sermons, as the constellating power of a single trait.

Today, critics tends to define the hobby horse as an "obsession," but Tristram himself glosses it as "ruling passion" in volume 2 (TS, 83).[58] The same phrase appears in "Sermon 9" in The Sermons of Laurence Sterne, which

instructs readers how to resolve apparent self-contradiction in the characters they encounter in life and literature. The immediate context is a study
of the biblical Herod, whose alternating gestures of humanity and cruelty,
Sterne thinks, threaten the "credit" of sacred history.[59] But, while Herod
may "appear with two characters very different from each other," they can
be reconciled through the right mode of analysis (*W*, 4.85). Sterne advises
the audience to "distinguish and carry in your eye the principal and ruling passion which leads the character—and separate that, from the other
parts of it,—and then take notice, how far his other qualities, good and
bad, are brought to serve and support that. For want of this distinction,—
we often think ourselves inconsistent creatures, when we are the furthest
from it, and all the varieties of shapes and contradictory appearances we
put on, are in truth but so many different attempts to gratify the same
governing appetite" (4.86). Repetition of the first-person plural pronoun
suggest that the way of reading that Sterne models is extensible. We practice it by isolating the "governing appetite" of the observed individual and
then tracking the way it arranges other characteristics. Particular traits
carry absolute moral valence—our characters are formed by combinations
of "good and bad" qualities—but in coming together they lead observers
to the false conclusion that humans are "inconsistent creatures." We can
observe the remarkable self-consistency of even such "complex characters"
as Herod if we identify the ruling passion (in Herod's case, ambition to
power) and watch how ostensibly contradictory qualities uniformly serve
that impulse. Compared to the more common practice of moral accounting, or organizing good and bad traits into two sides of a figurative ledger
and then subtracting the second column from the first, the method Sterne
proposes "brings us much nearer to the thing we want;—which is truth"
(4.86). Despite their differences of tone and rhetorical situation, *Tristram
Shandy* and "Sermon 9" conceptualize character in much the same way,
as complex but only apparently "contradictory" sets of qualities. Because
they are structured by an identifiable essential nature, the characters of
other people are finally amenable to the pursuit of "truth."

In keeping with the qualifier in Tristram's initial description of his
method, this truth turns out to be "pretty exact," though not comprehensive. A sentimental vignette in volume 2, chapter 12 introduces an entirely

separate register of Toby's character. Tristram relates the indelible impression that his uncle's gentleness toward a fly made on him as a child: "How far the manner and expression might go towards it;—or in what degree, or by what secret magick,—a tone of voice and harmony of movement, attuned by mercy, might find a passage to my heart, I know not;—this I know, that the lesson of universal good-will then taught and imprinted by my uncle *Toby*, has never since been worn out of my mind" (*TS*, 100). The uncertainty building with the addition of possible causes of sympathetic communication between uncle and nephew—Toby's tone or manner of expression? Some "secret magick," such as the way pleasure reverberates between bodies?—prepares the ground for a concession about the limits of characterological knowledge under his cherished hobby-horsical model. On the next page, Tristram admits that "I could not give the reader this stroke in my uncle *Toby*'s picture, by the instrument with which I drew the other parts of it,—that taking in no more than the mere HOBBY-HORSICAL likeness;—this is part of his moral character" (101). Moral character is a lot to leave out, of course, as the ironic force of the negation ("no more than mere") indicates.

Taken in context, however, the admission points more emphatically to the function of Tristram's primary method as part of a larger, open system of representation than it does to the errancy or inadequacy of the method. In this system, "character" refers to the sum of particularizing brushstrokes inside a bolder, more general outline. To give the full picture, Tristram has only to reach for another brush. The supplementary instrument in this case is the descriptive language of sentimentalism, an aesthetic that, as Barbara M. Benedict has argued, reinvigorated the value for symmetry between "material and moral reality" in the late eighteenth century.[60] Hence Toby's tone of voice and physical gestures harmonize not only with his good moral nature but also with the child Tristram's heart, producing affect as well as somaticizing emotion.

Complementarity with other techniques and openness to suspense distinguishes Tristram's approach from the system, based on nominal determinism, favored by his father. Parnell classes Walter Shandy among the "arid rationalists" whom Sterne satirizes.[61] Instead of the hubris of rationalism, however, Walter's view on the importance of Christian names shows submission to anxious, predestinarian faith. Tristram relates that "his opinion, in this matter, was, that there was a strange kind of magick bias, which good or bad names, as he called them, irresistibly impress'd upon our characters and conduct" (*TS*, 47). His rehearsed, repeatable demonstration of the theory intensifies an implicit, surprising connection to Calvinist soteriology: "How many CAESARS and POMPEYS, he would say, by mere inspiration of the names have been render'd worthy of them? . . . Was your son called JUDAS,—the sordid and treacherous idea, so inseparable from the name, would have accompanied him thro' life like his shadow, and in the end, made a miser and a rascal of him" (47–48). Walter's system encompasses both Mr. Honest's hope in *The Pilgrim's Progress*, that he will achieve the nature signified by this name, and Bunyan's obverse fear, in *Grace Abounding*, that he is a type of the apostate Judas. In Walter's formulation the coincidence of name and idea premised by allegorical personification is both stabilized and realized in the world; their inseparability guarantees the worthiness of a Caesar but damns a Judas. Walter's understanding of character, unlike Tristram's, is meant to be totalizing: "He was serious,—he was all uniformity;—he was systematical, and, like all systematick reasoners, he would move heaven and earth, and twist and torture every thing in nature to support his hypothesis" (49). Systematic "reasoning" is anything but reasonable. Rather, it entails a misguided violence of thought. Walter attempts to "twist and torture" the evidence of the created world into uniform agreement with his determinist system, and even attempts to dislodge the firmament.

Together with the novel's parody of inside-outside symmetry, Tristram's critique of Walter's predestinarianism evokes the character regime that, as I have been arguing, shapes the early history of the novel. Specifically, Sterne evokes this regime to highlight the flexibility of his own, opposed theory of character. In keeping with those claims to flexibility, Sterne also draws on the Calvinist notions of character that he ridicules here in an interpolated sermon on conscience. Redeemed from the kind of systematicity that Walter exhibits, Calvinism's typological structure proves useful to his argument for the propriety of liberal Anglicanism. Having tried to demonstrate that *Tristram Shandy* develops a form concomitant to Sterne's religious thought, I dedicate the remainder of this chapter to supporting my claim that these open religious and literary forms insinuate a Protestant imperialist ideology.

Bad Consciences vs. "Good Belief"

Tristram's methodological self-reflections constitute one of Sterne's counters to "systematick" presumption. They replicate Anglicanism's relativist epistemology, bringing us as near as possible to the "the thing we want," characterological truth, through an array of complementary strategies and with acknowledgment of the incompleteness—the ongoing-ness—of character's formation and representation. *Tristram Shandy* offers another, more direct assertion of this religious epistemology, as well, in the interpolated sermon on "Abuses of Conscience." An almost verbatim reprinting of a sermon Sterne himself delivered at York Minster in 1750, the text that Corporal Trim reads in volume 2, chapter 17 purports to solve the problem of spiritual-moral self-evaluation, a process impeded by the human propensity toward self-deception. Conscience "is not to be trusted alone," Sterne warns, but there is a way to compensate for its inadequacy (*TS*, 116):

> If you would form a just judgment of what is of infinite importance to you not to be misled in,—namely, in what degree of real merit you stand either as an honest man, an useful citizen, a faithful subject to your King, or a good servant to your God,—call in religion and morality.—Look,—What is written in the law of God?—How readest thou?—Consult calm reason and the unchangeable obligations of justice and truth;—what say they? Let CONSCIENCE determine the matter upon these reports;—and then if thy heart condemns thee not, which is the case the Apostle supposes,—the rule will be infallible. (117)

Despite the limits of human understanding, "infallible" knowledge of our own character is within reach. To "form a just judgment" of our standing at the intersection of social, political, and religious metrics, we need only apply "calm reason" to scripture, or "what is written in the law of God." This conceptualization of the proper operations of conscience reconciles Sterne to "the Apostle," Paul, who encourages us to trust our consciences.

We may, in fact, do so—we may regard its determination of our "merit" as reliably "just"—where conscience functions to check our interiorized sense of guilt or innocence against a fully legible, unchangeable moral code. His modest appraisal of the reasoning faculty is consistent with Anglican fideistic skepticism as Parnell defines it and applies it to Sterne's fiction.[62] Reason is a tool of application rather than invention, dependent on an external, objective order. As Sterne argues for the singular propriety of this idea of conscience, juxtaposing it to Catholic amorality and the arbitrariness of Islamic theocracy, he shows how skeptical rhetoric could serve the cause of secularist distinction.

Although it begins with a rejection of the Lutheran tenet of trusting conscience and thus proceeds from a sense of the danger of Nonconformist subjectivity, Sterne's sermon offers a much more sustained critique of Roman Catholicism. The piece mobilizes several of the strategies of characterization observed elsewhere in *Tristram Shandy*. Proving that his ridicule of Walter's nominal determinism targets not typology in general but its application as a totalizing system, Sterne crafts a social taxonomy similar to the one in Fielding's "Essay." Rather than kinds of hypocrite, Sterne enumerates categories of bad conscience. The first two character types he lists, the "shameless man" and the "selfish wretch," are defined by particular moral traits, while the third, the legalist, is defined by a disingenuously literalist interpretation of morality (*TS*, 110–14). The final type encompasses an entire religious tradition. "The good Catholick," Sterne writes, performs superficial acts of devotion in return for "absolution" at the hands of a confessor, artificially salving the needful "wound" of conscience: "believe in the Pope;—go to Mass;—cross himself;—tell his beads" (115). Through apostrophe, Sterne imagines the religion itself as an agent in need of atonement: "O Popery! what has thou to answer for?—When, not content with the too many natural and fatal ways, thro which the heart of man is every day thus treacherous to itself above all things;—thou hast willfully set open this wide gate of deceit before the unwary traveler, too apt, God knows, to go astray himself" (115–16). The sin of "Popery," compounded by cognizance of sinning, is seduction. Catholicism "willfully" exploits its adherents' natural tendency toward self-deception as well as promulgating a transactional model of absolution.

Personification and sentimental-physiognomic language intensify this anti-Catholic sentiment as the sermon proceeds. To illustrate his claim that the "history of the *Romish* Church" is essentially a record of imperial violence "sanctified by a religion not strictly governed by morality," Sterne once more invites readers to imagine Catholicism as a character (*TS*, 122). "In how many kingdoms of the world," he asks, "has the crusading sword of this misguided saint-errant spared neither age, or merit, or sex, or condition?—and, as he fought under the banners of a religion which set him loose from justice and humanity, he shew'd none; mercilessly trampled upon both,—heard neither the cries of the unfortunate, nor pitied their distresses" (122). As in the apostrophe to "popery," Sterne represents the Church as an individual subject. Specifically, "he" is a missionary deluded by religious zeal. The compound "saint-errant," of course, evokes "knight-errant" and, by extension, the misguided hero of Cervantes—long recognized as one of *Tristram Shandy*'s most important intertexts.[63] Rather than comic misadventure, however, this religious quixotism produces indiscriminate violence throughout the world.

Not satisfied with the generalized, historical evidence of crusades, Sterne extends his personifying gesture as he transports us to "the prisons of the inquisition" (*TS*, 123). There our gaze is directed to several spectacles of suffering unfolding simultaneously but at different levels of abstraction. The first entails an allegorical vignette, in which institutionalized cruelty enabled by Catholic amorality subjugates positive abstract values: "Behold *Religion*, with *Mercy* and *Justice* chained under her feet,—there sitting ghastly upon a black tribunal, propp'd up with racks and instruments of torture" (123). "Inquisition," the antecedent of "her" in the above sentence, physically dominates the concepts of religion, mercy, and justice at her feet. Establishing an analogy to carceral suffering, this descriptive technique helps readers understand the force of conceptual violence enacted by Catholic votaries at the same time that it recalls the actual harms of Spanish and Portuguese imperialism under the inquisition.

The second and third spectacles, Trim's sympathetic response to the sermon's presentation of embodied suffering and his auditors' reaction to *his* vicarious pain, rely on the sentimentalized logic of physiognomy.

We are called from the image of Christian values prostrate before a "black tribunal" to a more livid scene of human pain:

Hark!—hark! what a piteous groan! [Here *Trim's* face turned as pale as ashes.] See the melancholy wretch who utter'd it—[Here the tears began to trickle down] just brought forth to undergo the anguish of a mock trial, and endure the utmost pains that a studied system of cruelty has been able to invent.—[D—n them all, quoth *Trim,* his colour returning into his face as red as blood.]—Behold this helpless victim delivered up to his tormentors,—his body so wasted with sorrow and confinement—[Oh! 'tis my brother, cried poor *Trim* in a most passionate exclamation, dropping the sermon upon the ground, and clapping his hands together—I fear 'tis poor *Tom.* My father's and my uncle *Toby's* hearts yearn'd with sympathy for the poor fellow's distress,—even *Slop* himself acknowledged pity for him.— Why, *Trim,* said my father, this is not a history,—'tis a sermon thou art reading;—pri'thee begin the sentence again.]—Behold this helpless victim deliver'd up to his tormentors,—his body so wasted with sorrow and confinement, you will see every nerve and muscle as it suffers. (*TS,* 123).

In adapting his sermon for publication as part of *Tristram Shandy,* Sterne reaffirms an aesthetic in which involuntary signs create a text that, in turn, facilitates the communication of social passions. The original version includes verbatim the description of the prisoner's emaciated body, which registers the minutest details of pain and, in doing so, intensifies the experience of witnessing it: "You will see every nerve and muscle as it suffers." What had been the bad object of Tristram's satirical catalog of representational technologies, the cultural ideal of transparency, here serves Sterne's unironic purpose. The earlier chapter parodies authors' ambition to expose the soul to view through literary characterization; his sermon pursues that goal exactly, conjuring a see-through body, in order to vivify the widely reported horrors sanctified by Catholic doctrine. Bracketed descriptions of Trim's somaticized, sympathetic response and the other characters' second-order reactions are, of course, original to the novel. They appear intended as models of sentimental-physiognomic reading; Trim's alternately blanched, tear-streaked, and flushed face charts our emotional path through pathos to anti-Catholic rage. His auditors then show the appropriate response to Trim's category error when, in his effusions, he confuses the rhetorical strategy of a sermon for the truth claim of "history." Walter and Slop join the sentimental hero, Toby, in "yearning" with pity for Trim even as they correct his misapprehension that he's reading a factual account of his missing brother's murder. It is at worst a kind of patronizing indulgence, through which, perhaps, Sterne grants us permission to admire (or, at least, compassionate) the flights of sympathetic projection that make inquisitorial violence real to Trim.

We might recognize in these attempts to characterize the effects of false, fanatical religion both the outlines of Calvinist semiotics and the awakenings of the empire of liberalized Protestantism. The sentimental-physiognomic model operative in the account of Trim's reading revives, this time without irony, Calvinism's ideal of two-dimensional reading. And it does so in view of validating anti-Catholic sentiment. Sterne stops short, in the sermon and at any other point in *Tristram Shandy*, of arguing for British imperial expansion on religious grounds, but his presentation of centrist Anglican morality nevertheless prepares the ground for such articulations of Christianity's civilizing mission. He wields the high ground of relativism as a cudgel, juxtaposing the Anglican episteme's responsiveness to the limits of human knowledge production, and its consequent deference to an objective order, to the irrationality of its theological others. The superiority of his model of conscience, its explicit status as "good belief," is grounded not on theological "arguments" but on the simple, universal logic of causation (224). *"By their fruits ye shall know them,"* Sterne quotes Matthew. I've tried to show, contra scholars who would soften Sterne's anti-Catholicism, that the sermon examines the "fruits" of the Catholic system of faith as a way to bolster Anglican-Protestant hegemony (224).[64]

The Catholic other shares space with another figure of the unruly outside of the liberal Protestant imaginary—the Islamic theocrat. Sterne's sermon concludes with the following comparison: "Your conscience is not a law:—No, God and reason made the law, and have placed conscience within you to determine;—not like an *Asiatic* Cadi, according to the ebbs and flows of his own passions,—but like a *British* judge in this land of liberty and good sense, who makes no new law, but faithfully declares that law which he knows already written" (*TS*, 125). Here the British justice and

"Asiatick Cadi," or magistrate of a court of sharia law, operate in a familiar antithesis. But Sterne's jurisprudential ideal spotlights faith rather than reason. He shows "good sense," it's true, but the British judge does so by enforcing a code "already written." As a theory of conscience, Sterne's formulation glorifies deference to an immutable, objective order. The qadi's subordination of justice to the tides of passion defines Christian-skeptical conscience as well as its concomitant, and distinctively British, model of jurisprudence through contrast. Secular self-legitimation, in its eighteenth-century as well as its contemporary iterations, depends on such constructions of the character of Islam.

The sermon's thoroughgoing repudiation of Catholicism and more off-handed dismissal of Islam serve a claim about Anglican-Protestant propriety that could transform—that, the intervening centuries confirm, *has* transformed—relativism into a rationale for European imperialism. Sterne asserts Anglicanism as a commonsense episteme that stands above doctrinal dispute and theological argumentation and, thus, above any proper system of faith. The evidence of *Tristram Shandy* suggests a genealogical relationship between the relativist epistemology of Anglican centrism and the discourse of contemporary secularist ideology, which continues to impose Protestantized belief and practices under a new name and that promises to liberate its adherents from despotic unreason while it absolves them of the sin of colonialism.[65] Was this outcome inevitable, thus foreclosing the potential of doctrinal latitude to imagine social and political arrangements beyond the parameters established by imperial liberalism? My last two chapters attempt to answer this question through analyses of abolitionist and Gothic novels from the late eighteenth and early nineteenth century. Together, these works show the broad discursive reach of the character of liberal Protestantism that *Tristram Shandy* predicates. They also struggle, in different ways and with varying effects, to separate that character—in both its literary and religious iterations—from the mutually reinforcing, disciplinary mechanisms of patriarchy and empire.

4

The "True Religion" of Abolitionist Fiction

"THREE-FINGERED JACK" MANSONG, hero of William Earle's *Obi,* meets his match in a Maroon mercenary named Quashee. The final pages of the novel recount Quashee heading up a small party in pursuit of Jack, a fictionalized version of the self-emancipated enslaved person turned highwayman who famously hectored white planters in Jamaica in 1780–81.[1] Quashee takes a final preparatory step before departing Maroon-Town for Jack's den in the Blue Mountains: he "got himself christened, and changed his name to James Reeder" (156). As Reeder, he wields Christianity like a countermeasure against the magic of Obeah, the African-Caribbean religion that is supposed to have made Jack invincible. Jack's earlier evasion of Quashee's ambush persuades the enslaved population of his invulnerability, and "many of the Europeans believed in the fancied virtues of his Obi," as well (140). But when the two face off in their decisive battle, Quashee-Reeder boasts that Jack's "Obi had no power over him, for that he was christened, and no longer Quashee, but James Reeder. Jack started back in dismay; he was cowed; for he had prophesied that White Obi should overcome him, and he knew the charm, in Reeder's hands, would lose none of its virtue or power" (156). Quashee-Reeder and two of his followers eventually overpower Jack, dismember him, and then carry his severed head and hand to colonial authorities in order to collect the bounty on his life.

Their combat is a microcosm of the larger struggle between Christianity and Obeah for dominance in the British Caribbean, as Jhordan Layne has argued. Earle may "stag[e] Christianity as the winner," but it is not a triumphal performance.[2] His narrator laments that Jack did not die "like a man," but was "basely murdered by the hirelings of the Government" (*OBI*, 157). What version of Christianity sanctions this inhumane, mercenary killing? Layne cites this passage as evidence that *Obi* "blurs the categorical distinction between superstition and religion," as a way of reminding readers that both Obeah and Christianity "rely on belief in the supernatural."[3] Jack credits the "power and virtue" of "white obi," but does Quashee *believe* in the Christianity he adopts in order to become Reeder? The narrative relays his words and actions but not his thoughts; we know that he vaunts the superior force of his "charm," and that his Christianization is tactical, a preparatory measure. Earle is less interested in the sincerity or nature of Quashee's belief than its (and his) instrumentalization. Just as Jack adopts Obeah as his strategy of resistance, Quashee converts to Christianity in view of self-interest, which in this case overlaps with the colonial administration's interest in restoring Jamaica's theo-racial order. He follows the example of the novel's real villain, a slave trader named Captain Harrop, who deploys Christianity in the service of racial domination.

Obi's ending caps a sustained critique of missionary Christianity in the novel, while connecting Earle's work to other late eighteenth- and early nineteenth-century antislavery texts. When we read *Obi* alongside Ottobah Cugoano's *Thoughts and Sentiments on the Evil of Slavery* and *The Woman of Colour*, a trend emerges. British abolitionist writing from this period tends to repurpose the machinery of secular differentiation for internecine conflict—a struggle for the soul of Christendom. Antislavery writers distinguish the "true religion" of Christian abolitionism from the errant beliefs of antiblack racists and defenders of slavery. Although these texts share a progressive view of slavery, their constructions of true religion show some variability; they are all liberalized, albeit to different degrees. Cugoano reasserts the singular doctrinal authority of Calvinism, as I explore in my introduction, when he articulates his religious theory of racial difference, but he eventually widens the parameters of orthodoxy to include a monolithic, expansionist, antislavery Protestantism. Earle's idea of good belief is theistic but doctrinally nonspecific; real Christianity opens the gates of heaven to Obeah-professing insurrectionists like Jack's mother, Amri, as well as to liberal Protestants. The anonymous author of *The Woman of Colour* sees properly oriented Christianity as rooted in formal worship (at one point they contrast the heroine's regular church attendance to the lazy natural theology of an English nabob family) and resignation to providence, but primarily as evidence of moral rectitude. What these conceptions of belief have in common is their prioritization of moral over doctrinal orthodoxies, as well as their recourse to the two-dimensional model of personal and literary character that we have been tracing from its origins in Calvinist Protestant dissent. The secularized form of Calvinism that acts as the throughline for my previous chapters provides *Obi* and *The Woman of Colour* with a hermeneutic by which to reinterpret the spiritual meanings that attach to bodies, and with an ideal of legibility by which to judge the immorality and theological errancy of Christian missionaries and East Indian Company officers.

Earle uses footnotes and inset narratives to convey the parallelism between Obeah and the apostate Christianity of West Indian slavery, which consists in their shared capacity to disrupt the semiotic coherence normative to true religion. Obeah's "anomalous" symptomaticity is mirrored by the villainous Captain Harrop's double alienation of signs from signifieds. Like Talkative in *The Pilgrim's Progress* and Blifil in *Tom Jones*, Harrop performs inward experiences he does not feel, dislocating somatic signs from internal meanings, and purports to use natural theology to generalize from observations of the created world. But his religious interpretation, like his insincere performances of benevolence, depend on false correspondences to sanctify slavery as an extension of the religious and economic columns of civilization's advance from Europe to the black Atlantic. Semiotic incoherence thus links the notionally rationalistic, imperial theology of natural religion to the epistemological threat of Obeah as it is described by Earle's colonialist source materials.[4] Meanwhile, Earle subtly affirms Obeah's power through his characterization of the title character, who unites the terms of semiotic relation so perfectly that his name has the power to summon his being, even after death. Taken together, *Obi*'s characterization of Harrop and Jack represent the missionary Christianity of Jack's oppressors, or "white Obi," as the more consistent and unambiguous evil in colonial Jamaica.

The Woman of Colour also criticizes Christianity from the inside. How, the novel asks, might the values of racial and gender equity be made to harmonize with the strains of secularized Protestantism? Its provisional solution is to attempt to use a series of evaluations of the character of its protagonist, Olivia Fairfield, to sever the black-white dyad from the chain of binaries that structures secularist discourse. The epistolary form of *The Woman of Colour* makes Olivia a character-writer as well as an object of interpretation. In the first capacity, she abstracts race from semiotic activity, freeing markers of racial difference of their representational qualities. In the second capacity, she resists another kind of abstraction. Olivia's male benefactors and suitors make her the divinity of their eroticizing belief, abstracting her in the sense of decoupling her idea from her concrete attributes, her social value from its grounding meaning in inherited spiritual purity. Although Olivia denies its connection to race, she affirms the semiotics of character in its other applications.

Both *Obi* and *The Woman of Colour* uphold this system of character, then, evincing their participation in a novelistic tradition that includes such temporally and tonally different texts as *The Pilgrim's Progress, Oroonoko,* and *Tom Jones.* The ideal of two-dimensional coherence informs their characterization, as well as their entanglements with secularizing discourse, as we have seen. Here, though, the ideal is normative. True religion, which Bunyan articulates through the unstable dynamic of intrinsic and extrinsic character, and that Fielding and Sterne construct by multiplying epistemic and formal possibilities, in *Obi* and *The Woman of Colour* consists, in part, of a representational schema that realigns signs and signifieds while revaluating the spiritual import of race. This approach to character connects these novels not only to earlier examples of the form but also to the tradition of black antislavery intellectualism. Cugoano, we've seen, sets the precedent for theorizing race within Calvinist Protestant hermeneutics but outside of the aesthetic hierarchy of antiblackness.

A further affinity manifests, I argue in the conclusion to this chapter, through Cugoano's antimony between good belief and what he calls "antichristian" religions. His arguments, too, unfold within the discursive perimeter of secularism. This shared, secularist rhetoric suggests a new way to think about the affiliation between novels and early black critique, firmer grounds for connective analysis than, for example, speculation about the racial identity of the author of *The Woman of Colour*.[5] These genres of thought and expression are held together by a nuanced engagement with secularist ideology, an effort to claim the moral authority of true religion for abolitionism.

Obeah and Apostate Christianity in *Obi*

Obi does not appear in Alan Richardson's otherwise extensive survey of early Romantic-era literature of Obeah. His historicizing argument would need adjustment if it were to accommodate Earle's portrayal. According to Richardson's thesis, Obeah focalized British anxieties "about fluctuations of imperial power, the power of slaves to determine their fate, the power of democratic movements in France, in England, and in the Caribbean."[6] Despite appending long swaths of the same colonial histories that Richardson cites to its narrative, *Obi* relegates colonial fears about the power of Obeah to the literal margins of the page and foregrounds instead the delusive and destructive influence of errant Christian theology. To the extent that the text reproduces nonfictional accounts of Obeah's harms, as Kelly Wisecup holds, it does so in ways that set off Earle's criticism of Captain Harrop's bad-faith applications of natural religion.[7] Obeah "evaded and challenged" colonial forms of knowledge and being, but the construction of religion that Harrop promotes—and to which Three-Fingered Jack eventually succumbs—perverts the liberal principles of secularized Protestantism into a pro-slavery, antichristian practice.[8]

"Anomalous Symptoms": The Meaning of Obeah

After his first reference to "Obi-Man," Earle inserts a lengthy explanatory note that distills the colonial discourse on Obeah in the British Caribbean. The footnote reprints sections of the House of Commons Sessional Papers of 1789, which themselves record the testimony of West Indian planters and colonial historians such as Edward Long and Bryan Edwards.[9] Earle makes only minor changes to the original, editing lightly for formatting and punctuation, and offers no elaboration. If we take this reproduction as an endorsement of the Sessional Papers' account of Obeah practices, then *Obi* is concerned as much with that religion's variance from secular-Protestant signification as with its role in fomenting insurrections by enslaved people. The passages Earle selects from the longer text relate to the difficulty of identifying Obeah practitioners on Caribbean plantations, a tertiary consequence of "infatuation" that disrupts the categories of body and mind, the chain of signification assumed by Western medical semiotics, and the evidential protocols of colonial discipline.

Obeah's "power of delusion" extends beyond practitioners and professors to all enslaved Africans, according to colonial historians. Their credulity inhibits surveillance and control. Sufficiently "infatuated" to fear reprisal by "the Obiah-Men," enslaved people show great hesitancy to "reveal their suspicions," making it "very difficult" to "distinguish the Obiah professor from any other negro upon the plantation."[10] Earle's source observes the infrequency of detection and prosecution of Obeah practice in Jamaica following its prohibition after Tacky's Rebellion in 1760. "Detections are rare," the Sessional Papers record, because "the secrete and insidious Manner in which this Crime is generally perpetrated, makes the legal Proof of it extremely difficult."[11] Earle cuts this reference to "legal proof" but preserves the explanation of the "secrete and insidious" operation, which adopts the vocabulary of a corollary evidential paradigm—that of medical science.

Conceptualized as a disease or "distemper," Obeah confuses the relay between environment, mind, and body. The pathology has origins in the social networks and the system of retributive justice of enslaved populations: "When a negro is robbed of a fowl or a hog, he applies to the Obiah-man or woman; it is then made known among the fellow-blacks that Obi is set for the thief, and, as soon as the latter hears the dreadful news, his terrifying imagination begins to work."[12] Their physical and mental health deteriorate as they begin to interpret everyday maladies—headache, stomach pain—as evidence of the workings of a malevolent, supernatural force. The papers proceed:

The slightest painful sensation in the head, the bowels, or any other part, any casual loss or hurt, confirms his apprehensions, and he believes himself the devoted victim of an invisible and irresistible agency. Sleep, appetite, and cheerfulness forsake him; his strength decays; his disturbed imagination is haunted without respite; his features wear the settled gloom of despondency; dirt, or any other unwholesome substance, become his only food; he contracts a morbid habit of body, and gradually sinks into the grave.

A negro who is taken ill, enquires of the Obiah-Man the cause of his sickness; whether it will prove mortal or not, and within what time he shall die or recover. The oracle generally ascribes the cause of the distemper to the malice of some particular person, by name, and advises to set Obi for that person; but, if no hopes are given of recovery, immediate despair takes place, which no medicine can remove and death is the certain consequence. Those anomolous [sic] symptoms, which originate from causes deeply rooted in the mind, such as terrors of Obi, or from poisons, whose operations are slow and intricate, will baffle the skill of the ablest physician.[13]

The hedging in the last sentence—the affected party may suffer from "causes deeply rooted in the mind," or they may suffer "from poisons"— illustrates a tension that, according to Wisecup, pervades colonial Obeah discourse. That is, the openness of the text to natural and psychological causes bespeaks the ultimate failure of colonial historians to contain Obeah by "naturalizing it," or attributing its effects to an anachronistic botanical science transported with Obeah professors from West Africa.[14] But the preternatural operations of Obeah command the preponderance of attention here, with the natural effects of poison consigned to an appositive phrase at the close of the paragraph. Believers in Obeah's "irresistible and invisible agency" somaticize fear; this embodied response is "anomalous" in the sense that the symptoms, while real and degenerative, even deadly, do not have a determinate external cause. Obeah "baffles" the colonial physician who either lacks the specialized knowledge of the Obeah-man or Obeah-woman or confronts the therapeutic inadequacy of Western medicines in the face of a self-reinforcing, psychosomatic anomaly.

In the Sessional Papers that Earle cites, Obeah produces an eventual crisis of character. Although the document does not say as much explicitly, the initial example suggests some measure of social benefit to the operations of Obeah on a criminal. The "thief" internalizes fear of social repercussion, rooting it in the mind, and then begins to project the feeling outward, to the surfaces of the body: "his features wear the settled gloom of despondency" and present a "morbid habit," or unhealthy constitution. By this means, perhaps, the victim of theft might identify the perpetrator—and, in any case, the thief is subject to a severe penalty for his crime. The second, more general example of "a negro who is taken ill," however, shows an Obeah practitioner randomly assigning "malice" to "some particular person, by name."[15] Obeah enables a scheme of one-for-one retribution in the first instance, but its effect in the next case is to mark another member of the community with a malign character, presumably continuing the cycle of revenge when an "obi" is set for the "particular person" identified as the cause of the first party's suffering. In this respect, the workings of Obeah among the enslaved population create a problem similar to the one faced by enslavers, who cannot reliably distinguish the responsible individual (i.e., the "Obiah professor") from the totality ("any other negro").

By attaching this account of the workings of Obeah to his narrative of Jack Mansong, Earle defers to the authority and perpetuates the biases of imperialist discourse. His decision to cite the Sessional Papers implicates him in the colonialist representation of bad belief as a "superstition" or "fascinating mischief," which depends on the credulity of "deluded negroes" while confounding colonial ways of knowing other people. Yet the text of *Obi* is more agnostic than the purported experts it cites. When he addresses Obeah directly, the narrator, George Stanford, expresses suspicion and moral judgment consistent with the colonialist perspective. Stanford describes Jack's mother, Amri, as "self-deluded" when she turns to Obeah as a means of revenge against Harrop, and calls the hovel of Bashra, an Obeah practitioner, a "horrible cell of iniquity" (105). Stanford similarly rejects the supernatural explanations for Jack's escaping gunfire from Quashee and his men, deviating from widespread public credulity: "But Jack was not invulnerable, as was proved by Quashee, who wounded him in several places, and deprived him of two of his fingers" (140). All of the enslaved people and "many" of the colonists believe in the power of Obeah to render Jack invincible, but Stanford cites empirical evidence in refuting their conviction. He offers the alternative explanation that Jack's feats are superhuman in the exact proportion that his "cause" is "noble": Jack "fought for the liberty of his countrymen; he fought to avenge a father, and this endowed him with strength superior to the vaunting of his antagonists" (140). His prowess in combat reflects the intensity of the entwined imperatives he feels, to avenge the death of his father, Makro, and to emancipate his oppressed African "countrymen." Such a combination of Achillean virtue and emancipatory politics would have been more easily assimilable into the worldview of Earle's audience by 1800—even those readers who did not share his Jacobin sentiments—than the supernatural operations of Obeah.

The novel does not always reject Obeah's supernaturalism, however. Earle introduces ambiguity through Stanford's explanation of his compositional method. On the one hand, Stanford's method aligns him with colonial discourse. On the other hand, his narrative proceeds from an acknowledgment and an embrace of a powerful magic that works much like Obeah. He begins the correspondence that structures the narrative by confiding in his friend that he writes under a strange, irresistible influence:

> I'll tell you what, Charles—I have just read your letter for the hundred and
> first time, and upon my soul, cannot see that the business it is about is of
> such great importance; so, with, or without your leave, I shall put off answer-
> ing it, until I have eased myself of my insufferable burthen, by dispatching
> Jack, his three fingers and his Obi, and all that belongs to him; for, positively,
> I can think of nothing else. . . . If any of my neighbours, calling his servant,
> says; "Jack, come here," I start and stare about, in expectation of seeing the
> three-fingered one make his appearance. Nay, there is not a *thing* called jack,
> whether a smoke-jack, a boot-jack, or any other jack, but acts as a spell upon
> my senses and sets me on the fret at the bare mention of it. (*OBI*, 70)

Impelled to respond to Charles's unspecified "business" by the structure of expectations that obtains to epistolary exchange, Stanford nevertheless turns his attention to Jack's history, for he "can think of nothing else." What consumes Stanford's mind and determines the act of composition is not a story, precisely, but a character: "Jack, his three fingers and his Obi, and all that belongs to him." The sequence of terms in this list betrays an intensifying desire for comprehensiveness; neither the synecdochic maimed limb nor the religion of Obeah may stand in for Jack. To unburden his mind, Stanford must communicate "all that belongs to him," representing the whole rather than representing him by a part or an association.

Stanford's choice of verb, "dispatch," briefly hints at violence or dismissal, but, read back against his exculpatory narrative, the diction signals a frantic wish to send off Jack reconstructed in the form of letters. Stanford concludes his preamble: "As I have made it my business to collect every particular relative to him, I believe I shall have it in my power to give you a circumstantial account of all his actions. In fact, what I am now going to write is nothing more than a copy of what I had some time ago begun to put into a regular story, out of several memoranda collected at different times" (*OBI*, 71). His practice invites comparison to the practice of Obeah as it was understood by British writers at the turn of the century. When they are discovered, Obeah professors may be identified by the "implements of [their] trade," a farrago of objects consisting of, in one instance recorded by the Sessional Papers, "rags, feathers, bones of cats, and a thousand other articles."[16] Stanford *composes* Jack by rearranging the details recorded in his irregular memoranda into a "regular story." His plan of characterization is not unlike the interpretive labors of physicians, planters, and writers who impose orderly meaning onto the confused mixture of objects as part of their program of demystification and discipline.

While Stanford does not remark their similarity, the nature of his compulsion to write Jack's character closely resembles the effect attributed to Obeah in colonial discourse. The charm carried by the word "Jack" alters his perception—it "acts as a spell upon my senses"—and, with that, his apprehension of language. Three-Fingered Jack, the character, becomes the referent for all enunciations of the phonetic sign "Jack," replacing other persons, like "my neighbour's servant," as well as a variety of "things." Because it summons Jack's presence through the mere articulation of his name or even the unrelated words with which it shares a sound, the "spell" under which Stanford composes his letter resolves Obeah's tendency to unsettle conventional semiotic dynamics. Similar phonetic signs become disjoined from their original ideas, but they then coalesce in a single, repeated act of signification. They all now mean one thing, Jack Mansong. Stanford reacts ambivalently to this magic. He is discomfited by the way Jack coopts meaning (it "sets me on a fret"), yet he is unwilling to discharge the burden another way. He declares, "By heavens! it is too much, and I wish . . . Nay, I do not—I cannot find in my heart to form the same wish that most of the inhabitants here express every day" (*OBI*, 70). What is the ineffable desire that Stanford resists? Since the narrative is retrospective, the event of Jack's death precedes Stanford's writing and cannot be the object of Stanford's suppressed "wish." Perhaps he (almost) wishes that he could reclaim his senses and language, that he could break the spell without attempting this literary undertaking. Stanford himself provides no definitive answer, cutting off the train of thought and projecting his still-unnamed wish onto the figure of a "cruel hard-hearted planter" (70). The fictive planter attempts to rebut Stanford's argument that Jack's humanity takes precedence over his racial classification: "'Jack is a Negro,' say they. 'Jack is a MAN,' say I" (70). Through this imagined agon, Stanford exorcizes a desire that marks his participation in plantation capitalism and his assent to the fictions of African inhumanity upon which the institution of racial slavery is founded. In this way, he overcomes his ambivalence and accepts the implicit charge of the haunting spirit, the call to write Jack's character and send it to his addressee across the Atlantic. The passage implies that it is the charm of Jack's name, the ubiquity of the signs of his character, that facilitates as it also compels the act of composition.

A passing comment on the physical appearance of Bashra, the Obeah practitioner consulted by Jack's mother, tips the scales of narrative sympathy toward Obeah. Bashra carries the mark of a class of formerly enslaved Africans who are ostracized from plantations due to a highly contagious illness known as the yaws. He "was one of those deserted negroes, who, affected by a disorder prevalent in the West-Indies, are compelled to fly from the plantation on which they are engaged, and seek a retreat in the woods, where, unassisted, they are left to die or recover, at the will of Providence. . . . Those are the beings, who, in their seclusion most frequently practice Obi. The more they are deformed, the more they are venerated, and their charm credited as the strongest" (*OBI*, 119). Passive voice in the last sentence creates ambiguity about who, exactly, "venerates" and "credits" the Obeah-man's magic. It is unlikely, given the skeptical pose Stanford strikes elsewhere, that he includes himself or his fellow white West Indians among those who interpret physical disfigurement as a measure of the strength of a practitioner's "obi"; his syntax nevertheless keeps the possibility open. Moreover, the function of Bashra's marked body as evidence of spiritual status survives a shift to Stanford's Christian perspective. If those who fall ill survive only "at the will of Providence," then the "deformed" bodies of survivors are a visible record of divine favor. Viewed through either religious lens, Bashra and other yaws-afflicted, "deserted negroes" diverge from the colonialist accounts of Obeah that Earle cites in his footnote. They boast a bodily semiotics that hints at Earle's ambivalence. Bashra's body is a text with multiple meanings. His appearance distinguishes him from other enslaved people, marking him as a practitioner of Obeah and, thus, as the proper object of colonial discipline of the kind endorsed by the Sessional Papers and other historical documents. At the same time, Bashra's flesh is marked by the hand of God, at whose "will" alone he and others like him survive a ravaging disease. His legible character as an Obeah-man obviates the epistemic fear in the Sessional Papers' description of the religion. Inscribed on his flesh, Bashra's bad belief singles him out as a proper subject of colonial discipline, but it also renders him less threatening than the character the novel associates with liberalized Christian theology, Captain Harrop.

White Obi

Earle's footnote, as I say, reproduces portions of the 1789 parliamentary report on Obeah almost verbatim. One of his deviations from the language of the Sessional Papers hints at the novel's secularist framing. The passage in question describes the challenge of identifying Obeah-men and Obeah-women in the Caribbean. In the original text, the clause reads, "It is very difficult therefore for the White Proprietor to distinguish the *Obia Professor* from any other Negro upon his Plantation."[17] Earle's note substitutes "white professor" for "white proprietor."[18] It is, perhaps, an error of transcription. If so, it is a surprisingly appropriate and instructive slippage. The repetition of "professors," modified by the binary terms of epidermal race, creates a distinction not between social classes (the planter vs. enslaved people) but between deadlocked colonial religions. "Professor" further connotes characterological uncertainty; in previous fiction by Bunyan, Behn, and Fielding, the word often carries with it the stigma of hypocrisy, highlighting the potential gap between declarations of faith and sincere faithfulness. In *Obi*, it is the "white professor" more than "obiah professors" who most clearly illustrates this danger.

The bad object in Earle's antislavery argument is not Obeah, but Captain Harrop's false Christianity. In letters 2 through 5, Stanford copies out Amri's first-person narrative. It is a tale of abused credulity that she tells Jack to incite him to take revenge on Harrop and his fellow enslavers. Amri and Makro rescue Harrop and his apprentice from a wreck on the shores of the Gambia River, nursing the Englishmen through injuries and illness. Ostensibly motivated by gratitude, Harrop assumes the role of religious instructor to his African benefactors. He instructs them, specifically, in the principles of natural religion. The premise of this form of Christian thought is that the created world, viewed by the light of reason, reveals theological truths. Believers reason from observations of the natural world to what knowledge—of God's existence and law, for example—is required to achieve salvation. Isabel Rivers finds an emphasis on natural religion in writings by members of the progressive arm of the Anglican Church, Latitudinarianism, as well as more radical deists. Its prevalence reflects the general trend she observes in her expansive history of religious thought between 1660 and 1780—that is, an increasing prioritization of the operations of right reason over the precepts of revealed religion and of the capacity of the rational agent to choose "the good" over the workings of grace.[19] In other words, natural religion is a link between progressive forms of Protestant thought and the putatively secular intellectual tradition of moral philosophy—and a step toward the actualization of liberal subjectivity. From its inception, natural religion was tied to a left political orientation. Among its proponents were influential English freethinkers (John Toland; Anthony Collins; Anthony Ashley-Cooper, the third Earl of Shaftesbury; Matthew Tindal) sympathetic to the republican ambitions of the 1650s and hostile to the authority of the established church.[20] By implicating natural religion in Harrop's activities as a West Indian slave trader, Earle acknowledges a pernicious legacy of this liberal religious tradition: its use as a screen for the fundamentally illiberal practice of slavery.

Natural religion facilitates the first step in Harrop's betrayal of Amri and Makro, establishing his false character of authority and trustworthiness. Amri once overhears his ejaculatory prayer and, confused by his address, asks, "Who was nature?" In his response, Harrop both repudiates Amri's pagan belief system and installs the type of the missionary atop a hierarchy of creation:

> "The great Creator," answered he; "He to whom you owe your being." I did not rightly comprehend him, but he soon gave me to understand that I worshipped a false god. I looked upon him with astonishment. He told me the glorious sun was but a substance created by his God, who was the great father of all. He told me of the enlivening power of the sun. "I," cried he, "feel its warmth in my heart; its splendor inspires me with an active spirit to fulfill the duties of this life and enjoy society. You yourself," applying to me, "feel the same influence; the sun cheers the herbage of the field, when drooping; it shed its enlivening rays, expands the opening leaf, which soon revels in prosperity. So the charitable man spreads his kind rays around, revives the depressed, becomes a father to the orphan, a husband to the widow; by him are the afflicted comforted, the ignorant enlightened, and the poor relieved. Oh! Amri, a charitable man is the noblest work of God." (*OBI*, 77)

Harrop corrects Amri's relation to the sun, which she apparently worships as a deity—"for the moment, he staggered my belief that I was doing right in worshipping, as he said, the servant of the real God," she reflects (77)—but that she should instead regard as an object of interpretation.[21] As he shifts from assertion to proof, Harrop bypasses pat deistical glosses on the sun's "enlivening power." He strikes that chord later, when he presents the contrast of sunrise and nightfall as an illustration of the completeness of God's works and wisdom (78). In this first pedagogical scene, though, he does not say that the sun's salubrious effects demonstrate God's benevolence; rather, he instructs Amri that its rays enable and figure the character of "the charitable man." The sun "inspires me with an active spirit to fulfill the duties of this life and enjoy society,"

Harrop claims, while its diffusion of warmth and light metaphorizes the social function of the man of charity. Although he stops short of explicitly claiming this sunlike character, the "noblest work of God," for himself, Harrop preemptively glorifies the civilizing ambition he initiates with this speech. He will act the part of the charitable man by "enlightening" his "ignorant" African hosts. Harrop's performance has the desired effect. Amri and Makro "thought him all virtue" and "wisdom," "entreating him never to leave us" (78). Harrop doesn't leave them, of course, instead springing a trap once they board an English boat and then carrying them to a slave ship headed to the Caribbean.

There is historical and literary precedent for Harrop's approach to evangelism. The program for Christianizing Native Americans and free and enslaved black people laid out by the Society for the Propagation of the Gospel in Foreign Parts (SPG), a prominent Anglican missionary organization in the eighteenth and nineteenth centuries, begins with instruction of natural religion.[22] Unca Eliza Winkfield, the heroine of the popular Robinsonade *The Female American* (1767), follows this plan to convert the Indigenous people who visit her otherwise deserted island. Hiding inside a giant idol, Winkfield "began to discourse upon the nature and attributes of the Deity, from what are usually called the principles of natural religion; though I believe, strictly speaking, all religion to be revealed."[23] In both cases, the usefulness of natural religion in promulgating Anglo-Protestantism permits a temporary deviation from the Anglican investment in revelation. They hint at the instrumentalist approach to religious precepts that, in *Obi*, becomes outright mercenary deception. The difference coincides with a larger contrast of attitudes toward the missionary enterprise. While the papers of the SPG and *The Female American* endorse Christian imperialism, *Obi* represents the Christian ambition to colonize the world as a villainous perversion of true religion.[24]

Harrop, like the SPG and Winkfield, harnesses the complementarity of nature and revelation. Rivers explains that the place of revealed religion in a writers' arguments helps to distinguish their place on the theological spectrum of the long eighteenth century. Freethinkers (a group that, in her taxonomy, includes deists) regarded revelation as redundant with nature. Latitudinarians, the dominant school of Church of England theology by the turn of the century, invested natural religion with weight but saw revealed religion as a distinct (and either opposing or corroborating) concept.[25] Although his instruction of Amri and Makro consists entirely of rational engagement with "the works of the infinite Creator of all things" (*OBI*, 79), Harrop later alludes to scriptural teachings in his first encounter with Jack. He sees Jack toiling in the sugar cane fields and accosts him as "a material acquisition to the plantation of Mr. Morton" (106). Then, unprompted, Harrop pontificates about what he takes to be the spiritual advantages of enslavement:

> But you feel a pleasure in cultivation, that fully rewards your labor. The sun shines and assists you in your toil; a glorious opportunity presents itself to you to contemplate the various beauties of Nature, and the soft zephirs that play around you keep your body in a moderate degree of warmth.
>
> How happy is your situation, how truly enviable! You can contemplate the vast expanse before you, and can say in private to your heart: "My God, I have answered the end of thy creation; for I, with the sweat of my brow, diffuse thy beneficence around, extract from the earth the produce thereof, and help to render the comforts of life complete." (106)

In this idealized account, the work of "cultivation" is pleasurable and "fully rewards" the laborer in a closed circuit of extraeconomic compensation. Harrop declares that enslaved labor carries an additional, spiritual reward: the "opportunity" to "contemplate" nature and, through that reflection, to achieve a sense of divine purpose fulfilled.

His description of enslaved labor, and specifically his use of the phrase "sweat of my brow," combines the logic of natural religion with the authority of revelation. The ventriloquized, spontaneous prayer of the enslaved puts a celebratory spin on the punishment for original sin: "Cursed is the ground for thy sake; in sorrow shalt thou eat of it all the days of thy life; Thorns also and thistles shall it bring forth to thee; and thou shalt eat the herb of the field; In the sweat of thy face shalt thou eat bread, till thou return unto the ground; for out of it wast thou taken: for dust thou art, and unto dust shalt thou return."[26] Having forfeited the superabundance of paradise along with eternal life, Adam and his posterity are "cursed" to extract their subsistence from the earth through strenuous labor. Sorrow, not pleasure, mingles with the sweat of his toil. Harrop adapts the language of scripture to promote a sanguine image of postlapsarian experience, but his reinterpretation of labor outside the walls of paradise promotes a stark inequality. Jack's "end" is to act as a conduit of divine benevolence, to "render the comforts of life complete." What, according to this self-serving religious argument, is the planter's purpose?

As Harrop describes his relationship to Amri, still unaware that he speaks to her adult son, he clarifies that the enslaver, too, cultivates. His harvest is the uncivilized mind of the African: "She was ignorant, and I matured her understanding; her good heart was encircled by weeds of savage growth; I plucked them by the roots and implanted in their stead seeds of a more refined nature; by my daily perseverance, and the susceptibility of a heart that owned all tender feelings from her birth, they soon expanded and ripened into blossom. I felt a pleasure in the culture of her mind, such as you must feel, when raising from the ground a nutriment to life" (OBI, 107). Through metaphor and the proposition of a shared feeling of pleasure-in-fulfillment, Harrop posits a false equivalence between the missionary's "culturing" of "savage" character and the agricultural labor of the enslaved person. He misrepresents a structure of domination as parallelism; in fact, a causal relationship obtains between the civilizing enterprise of conversion and enslaved labor. The refinement of Amri's mind and heart by way of instruction in natural religion ends with her enslavement, and the work Jack now performs is the hereditary curse of chattel slavery.

Harrop's characterization indicates that the novel does not reject natural religion absolutely. He is a hypocrite, as Amri reflects and Stanford later confirms, scheming to sell Amri and Makro into slavery while he "daily habituated our ears to tales of humanity" (OBI, 79). When Amri laments their "credulity" as the cause of their suffering, she refers to faith in Harrop's performed goodness rather than assent to his theological teachings (79). Stanford's "sketch" of Harrop corroborates the one contained in Amri's interpolated narrative and suggests that her and Makro's trust is an excusable error (126). Harrop is another Blifil: "He had a smooth tongue, which gained him the good will of all. Artful and cunning, he could disguise the sentiments of his heart with the greatest ease" (126). Beyond smooth talk, Harrop shows a talent for displaying emotions that are beyond his actual capacity to feel. He combines a coldly analytical knowledge of "the human heart" with an ability to feign somatic clues, carrying on the novelistic tradition of characters who disrupt the relationship of moral disposition (here, of insensibility, "a man dead to every tender feeling") and exterior evidence (the "well feigned tear and extreme agitation" of a sympathetic lover) (129–30). Earle's characterization of Harrop once again raises the issue of two-dimensionality—the shifting relationship between exteriority and interiority—that originates in the Calvinist tradition of reading character. Like Behn, Earle adapts this tradition, which begins as an acknowledgment of the inherent difficulty of knowing fellow adherents within a relatively insular English religious community, as the idiom for her critique of colonial encounter. Secularized in the sense of untethered from specific doctrinal codes, the Calvinist model illustrates the insincerity and deceptiveness of the Christian missionary in Jamaica, another colonial counterpart to Bunyan's false professors. In this way, the model perpetuates the machinery of secularist distinction, marking adherents to the false religion of imperialist ambition.

Among the "sentiments" Harrop dissembles is reverence for commerce. Stanford narrates that, "by his flattering tongue, he had gained the hearts of the two unsuspecting Feloops; but, while he remained here, he was ruining his own interest; trade was his idol, and there was no relief to his busy mind" (*OBI*, 128). Comparing this gloss of Harrop's deception to Amri's account of his teachings clarifies the purpose of his advocacy for natural religion. Stanford (whose access to Harrop's interiority goes unexplained) dismisses his teachings as silver-tongued flattery. "Flattering" can mean "adulatory" or "gratifying to the self-esteem" of the hearer.[27] But a "flattering tongue" may also deliver "pleasurable (usually, delusively) anticipations or beliefs." Given what readers already know about the intercourse between Harrop and Amri and Makro—namely, that religious instruction is the primary means by which he insinuates himself to the couple—the latter denotation makes the most sense in context. He offers them "delusively" pleasing ideas, not only of his warm friendship but also of his adoration of the works of God. Harrop, too, through his insincere expression of belief, dissembles the true object of his devotion, the "idol" of trade.

The novel's structure facilitates this interpretation by layering Stanford's authority onto Amri's relation. Her narrative comprises chapters 2 through 4, while chapter 9 covers the same events, with greater emphasis on and access to Harrop's motivations. As Katherine G. Charles has recently pointed out, the "formal device of the interpolated tale" confers "vigor and moral authority" on Amri, allowing her to emerge "as one of the most powerful female speakers in late eighteenth- and early nineteenth-century novels."[28] The same device lends certainty to Harrop's religious character and, thus, specificity to Earle's antislavery critique of religion. Stanford's character sketch corroborates Amri's portrayal. For Amri, Harrop's hypocrisy is typical of the "character of the Europeans" and "the christianity of the Europeans who profess humanity" (*OBI*, 79, 84). Stanford, too, suggests that Harrop's hypocrisy is representative; his goal in copying out Amri's narrative is to "delineate the character of an European West-Indian" for his friend, who resides in England, thereby putting flesh on the type from his dialogue in the first letter (82). In letter 9, Stanford elaborates on Amri's charge of hypocrisy, stating that Harrop's profession of Christian humanity disguises his acquisitiveness and iniquity.

Such vices are not endemic to Christianity, but to the false idol of trade that Harrop and the settler class he typifies worship under the affectation of humane feeling. Through Makro's apparent conversion, Stanford's sentimentalist editorializing, and Amri's fate, *Obi* provides the bare outlines of good belief. True religion differs from the "christianity of the Europeans" whom Amri decries less on theological than political grounds. Natural religion features in this construction, but it has an antislavery orientation. Aboard the slave ship, shortly after Harrop's betrayal, Makro explains to his wife why he chooses death over slavery. "Amri," he says,

> 'tis not that I fear to live, but that I have resolved never to acknowledge a master. I do not seek death because I fear buffet with those Europeans, it is because I never can own a superior but my Creator. Man was His noblest work, and I am a man. He did not make slaves of one half of this globe, nor order the black to bend subservient to the white man's yoke; nor will I, a created being like them, be bought and sold, and toil like a beast of burden, that they may enjoy the fruits of my labor. (90)

Makro never refers to a moment of conversion, but the diction and logic of his speech indicate that Harrop's teachings, however insincere and self-serving, have in fact Christianized him. When Amri remains steadfast in her adherence to their native paganism until turning to Obeah after arriving in the Caribbean, and when she speaks of divinity, it is frequently with a possessive pronoun ("our God" [74, 90]) or identifying prepositional phrase ("the God of Africa," [xx, 76]). Makro, though, refers to "my Creator." More substantively, Makro concludes that slavery violates the order of creation because it would require Makro to "own a superior" other than God. Drawing entirely on natural religion—we recall that Harrop, like the missionaries of the SPG, instructs him entirely in Christian-rationalist principles rather than through lessons of scripture—Makro arrives at the truth of human equality. Natural religion reveals itself even in the face of the false intentions and duplicity of Harrop. Earle's faith in natural religion is best attested by the fact that Makro is converted even though he learns religion from Harrop, the quintessential villain.

True religion extends grace to unconverted Africans, as well. After describing a poignant exchange between Jack and his friend-at-arms, Mahali, Stanford cites their heroic sensibility as a contradiction of stereotypes and an example for Christians to follow. "Oh! thou great Creator," he exclaims, "look down upon those *unenlightened savages!* See them entwined within each other's arms, while the mingled tear of friendship, the grateful effusion of two noble hearts, deprives each of the power of speech. But these are savages and worship an imaginary god; they are black men, and slaves, unworthy the appellation of men. Ye sons of christianity, versed in enlightened schools, that teach you to distinguish and to adore the great Creator, emulate their great example, for ye have no such heroes among you" (*OBI*, 146). As in his dialogue with a typical planter in letter 1, Stanford counters racism first by ventriloquizing it. "Sons of christianity" would exclude Jack and Mahali from the category of the human based on their religious, racial, and social identities. They are "unworthy the appellation of men" because they "worship an imaginary god," "they are black men," and they are "slaves." Speaking in his own voice, Stanford argues for the superiority rather than the mere equality of the "unenlightened savages" in his sentimental vignette. To better realize the teachings of the "enlightened schools" of Christianity in which they are trained, Stanford's interlocutors should "emulate" Jack and Mahali's heroic sensibility. Grammatical parallelism—"great creator" and "great example"—conveys their proximity to divine nature. Through his narrator, Earle issues a directive to recognize the visibility of character. Nominal and implied addressees, professing Christians and readers alike, should "look down upon" Jack and Mahali's embrace and "see" them as models of Christian-heroic virtue rather than as theo-racial stereotypes.

Stanford calls on God, too, to witness their display. Without quite accusing the Christian deity of complicity in Amri and Makro's mischaracterization, Stanford's address hints that the two men occupy a blind spot in providential vision. Asking God to "see" the friend's intimacy is tantamount to asking that divine omniscience and judgment be extended to those who demonstrate the virtue of sentimental masculinity outside the formal precincts of Christian belief. Stanford imagines this prayer answered through Amri's death. He deviates from the flimsy claims to narrative authority that, at first, ground the earlier retelling of her history. As he begins, he informs Charles that "the narrative was imparted to me by a negro, well acquainted with Amri," and "I set down her own words as near as memory can trace" (*OBI*, 73). Now, he purports to see beyond the border between life and death: "The last breath was trembling on her lips when Jack appeared; she opened her eyes, beheld her son, who with filial ardor grasped her hand, and she expired. Heaven received her amidst a choir of angels" (148). Apart from *Obi*'s tenuous relation to realist fiction, this passage expresses a conception of Christianity as inclusive even of Obeah practitioners and insurgents. Despite her crimes and her unbelief, and, as a matter of straightforward narrative fact, Amri ascends to heaven.

Quashee arrives several pages on, brandishing his new religious identity, to concretize the distinction between the expansiveness of authentically "enlightened" Christianity and the violence of Christian imperialism. Narration of Quashee's christening as James Reeder is sparse, but it illuminates his relationship to the Christian faith:

The reward of three hundred pounds, and liberty, was a great inducement [to kill or capture Jack], and worked upon the hearts of many; but Jack's malefic Obi in the opposite scale, was a tremendous evil, and their courage failed them. But the bold and lion-hearted Quashee was not to be intimidated by his imaginary spell, and, accompanied by another daring fellow, Sam, of Scot's-hall Maroons-town, they set out, determined to bring in the head and hand of Jack, or die in the failure of the expedition. Quashee first got himself christened, and changed his name to James Reeder. A great party of the towns-people accompanied them, and the expedition commenced. (*OBI*, 156)

Quashee's Christianization consists of a single ritual, nominally transformational but motivated by the rewards of cash and manumission and undertaken as if it were a simple logistical concern, a step preparatory to battle. Christianity is a "charm" that differs in relative force but not in kind from Jack's "imaginary spell." It is a superstition that makes of Quashee an effective instrument of state violence, enabling him to restore plantocratic order by overpowering Jack. Stanford remarks that Jack's crimes warrant capital punishment, but not the indignity of being "basely murdered by the hirelings of Government." Those hirelings, Quashee and another Maroon named Sam, "beat his brains out with stones" (157). Earle thus depicts the triumph of Christian-secularist hegemony in Jamaica. The capacity of this anti-Christian Christianity to assimilate black enslaved people, its framing as the privileged term in a religious dyad with Obeah, its concomitance with the interest of the West Indian planter class, and its function as a rationale for grisly violence are all figured by Quashee's conversion and subsequent murder of Jack.

Most immediately, Earle's narration of Jack's death represents a conflict between professors of Obeah and Christianity. However, read in light of its earlier articulations of true Christianity (Makro's appeal to natural religion as justification for black self-determination; Stanford's apostrophe to God and reader; and the narration of Amri's admission to heaven), the ending punctuates a conflict between two strains of Christian faith in the British Caribbean, each liberalized with respect to Protestant doctrine. These schools differ not according to theological argument or institutional vision—each focuses on reason instead of doctrinal specificity or ritual program—but according to their relationship to the evil of slavery.

Abstracting *The Woman of Color*

There has been an explosion of interest in *The Woman of Colour,* particularly after the publication of Lyndon J. Dominique's Broadview edition in 2008. The novel relates Olivia Fairfield's negotiation of Caribbean and English identities. Olivia, the daughter of a white enslaver and an enslaved African, travels from Jamaica to England in order to fulfill a condition of her father's will: she must marry her cousin, Augustus Merton, to secure her inheritance. Olivia and Augustus do wed, and they enjoy a brief period of domestic happiness. When Augustus's first wife is discovered alive, however, the union is delegitimized, and Olivia's fortune passes to Augustus's brother and scheming sister-in-law. After rebuffing several further proposals of varying degrees of propriety, Olivia decides to return to Jamaica. Scholars are divided on the question of how to interpret the end of the novel. Olivia's refusal to marry for a second time, coupled with her imminent return to the West Indies, signals to some readers the novel's radical politics. Dominique positions *The Woman of Colour* as the telos of a progressivist literary history; Olivia "embodies," more fully than previous African characters and white abolitionists alike, the spirit and subjectivity of "resistance."[29] She chooses not to remarry because she is an "independent black female activist dedicated to her own emancipation" and that of other enslaved people.[30] Victoria Barnet-Woods similarly describes Olivia as the "embodied critique of moral corruption" under empire and the pattern for a new kind of bildungsroman, in which women develop toward self-actualization against the model prescribed by patriarchal capitalism.[31] Emphasizing external (i.e., narrative and social) forces rather than Olivia's personal agency, another train of scholarship reads Olivia's exclusions from marriage and the metropole as confirmation of contemporary racial and colonial attitudes. Jennifer De Vere Brody speaks forcefully for this position when she argues that, "if the 'departed father' is read also as the law or as laws of nature racially inflected, it is the fate of the woman of colour to disappear in order to sustain the fiction of the pure, white family and the family of man, which functions as a homologue for the English nation."[32]

Attending in equal measure to the potential of and the constraints on the novel's radical undertaking, the following section navigates the extremes of existing scholarship and, in the process, shows *The Woman of Colour*'s complicated engagement with secularist ideology.[33] The novel seeks to uphold the representational and devotional schema of secularized Protestantism while also delivering criticisms of slavery and marriage and revising the concepts of gender and racial capacity that buttress those institutions. The resulting ideological tension plays upon Olivia's features. Although they overstate the novel's interest in subjectivity per se, scholars like Dominique and Barnett-Woods rightly draw attention to how and what Olivia signifies inside the text and beyond its diegetic parameters. The word they both choose, "embodiment," captures something of the novel's preoccupation with inside-outside convergences. Centering this interest clarifies the *The Woman of Colour*'s oft-discussed but elusive relationship to contemporary racial constructs, as well as their entanglement with secularizing premises.

The Woman of Color as Resisting Object

The Woman of Colour promotes a system of character-reading based on somatic clues but denies markers of racial difference a place in that system. While the stakes of Olivia's errand are financial, the primary obstacle to its success is characterological. To secure her fortune, she must teach the white Englishmen who serve as arbiters of her interpersonal value how to read differences of skin color—or, rather, how not to read such differences. Olivia worries, in the early days of her acquaintance with the Merton family, that "the good qualities, which I may possess, are not to be discerned in my countenance."[34] Since the disharmony she fears, between the surface and depth of her character, would derive strictly from the color of her skin, Olivia confronts an explicitly racialized instance of the hermeneutic crux that made its way from Calvinist theology to eighteenth-century novels.

The threat of essentialized religious difference is evident even in the character's name, which alludes to her "olive" complexion and suggests a set of linear connections between her identity (name), her outside (skin color), and her inside (religio-ethical status). Olivia cannot avoid these associations, so she responds to them directly. In one of the novel's more memorable passages, Olivia leads Augustus's nephew, George Merton the younger, in an antiracist religious interpretation of blackness. George begins the pedagogical exchange by literalizing the stigma of black skin. Shortly after Olivia's arrival in Clifton, George complains that her black maid, Dido, has "been kissing me, and dirtying my face all over!" (*WOC*, 78). Olivia begins with direct instruction, comparing their hands and declaring "mine is quite as clean as your own, and . . . that of the black woman's below, is as clean as either of them" (78). Before demonstrating her claim on George's literal terms, and perhaps because her audience includes not only the boy but also his mother (Letitia Merton), grandfather (Mr. Merton), and uncle, Olivia addresses the figurative, spiritual implications of his false equivalence between blackness and uncleanness. Here is their Socratic exchange, punctuated with telling interjections by their auditors:

"Oh now, what nonsense are you telling me!" said he, lifting up both his hands in astonishment.

"No," returned I, "it is very good sense: do you know who made you?"

"My grand-papa said God," answered he.

"Oh, if you mean that, he is very backward in his catechism," said Mrs. Merton: "I am sure I could not pretend to teach it to him."

"So I should imagine, if you think Miss Fairfield put the first question of it to him," said Augustus, rather sarcastically.

"The same God that made you made me," continued I—"the poor black woman—the whole world—and every creature in it! A great part of this world is peopled by creatures with skins as black as Dido's, and as yellow as mine. God chose it should be so, and we cannot make our skin white, any more than you can make yours black."

"Oh! But I can make mine black if I choose it," said he, "by rubbing myself with coals."

"And so can I make mine white by rubbing myself with chalk," said I; "but both the coal and the chalk would be soon rubbed off again."

"And won't yours and hers rub off?" said he.

"Try," said I, giving him the corner of my handkerchief; and to work the little fellow went with all his might.

"George, you are very rude and troublesome to Miss Fairfield," said Mr. Merton.

"Not in the least," said I; "it is right that he should prove the truth of what I have been telling him, he will then believe me another time."

"Yes, that I shall," said he, sighing and resigning his employment, as if it had wearied him.

"What do you sigh for, George?" asked Augustus.

"I could wish," said he, looking at me, "that God had made you white, ma'am, because you are so very good-natured; but I will kiss you, if you like."

"Thank you for the wish, my dear child, and for the favour conferred upon me," said I, pressing his cherub lips to mine. "I am not a little proud of this as I consider it a conquest over prejudice!" (78–79)

By challenging George to scrub her dark complexion with a handkerchief, Olivia "proves" the pure materiality of racial difference. Skin color can be permanent without countervailing monogenesis, or the theory of a single creation, because it carries with it no emblematic significance beyond the arbitrariness of providential determinism. The world is replete with peoples of darker complexions than George's, and this is so because "God chose it should be so." Given George's concluding wish that God had matched her "good nature" with white skin, we might doubt the completeness of Olivia's "conquest over prejudice." George has at least learned that the relationship between whiteness and good nature is contingent rather than causal. And, in any event, Augustus's internalization of the lesson has higher stakes. The questions Olivia asks provoke Letitia to declare that her ignorance of even rote Christian teachings has limited her son's religious education. Letitia's admission and Augustus's contemptuous retort mark a fault line in the Merton family, between Anglican orthodoxy and irreligion. Olivia co-opts the former position by leaving no room for religious justifications of racial hierarchy.

Her lesson in the impossibility of white washing is also a performance of blackness, and an example of what Fred Moten calls "resistant material objecthood."[35] George's racial disgust does not extend naturally to Olivia; it is she who calls attention to her exclusion from whiteness and her embodied affiliation with Dido. Repeatedly subject to English racism, including Letitia's attempts to humiliate her by feeding her rice, a food closely associated with enslaved Africans' labor and consumption, Olivia redefines the value inscribed on her body. She demonstrates, as much for the adults in the room as for the child George, a mode of objection resistant to meaning imposed from without. This resistance to racist interpretation works first of all through Olivia's direct refutation of the symbolic association, by way of Christian aesthetics, of blackness with spiritual impurity or inferiority. At the same time, if more subtly, it counts as an assertion of "radical materiality" as Moten describes its workings within the black aesthetic tradition.[36] Building on the scholarship of Hortense Spillers and Saidiya Hartman, among others, Moten defines the performance of blackness as a self-critical "revaluation" that disrupts the opposition of matter and spirit, as well as the theory of value that obtains to both racial capital and Marxist critique—that is, the thesis that value is not intrinsic. The "performative essence of blackness," Moten writes, is a materiality "infused with a certain spirit, a certain value not given from the outside." This "spirit" is the animating, bodily "trace of the maternal," the faded but durable link to both capitalist reproduction under slavery and African matrilineal culture.[37]

Avowing her blackness before the impressionable George, Olivia also directs the gaze of the assembled Merton family to the perceptible, literal marker of her kinship to enslaved black people. Earlier, she explains to Mrs. Milbanke, her white Creole governess in Jamaica, that she avows her "black brethren" because she recognizes the genealogical marker of her skin: "I say our, for though the jet has been faded to olive in my own complexion, yet I am not ashamed to acknowledge my affinity with the swarthiest negro that was ever brought from Guinea's coast!—All, all are brethren, children of one common Parent!" (WOC, 53). Olivia's "affinity with" the enslaved people is a material trace, to use Moten's vocabulary, the "jet" black complexion of the West African "faded to olive" yet not attenuating her connection to "the swarthiest negro." Olivia's participation in the category of the human, universalized according to the monogenist view of creation, gives her a claim to the love of "one common Parent," God. Meanwhile, her blackness—"faded" yet indelible, perspicuous—is straightforwardly a material trace of the maternal; it demonstrates her filial attachment to her black, enslaved mother, Marcia, and by extension the practice of revaluating blackness and spiritual beauty.

Olivia gives her mother's character sketch in the novel's opening letter. Her description of Marcia's physical appearance contrasts the inert, impenetrable quality of her black skin to the expressiveness of her eyes and shape: "The soul of my mother, though shrouded in a sable covering, broke through the gloom of night, and shone celestial in her sparkling eyes" and in the "symmetry and majesty of her form" (WOC, 54). Marcia's body is beautiful despite an aesthetic hierarchy that privileges "celestial light" over the "sable shroud" or "gloom of night." It furnishes signs of her inward perfections, restoring the mutually enforcing relationship between flesh and spirit at the heart of the eighteenth-century secularist character system and its sectarian Calvinist antecedents. Assigning grammatical agency to Marcia's "celestial" soul presents the alignment of form and content as inevitable. Instead of relying on the interpretive labor of the spectator, Marcia's personified religious disposition, her intrinsic spiritual value, "broke through" its covering. As an object, Marcia resists the meaning assigned from without—the shroud of signification thrown over black people. As a character-writer, Olivia shows attunement to this resistance, documenting the truth of religious character—the purity of soul—that Marcia bodies forth in defiance of the meanings imposed on her from the outside. Although this passage does not, like the one quoted above, directly refute the alignment of blackness with negativity or evil, it does assert a correlation between Marcia's inward goodness and her outward beauty, specifically her symmetrical features and sparkling eyes. Those beautiful features just need to be isolated from the color of her skin.

Brigitte Fielder makes a persuasive case for extending our reading of The Woman of Colour "beyond the text's heterosexual relations" to Olivia's relationship to both white women like Mrs. Milbanke and other women of color, like her slave-turned-servant, Dido.[38] Doing so, Fielder contends, illustrates "Olivia's shifting positions of relative power[,] her privilege and her oppression" and, in turn, helps us to see how the novel depicts the movement constitutive of the black Atlantic.[39] While Fielder focuses her discussion of Olivia's relation to black women on Dido, contrasting the "Africanist presence" of the latter to the "shadow" of Olivia's "dead, enslaved mother," I have tried to show the importance, and the materiality, of the posthumous mother-daughter connection.[40] The material trace of maternity, not a shadow but blackness faded to "yellow" or "olive," shapes Olivia's self-characterization. And it also appears to shape the way her cousin and love interest, Augustus, interprets her character. Proceeding from the female relationality that Fielder so productively centers back to the heterosexual romantic relationship on which the novel's plot turns further clarifies the nature of the fantasy that Olivia briefly realizes through marriage.

It is a dream of white male attunement to the object's embodied, intrinsic value. When Augustus takes his own, brief turn characterizing a woman of color, he uses the same terms in which Olivia describes her mother. Perhaps it is no coincidence that Augustus overcomes his own prejudice after having observed Olivia's lesson in the proper religious reading of racial character, her reproduction of her mother's performance of blackness. Olivia is the author of nearly all the letters that comprise *The Woman of Colour,* but, in a rare glimpse of another character's perspective, Augustus explains to a friend how his feelings toward Olivia have evolved. He writes,

> The moment when my eyes first cast on the person of my cousin, I started back with a momentary feeling nearly allied to disgust; for I beheld a skin approaching to the hue of a negro's, in the woman whom my father introduced to me as my intended wife! I that had been used to contemplate a countenance, and a transparent skin of ivory, where Suckling's expression of "even her body thought" might have aptly originated. . . . A very few hours served to convince me, that whatever might have been the transient impression made by the colour of Olivia, her mind and form were cast in no common mould. She has a noble and a dignified soul, which speaks in her words and actions; her person is raised above the standard of her sex, as much as her understanding and capacity. In her energy, her strength of expression, in the animation of her brilliantly black eye, there is something peculiarly interesting. (102)

The color of Olivia's skin initially gives Augustus an "impression" of her identity with the "negro," but his revulsion has as much to do with the perceived opacity of her body as with her proximity to a racial-ethical category. Sharply contrasting the "skin of ivory" that Augustus is accustomed to "contemplate," Olivia's "hue" registers at first as incommunicative and inert. Synecdochic reference to Angelina, the first wife he believes to have died, underlines the operative semiotic ideal, one that Augustus recovers by shifting his attention from the color of his cousin's skin to the "form" of her person.

Augustus becomes romantically "interested" in Olivia, in other words, when he learns to see her the way Olivia saw her mother, Marcia—in outline. The qualities of her soul, too, shine through the seeming opacity of its covering. Olivia's body furthermore realizes the poetic image that he at first identifies exclusively with the porcelain Angelina: a female form that collapses the body/mind distinction so completely as to make ethical-intellectual capacity an anatomical function and, thus, apprehensible to the male gaze.[41] Augustus now recognizes in Olivia a congruent elevation of beauty and virtue; he sees her as "one of that sort of people whose mind is revealed in the countenance," as he later declares at a ball (WOC, 117). This recognition becomes possible only after Augustus abstracts Olivia's racial difference in the specific sense of divesting it of representational properties, much as Olivia herself had done in her tutorial for young George. Beyond potential assimilation into English society, the relationship between Olivia and Augustus represents the possibility of a responsive white male interpreter. Augustus joins or, rather, follows Olivia in the imaginative work of revaluating race.

Abstraction as False Religion

Together, Olivia and Augustus's readings of racial difference disentangle black bodies from the stigmas of sin and illegibility. These episodes reverse a process of racialization that Jared Hickman takes to be synonymous with modernity, whereby religious variety solidifies into ontology—into sex and race.[42] For Hickman, "variety" refers to the lists of cosmic warfare, a matrix of competing, territorialized mythologies. The Woman of Colour reveals, through a kind of back-formation, the ontological solidification of categories of difference internal to secularized Protestantism.

By extruding racial difference from the layered oppositions of real religion and bad belief, the saved and the damned, the novel gives evidence of prior coincidences of religious and corporeal difference. What these episodes of character-reading neither achieve nor attempt is a challenge to secular dialecticism in general. The novel's progressive arguments about race, slavery, and marriage travel through that logic, contrasting Olivia's Anglican orthodoxy to the malign belief or skepticism of English characters.

One Sunday morning conversation during Olivia and Augustus's brief marriage exemplifies this dynamic. The couple return from church service to find Letitia's partner in irreligion and racial prejudice, Miss Dansby, with Lady Inglot and her son, all enjoying a languid breakfast at their home. When Lady Inglot, a wealthy neighbor newly returned with her family from India, registers surprise at the absence of servants, Augustus explains the phenomenon as a testament to Olivia's contagious piety. "My Olivia," he declares, "is not content with being good herself, she makes others so likewise, and all our male servants go to church on a Sunday" (*WOC*, 121). Miss Dansby dismisses the Fairfields' punctual attendance at church as the effect of "methodist" enthusiasm, and Lady Inglot responds by expatiating on the inconveniences and superfluity of organized religion (123). "I never set foot in that church but once," she says,

> and then I was absolutely starved to death. I told Sir Marmaduke it was hazarding the very existence of our tender one there (looking at her son), if he ever let him enter it, unless he could portion off a large space for our separate use, and have it well stuffed and carpeted, and a chimney built, and a good register stove put in; but it seems there are great difficulties, in the way to all improvements in country parishes:—what with their rectors, parsons, their graziers and yeomanry, who talk of "my pew," and "mine," with as much tenacity as if one wanted to deprive them of anything worth retaining. Sir Marmaduke has had so many things of consequence to attend to since we came to the Pagoda, that he has not had leisure to settle a plan for a little sequestration (as I term it); for his family's accommodation at church; and for my own part, I do not much trouble about it. My own religion, is the religion of nature! I can put up my aspirations, while walking in the fields or driving on the road, just as devoutly as if I was kneeling on the moist and humid pavement of some time-worn, superstitious structure,

and catching a sudden death at the very moment when I was praying to be delivered from it,–for nothing short of a miracle could preserve me! (121–22)

With an eye toward worldly comfort, Lady Inglot envisions an act of enclosure that extends the rapacious model of colonization practiced by the East India Company at the same time that it extends the family's property lines.[43] She imposes social hierarchy and an attendant conception of private property onto a parish ground governed, ideally, by more egalitarian principles. If Lady Inglot does not insist on the execution of her plan, it is because her "religion" is just as aggressively privatized as her conception of ecclesiastical space. Her profession caricatures natural theology, emphasizing a spontaneous connection between the believer and the created world while also reducing the church to a ruin of "superstition" and anchoring prayer and "miracles" to the temporal good of physical health. Of course, Lady Inglot's rhetoric of natural religion is a form of excuse-making, a logic that validates her priority of worldly comfort and pleasure while making no claims on her. Because she is the only character in *The Woman of Colour* who espouses the "religion of nature," I would suggest that the novel ascribes this primacy of conveniency and worldliness to natural religion as such. The character of Lady Inglot unites harm to ecclesiastical community and doctrinal impoverishment. Her juxtaposition of the Anglican church's inhospitable environment to the comforts of the family "pagoda" also links Lady Inglot's religiosity, such as it is, to the syncretic architectural and spiritual practices of East India Company factors. Bad religion follows from bad methods of colonization.

In addition to serving, more passively, as the counterpoint to Lady Inglot's errant theology, Olivia evinces a defensively secularist self-understanding. She does so, specifically, by insisting on her two-dimensionality. When Angelina reappears in volume 2—Letitia contrived to fake her death to avenge her own thwarted desire for Augustus—Olivia must be reinterpreted according to the norms of patriarchy. The men who seek, variously, to counsel or court her abstract Olivia's "idea" from her embodied presence, her past, and her Protestant devotion. Stirred by her display of fortitude after her separation from Augustus, Mr. Lumley, the minister, projects an audience of racist strawmen:

"Oh, come here, ye prejudiced, narrow-minded beings!" said he, apostrophizing from the feelings of the moment, and entirely losing the idea of my presence in them:—"Oh come hither, ye advocates for slavery!—ye who talk of the inferiority of reason, which attends a difference of colour,—oh, come here! And see a woman,—a young—a tender woman, who, in the contemplation of her own unparalleled misfortunes, and with a heart almost broken by affliction, yet rises with unexampled preeminence of virtue! See here a conquest over self, which ye would vainly try to imitate!" (WOC, 148)

Lumley's address renders Olivia grammatically secondary, centering imagined opponents instead of the objective correlative, Olivia, of his "feelings of the moment" (his ecstasy of abolitionist triumphalism). His apostrophe to proslavery Britons assimilates "the idea of [her] presence" within the universal ideal that, in his view, her behavior represents: a protoliberal fantasy of rational agency. According to Lumley, her singular virtue consists in self-regulation, a triumph of reason over heartbreak that disproves an eighteenth-century commonplace that the emotions of African-diasporic peoples exceeded their capacity for self-regulation.[44]

Olivia offers an alternative gloss on her "conquest over self," once again invoking Marcia's character. "I had a glorious example in my mother, Mr. Lumley," she begins. "My mother, though an African Slave, when once she had felt the power of that holy religion which you preach, from that hour she relinquished him, who had been dearer to her than existence! And shall I then shrink from a conflict which she sustained? Shall I not go on, upheld by an approving conscience, and the bright hope of futurity?" (WOC, 148). Christian theology provides the logic and her mother the pattern for her virtuous endurance of suffering. Olivia emphasizes precedent, assigning more weight to the "glorious example" of her mother's lived piety than to her own rational faculty or even the compensatory function of the rewards of "futurity," or the afterlife. She holds herself first of all to the standard Marcia had set in ending her relationship with Mr. Fairfield after her conversion. Where Lumley insists on Olivia's exceptionality—her misfortunes are "unparalleled" and her forbearance both "unexampled" and inimitable—Olivia inserts herself into a system of reference. She asserts her place in a typology of Christian self-denial that, in its explicit inclusion of an "African Slave" as well as a mixed-race West Indian, makes Lumley's rhetoric of racial equality more widely extensible.

Much has been written, I have already observed, about Olivia's refusal of Mr. Honeywood's proposal at the end of the novel. Her singleness functions, for some scholars, as an assertion of autonomy and, for others, as implicit confirmation of prevailing biases about race and gender. Dominique's interpretation is representative of the former train of criticism: "*The Woman of Colour* advocates that the most virtuous black woman should never try to transform herself to fill the space of an angelic white wife" because outside the form of the couple she "represents a more actively liberatory challenge to hegemony."[45] Jennifer Reed assigns an antithetical ideological function to the same narrative circumstances, arguing that Olivia's exclusion from marriage reflects the novelist's wish to "remove the reminder of the source of Caribbean wealth" and, with it, the reminder of Britain's material dependence on slavery.[46] Parsing the terms of Honeywood's declaration of love for evidence of the specific danger his desire poses may help us to move beyond this either/or framing.

Honeywood's desire is less threatening to Olivia's mobility or agency than to the mode in which her outward character signifies. He worships Olivia as a "sylvan goddess" and "benign genius" (*WC*, 164). "While daily present with you," he effuses,

> while listening to your melodious voice—to your noble sentiments—to the delicate purity of your conversation, I drank deep draughts of a passion which was as violent as it was hopeless. Vainly did reason and reflection urge me to break my bonds; I loved my fetters, and, to contemplate your dear idea, to turn with retrospective eye on those blissful hours of friendly intercourse was my utmost pleasure; even when I knew that you were to become the wife of another; even when I knew that duty and propriety bade me fly your presence. The loss of my ever-to-be-lamented mother, though it plunged me in sorrow, did not erase your image from my heart; I still remembered how you had, in the soft voice of friendship, tried to prepare me for this cruel stroke; and on retirement to this sequestered country, you were still the sylvan goddess of the shades I visited,—you were the benign genius of all my avocations! (164)

Desire intensifies with the impossible remoteness of the object because it has engraved Olivia's "image" in memory, allowing Honeywood to conjure her "idea" at his pleasure. Olivia replies that accepting his proposal would violate the "consistency of [her] character" in several senses of the phrase, including the concordance of her actions with her judgment and with the public character—de facto widow—she has assigned herself (165).

But Honeywood's declaration also presents a potential disruption of semiotic relationality. He abstracts Olivia's character in the sense of uncoupling phenomenal signs (her body and voice) from the virtues (her "noble sentiments" and "delicate purity") they signify. This devotion is menacingly anti-Protestant not only because it divinizes Olivia but also because it changes that tradition's precisely calibrated relation between signifier and signified. In the novel's conception of true religion, as in Brown, Butler, and Mahmood's idea of secularized Protestantism today, signs and the meanings they convey should be discrete yet correspondent. They stand apart within a system of reference that privileges mediation over immediacy, universal meanings over phenomenal forms. Honeywood's "violent" passion becomes bad belief as it severs the correspondence between these terms, working in the inverse direction of religions, like Catholicism and Islam, alleged to fetishize signs. His desire exaggerates rather than closes down the prescribed distance between "revered object" and "reverential subject."[47]

Olivia's tacit preservation of two-dimensionality and her explicit participation in an ameliorationalist, civilizing mission betray her commitment to a discourse of secularism forged through empire and disseminated through a semiotic model of character. Olivia informs Mrs. Milbanke of her return to Jamaica shortly after rejecting Honeywood's marriage proposal. For Fielder, this resolution is unambiguously positive. She writes, "If an antislavery and antiracist cause is Olivia's object, these are radical interracial endeavors in a slaveholding empire. . . . Olivia ultimately rejects the social reproduction of Englishness, whiteness, and empire, and embraces kinship with the African diaspora of the colonies."[48] Fielder's interpretation rests on a tenuous equation of abolitionism and amelioration. Here is Olivia's stated "object:" "I shall again zealously engage myself in ameliorating the situation, in instructing the minds—in mending the morals of our poor blacks" (*WOC,* 188). Rather than "the promise of abolitionist collaboration in the black Atlantic," Olivia articulates a moderate vision of religious and moral instruction. The word "again" indicates that Olivia sees her homecoming as a return to the social role she inhabited before her father's death, a role she may perform within rather than opposed to the institutions of slavery and plantation capitalism. It's not clear whether Fairfield Plantation is part of Olivia's patrimony—if the sum of sixty thousand pounds that's returned to her at the behest of a dying Mr. Merton includes real as well as mobile property—but it's possible that she returns to Jamaica as a reformist plantation owner rather than an abolitionist activist.

Fielder also exaggerates the force of Olivia's rejection of "Englishness, whiteness, and empire." It's true that Olivia's statement of purpose is accompanied by expressions of excitement: she "shall come back to the scenes of my infantine happiness," and she is "eager to be with you once more, I almost count the tardy minutes as they move along" (*WOC,* 188). But, after breaking off her epistolary journal, Olivia renews the topic through a melancholy apostrophe: "England, favoured Isle!—Happy country, where the laws are duly administered—where the arts—the sciences flourish, and where religion is to be found in all its beautiful purity. Farewell!—a long farewell!—Fain would I have taken up my abode in this charming clime,—but Heaven forbade it. Yet, England, I shall carry with me over the world of waters a veneration for thy name, a veneration for that soil which produced a Lumley—a Bellfield—and an Augustus Merton" (188). Olivia must forget in order to remember, efface a personal history replete with evidence of English prejudice and cruelty in order to preserve a national mythology. Self-forgetting enables her to venerate England as the junction of legal, cultural, scientific, and religious virtues and, therefore, as distinguished by God's favor. But her reverence also entails an explicit acknowledgment that this ideal, however nourishing to the white men she lists, proves uninhabitable to a woman of color. When Olivia addresses England, she speaks from the inevitably conflicted position of a "mulatto West Indian," compelled to cherish a promise from which she is excluded with the arbitrary fatality of providential decree (92). She would have preferred to stay in Britain, but "Heaven forbade it."

Novels, Secularism, and Black Critique

Dissonance between *The Woman of Colour*'s radical revaluation of physical difference and its anticlimax, with Olivia's outsider status affirmed and her politics moderated, speaks to the discursive constraints on literary resistance. Olivia refuses to invest corporeal difference with hierarchized spiritual meaning, but she cannot transcend the Christian hegemon that those values organize and serve. We leave her essentially where we met her, contemplating Atlantic transit and embracing a supporting but marginal role in imperial British mythmaking. Olivia helps preserve the ideal of England by sanitizing its colonial operations, making good on the insincere promise of pastoral care issued by white West Indian planters like Captain Harrop. *Obi*'s arguments, too, unfold within the parameters of secularism, the discourse through which certain conceptions of religion are imagined and legitimized at the expense of others. Earle, like the author of *The Woman of Colour,* perpetuates the distinction between good and bad belief, with semiotic coherence as the measure of theological truth or errancy. He portrays Obeah as bad belief in two ways: first, by reproducing a colonial discourse that foregrounds the Obeah professor's disruption of social, forensic, and medical forms of knowledge of character; and, second, by using narrative structure and characterization to compare it to the false Christianity of enslavers. The comparison favors Obeah, with its adherents included in God's care (as when Bashra survives the yaws, untreated) or welcomed to the kingdom of heaven (as when Amri passes into the afterlife), but the African-Caribbean belief system is still, at best, a mediating third term in the conflict between real and counterfeit expressions of liberalized Protestantism. Obeah is in Earle's novel, as in other, more reactionary entries in the catalog of Obeah literature, a delusive charm.

The arguments of *Obi* and *The Woman of Colour* are certainly progressive. Both texts criticize racism and chattel slavery, with *The Woman of Colour* also criticizing the asymmetries of heteronormative coupledom. But their critique travels through the structures of thought and character that obtain to eighteenth-century secularism. They direct the Protestant religion naturalized through this discourse—its doctrinal content

multiple or unspecified, its immediate stakes heightened but not independent of a system of deferred rewards and punishments, its undergirding
model of self adapted from the sectarian discourse of Calvinism—toward
the goal of a more humane colonial regime.

They have this objective in common with perhaps the most celebrated
early example of black critique, Cugoano's *Thoughts and Sentiments on the
Evil of Slavery.* In my introduction, I showed how that text's religious interpretation of racial difference appeals to the authority of Calvinist doctrine. Cugoano answers the bad exegesis of slavery apologists, who trace
an errant genealogy from Ham to the inhabitants of Africa or refuse to
contextualize properly the Bible's accounts of bonded servitude. *Thoughts
and Sentiments on the Evil of Slavery* applies the doctrine of double predestination to show that both white and black skin represent sinfulness,
albeit through a complicated mechanism of reciprocal looking. This part
of Cugoano's argument runs counter to the logic of secularism. In order to
prevent the solidification of salvific states into race, Cugoano affirms the
singular propriety of the doctrine of double predestination. Yet the overarching argument of *Thoughts and Sentiments on the Evil of Slavery,* which
Vincent Caretta pronounces "by far the most radical assault on slavery, as
well as the slave trade, by a writer of African descent," betrays a secularist
inclination.[49]

Cugoano equates the antislavery cause with "the only true religion that
was ever given to men," Protestant Christianity understood as a monolith
of general, "genuine principles" and duties.[50] "I would have my African
countrymen to know and understand," he writes, "that the destroyers and
enslavers of men can be no Christians, for Christianity is the system of
benignity and love, and all its votaries are devoted to honesty, justice,
humanity, meekness, peace and good-will to all men" (*ES,* 66). Whereas
Cugoano's theory of racial character relies on doctrinal specificity, a more
generalized understanding of Christianity animates his condemnation of
slavery and enslavers. Here, it is a "system" of moral values, and its "votaries" are distinguishable according to the moral character they exhibit.
His calls for abolition and emancipation gather strength from secularism's dialectical structure, its continuous enforcement of binary struggle
between "true religion" and bad belief, while advancing a familiarly

liberalized model of Christianity. To this version of Christianity Cugoano juxtaposes the "Antichristian" character of slavery and *its* votaries (67).

He classes all those who participate in, profit from, or grant political and legal sanction to racial slavery with Protestantism's prominent theological others, Muslims and Catholics, routing his antislavery arguments through the machinery of secular distinction. He adapts imagery from Revelations, which describes the iconography of the Devil as an idol "arising up out of the earth, having two horns like a lamb," to represent the infernal origin and influence of Islam and Catholicism (*ES,* 67). The persistence of slavery serves a secularist global view by demonstrating the falseness of Protestantism's rival religious traditions, according to Cugoano. If either tradition were "endowed with any real virtue and goodness . . . , then would not slavery and barbarity have been prohibited and forbidden" in their historically expansive domains (93)? Slavery in Islamic and Catholic societies is an effect of false religion, then, but in the British context the practice itself qualifies as a bad belief. Cugoano warns that "whatever else they may call themselves, or whatever else they may profess," the states and people who "support that evil and wicked traffic of slavery, however remote the situation where it is carried on may be, are, in that respect, as much Antichristian as any thing in the world can be" (67). Extending the allegory from an interpretation of scripture to a representation of the world, Cugoano imagines that a third horn of apostasy grows from the British Atlantic.

The critique that *Thoughts and Sentiments on the Evil of Slavery* mounts is prescriptive as well as descriptive. At the end of the text, Cugoano outlines measures for spiritual and political reform that are specifically aimed at expunging the sin of slavery without controverting the imperial bent of secular-Protestant thought. While Britons reflect and repent, their leaders should legislate a gradual but "universal emancipation," then enforce the law internationally through military action (98–102). Britain should thereafter practice a "more honorable way of colonization," one that pursues the religious conversion of African people and the economic development of Africa as principal aims (105). On that model, naval patrols of the Guinea Coast create the conditions required for human liberty to flourish and, simultaneously, extend the circumference of Christian dominion. Jeffrey Hole regards Cugoano's favorable view of "the force of the state" as evidence of his support for an incipient liberal political order.[51] *Thoughts and Sentiments on the Evil of Slavery* reinforces the same "ineluctable bonds between human liberty and state instrumentalities" that ligature the modern liberal order.[52] In elucidating Cugoano's "liberal principles," Hole reproduces the mainline secularization thesis in microcosm, arguing that *Thoughts and Sentiments* "shifts registers" from religious thought to secular exposition.[53] On my reading, Cugoano's affirmations of political liberalism and his religious arguments work in tandem to create a secular vision of Atlantic modernity. He explicitly links his emancipatory politics to Christian empire, writing that the dominions of "the true religion" must be extended alongside "the blessings of liberty" (*ES*, 92). The coordination of these ambitions in *Thoughts and Sentiments on the Evil of Slavery* confirms what Asad, Mahmood, and others have argued from more contemporary examples. Secularism and liberal orthodoxies are coconstitutive, rationalizing the Euro-Christian ambition of planetary domination by producing religious subjectivities in need of normalization according to the standards of true religion. The difference is that Cugoano attempts to separate what secularism in the present intertwines: false religion and unviable forms of life. Bad belief legitimizes the Christian imperial project, but according to a reformed "method of colonization" and without being inscribed on the flesh of its subjects (*ES*, 75).

This endeavor places Cugoano alongside eighteenth-century novels in a history of secularization in which writers variously attempt to weave together or disentangle two threads of the modern project, the fragilization of belief and the ontological solidification of cultural variety. In making this claim, I apply a different definition of secularity than Stefan Wheelock uses to center black antislavery intellectualism in North Atlantic modernity. Wheelock argues that black antislavery writing has been marginalized by the secularist histories of political modernity. In such accounts, "black prophetic declarations, sermonizing, and black autobiographical accounts of freedom" are considered "idiosyncratic" or residual while the "secular and elaborate philosophical systems of the enlightenment" are held up as key to the development of modern political self-understanding.[54] Working from a conventional definition of the secular as non- or anti-religious, Wheelock issues a call to attend to black Christian discourse as an offsetting intellectual current, as much a part of the "discursive foundations" of liberalism in Britain and the United States as the philosophies of the "secular 'Enlightenment.'"[55] Secular and Christian perspectives interact, even "overlap" in visions of political liberty and hope for the future, he argues, but they represent discrete schools of thought.

Yet what Wheelock tracks through antislavery texts by Cugoano, Olaudah Equiano, Mary Steward, and David Walker could actually be described as the operations of secularism. Wheelock emphasizes these writers' commitment and skill in correcting the "errant religious sensibilities" and "errant theologies" that form the basis of a culture that sanctioned and sanctified "black bondage."[56] My reading of Cugoano thus corroborates Wheelock's argument about early black critique while adjusting its theoretical frame according to the insights of new secular studies. Asad, John Modern, Peter Coviello, Joan Scott, and others have explored the mutual dependence of the secular and the religious. This relation is on full display in Cugoano's text, suggesting that black antislavery writing was, indeed, central to the evolution of modern thought. But, if *Thoughts and Sentiments on the Evil of Slavery* is representative, these writers exert their influence within the dominant ideology rather than through dialectic struggle with it.

The critical energies of all three texts considered in this chapter are contained by secularism. How, then, should we appraise their political achievements? Wheelock is instructive on this point. Reflecting on Cugoano's arguments and scholarly characterizations of his project, he warns against the zero-sum framing of resistance versus complicity. "Vindicationist" readings of *Thoughts and Sentiments on the Evil of Slavery* occlude "variations in the ideological temper of black literary resistance," but it is also unhelpful to hold black writers to the standard of transcending the "ideological limits of [their] historical moment."[57] Wheelock models "a fuller engagement with antislavery texts' *investigative* dimensions."[58] Following his example, we might hold up the shared imaginative project of *Thoughts and Sentiments on the Evil of Slavery, Obi,* and *The Woman of Colour* as an investigation of what is possible, in political and literary as well as religious terms, under imperial secularism. They illustrate the Atlantic futures that secularism's disciplinary valence could help to usher in and the forms of race-thinking its characterology could support. The late eighteenth- and early nineteenth-century fictions analyzed in my final chapter try to imagine what lies beyond those limits.

5

Gothic Postsecularism

I N THE FIRST FOUR CHAPTERS of this book, I tried to show how the play of two-dimensionality reflects a secularist ideology in formation in Britain and its colonies during the Restoration and eighteenth century. Across that period's variable fictional modes (allegory, romance, picaresque, satire, sentimentalism), unstable methods of characterization enact the unbinding of doctrinal orthodoxy and the subsequent countercodification of antiorthodoxy as Anglican moralism. They reveal the novel's tendency to naturalize the "true religion" of secularized Protestantism. The works of fiction discussed in previous chapters are not free from ambivalence, particularly with regard to the question of how forms of life relate to forms of belief. Earle and the author of *The Woman of Colour*, as I argued in chapter 4, disjoin errant devotionalities (Captain Harrop's natural religion as well as Three-Fingered Jack's Obeah) from markers of sexual and racial difference. But their criticism of plantation capitalism and slavery, like Cugoano's vision of a "more honourable way" of colonialism, are nevertheless contained within the aesthetic and discursive bounds of secularism; its semiotics of character and its Christian-dominionist ideology encompass forms of resistance to as well as rationalizations of colonialism.

But not all forms. The genealogy of fictional character that we have been tracing also comprehends a form of fiction that subverts rather than naturalizes the representational practices of secularism. In the final pages of this book, I turn to entries in the catalog of Gothic Romance by Elizabeth Inchbald, Charlotte Dacre, and James Hogg as examples of a genre that lays bare not only the harms of imperial secularism but also the novel's role in propagating that ideology. Redefined, in part, as an interrogation of the ways of writing and reading character that had constituted the novel until the turn of the nineteenth century, Gothic fiction achieves a level of self-conscious reflectiveness that represents the best possible recourse against secularism, even by the standard of critique in the present.

Rather than proceeding in chronological order, I begin with Hogg's engagement with the Calvinist tradition of character-writing in *The Private Memoirs and Confessions of a Justified Sinner*. It is in this 1824 novel that the link between Gothic fiction's immanent critique of the religious-technical dynamic that I have been exploring to this point is most obvious. Much as the eighteenth-century novels discussed in prior chapters had done, The novel's villain, an uncanny, shape-shifting Calvinist Presbyterian named Gil-Martin, secularizes fervent Nonconformist religiosity by coordinating its semiotics with the system of differentiation prescribed by liberal-rationalist sociability. Hogg links that phenomenon, the perpetuation of divisions between true religion and bad belief, to an epistemic corollary to colonial violence. Gil-Martin serves as a parable of secular authorship by "colonizing" the characters of other people.[1]

More than any of the familiar indicators of atmosphere, archetype, or emotional intensity, Inchbald's response to the interpretive problem that gave shape to novelistic character marks her first and best-known novel as "Gothic." In *A Simple Story*, the potential disharmony of "assumed" and "real character," as Fielding put it at midcentury, manifests as feminine subjectivity in need of domestication. The ever-tenuous harmony of extrinsic signifiers and prior, interior truths of salvific status or ethical content justifies paternalism on the scales of the family and the cosmos. Miss Milner's desires are disciplined into legibility by Mr. Dorriforth, a secular priest according to the technical definition (he lives outside of monastic orders) who also exhibits the secularist tendency to conflate female and theo-racial otherness. There is precedent for designating *A Simple Story* as Gothic, but the argument for including Dacre's *Zofloya, or The Moor* is even more straightforward: this work, an homage to Matthew Lewis's prurient tales, exhibits the full range of formal and thematic characteristics used to define the Gothic in existing scholarship, and its place in discussions of the sexual politics of the genre is secure.[2] *Zofloya* fulfills the criterion developed in this chapter, as well. Like *A Simple Story*, Dacre's novel depicts the disciplining of female sexuality via semiotic characterization, specifically that of an antiheroine, Victoria di Loredani, who repeatedly challenges the consolidated authority of aristocratic masculinity and the Venetian Inquisition. To a greater degree than either Inchbald or Hogg, Dacre also emphasizes the interrelation of sex and race under secularism. While the former writers engage with settler colonialism through form and figure, Dacre addresses the historical practice through her title character's origin story and his demonic possession.

Often measured against the politics of Jacobin feminism or "the female Gothic" and found wanting, the radical potential of these novels becomes clear when they are compared instead to the aims of a still-emergent body of critical thought: postsecularism. Recognizing the impossibility of liberating humanistic critique from the idiom of secularism, the only language we have to speak of belief and its discontents, John Modern calls for scholars to "inflect rather than affirm" its grammar.[3] In Julie Orlemanski's lucid synthesis, "postsecular critique and the scholarship informed by it have sought to disaggregate the interlocking binaries that structure secularist ideology: enchantment and disenchantment, nonmodernity and modernity, belief and knowledge, compulsion and freedom, immediacy and mediation, folklore and literature, fantasy and fiction."[4] *A Simple Story* and *Zofloya* exhibit both of these commitments. Their authors reinflect the discursive grammars by which secularism produces the subjects proper to it, the ways it assigns meaning to sexed and racialized bodies. Inchbald and Dacre repudiate the semiotics of character, but they also reconfigure the asymmetries that it enshrines. In the process, they unsettle several of the binaries from Orlemanski's extensible list (immediacy/mediation, compulsion/freedom) as well as those (male/female, white/nonwhite) through which secularism plots its abstract values onto axes of sex and race.

The subjectivities and devotionalities they explore may be spiritual, filial, erotic, or an admixture of kinds, but in each case they set body and self, subject and object of reverence, in relations askew of secularist rubrics. In Lady Matilda, Miss Milner's daughter, *A Simple Story* presents a model of filial piety that intensifies—or, in the vocabulary of secularism, "fetishizes"—phenomenal signs of divinity. Inchbald recasts fetishism as an achievement of feminine agency, not according to the universalizing definition to which liberal-secular feminism tends to restrict it, but to a revised understanding of the gendered experience of creatureliness. The alliance between Victoria and Zofloya, meanwhile, weakens the systems of reference that lend the secular body its organizing coherence. If these characters and the counterpossibilities to which they give expression are finally circumscribed within the concentric borders of liberal sociality and Christian mythology, they nevertheless point a way forward. They gesture, that is, toward the self-interrogatory, subjunctive mood of the postsecular.

Religious, Secular, Gothic

A small but distinguished body of scholarship identifies Gothic fiction with secularization. For E. J. Clery, the Gothic's "aesthetic revalorization" of the supernatural instantiates secular modernity's dialectical character within the sphere of culture.[5] "Given that there is no room for ghosts in a rationalistic world," Clery writes, "the making 'real' of ghosts . . . necessarily involves an enhanced sense of the possibilities of the aesthetic, and of its separateness. Only in art could ghosts have an affective afterlife. Valorization of the supernatural as a source of aesthetic pleasure, the awakening of a sensibility detached, not only from truth, but also from probability, is the sign of an autonomous sphere of art in the process of formation."[6]

This formation is secular in that it preserves the organization of the rational and the irrational, probability and sensibility, into separate spheres. Supernaturalist fiction and art more generally supply the place of religion in Clery's restatement of the mainline secularization thesis. Whereas Clery emphasizes autonomy, Diane Long Hoeveler understands Gothic media as sites of imbrication. The Gothic is a part of the "ambivalent secularizing process" that made it possible for "modern Europeans to inhabit an imaginative space in which both the material (science and reason) and the supernatural (God and the Devil) coexisted as equally powerful explana-tory paradigms."[7] The Gothic, on Hoeveler's account, not only represents but also helps to catalyze secularization as Charles Taylor explains it. The genre contributes to the nova effect, or the pluralization of belief. Clery and Hoeveler each describes the Gothic as a hybrid discourse ("economic theodicy" or "secularized theology"), and its supernatural elements as resi-dues of a past that is at once more fully religious and ultimately assimilable by the intellectual and historical conditions of modernity.

Alison Milbank has ascribed to Gothic writers a more straightfor-wardly adversarial posture toward the processes of secularization. Mil-bank's critical methodology parallels the imaginative agenda she sees in her objects of study. Just as Gothic writers endeavor to reenchant the matter of secular materialism, Milbank seeks to recover the authentic theological content of their texts. Chronicling the intensifying commit-ment of Gothic writers to this recuperative project over the course of the nineteenth century, Milbank proposes that "the Gothic genre points, like the Gothic arch, upward, toward transcendence."[8] Her study is illuminat-ing; it reveals the potency and theological specificity of belief in this body of literature. But it also exemplifies the trend, in research on Gothic reli-gion, to reinforce Taylor's structuring dialectic of immanence and tran-scendence.[9] The result is a literary history that unfolds, quite explicitly, within the frame of dis-/reenchantment.

Clery and, especially, Hoeveler successfully extricate supernaturalism from oversimplifying metanarratives. Because they emphasize thematic patterns over formal concerns, however, these scholars neglect the poten-tial of the Gothic as a vehicle for critiquing secularism discourse. This chap-ter brings form to bear on the historical question of how Gothic fiction represents secularism and secularization, with help from Eve Sedgwick's underappreciated theorization of the mode in *The Coherence of Gothic Con-ventions* (1980). Hoeveler's study also draws on Derrida—the supernatural is, for her, a "trace" of premodernity—but it's Sedgwick's self-styled "decon-structive insouciance" that proves most helpful in thinking through the relationship between Gothic fiction and secularity.[10] Attending to methods of characterization that Sedgwick regards as distinctively Gothic reveals writers' self-conscious, sophisticated engagement with secularist ideology.

Departing from an earlier consensus, Sedgwick proposes that writers in the Gothic tradition problematize rather than reproduce a depth model of character. The genre is defined by the play of two-dimensionality, a simultaneous insistence on and disruption of "the programmatic symmetry of the inside-out relation" (*GC*, 13). Because the content of character, the locus of the individual self, should pass to the outside, the "strongest energies inhere to the surface" (12). Hence the use of faces, in texts like Lewis's *The Monk* (1796) and Ann Radcliffe's *The Italian* (1797), as instances of *writing* in the Derridean sense. Sedgwick contends that Gothic faces are "half-way toward becoming a language, a code, a limited system of differentials that could cast a broad net of reference and interrelation" (159). "Half-way," she clarifies, because the "diacritical code" they constitute is both incomplete and dominant, excluding all "nonlinguistic discriminations" (159). Although Sedgwick doesn't relate her argument to the concepts of secularity or religion, her description of Gothic faces serves quite well as a restatement of the formal effect I have tried to capture in previous chapters of this book. Translated into signifying practice, a system of literary reference, the mechanics of secularist distinction produce a characterological language that teeters toward incomprehensibility yet carries normative force.

Sedgwick's description of Gothic fiction's externalizing mode of description enriches (indeed, enables) the readings that follow. Like her, I seek to explain the peculiar energy with which Gothic writers confront the instability of inside-out relations. We diverge, however, in the ways we contextualize such confrontations historically. Where Sedgwick sees idiosyncrasy—the problematics of character are supposed to distinguish the Gothic from other strains of novelistic fiction—I see a genealogical marker. As part of its ambition to historicize constructions of true religion, this book has argued that novels from the long eighteenth century dwell with evident concern on the "issue of what constitutes character," that their performances are as alive to the "drama of substance and abstraction" as are the Gothic fictions that succeed them (*GC*, 170).[11] What distinguishes the novels by Hogg, Inchbald, and Dacre considered in the following sections is not the prevalence of complicatedly flat characters, who pre-date this literary movement by more than a century, but the deployment of those characters as a way to illustrate the insinuation of secularist ideology into the very form of the novel.

The writers' engagements with specific religious forms clarifies the mechanics of their critiques of secularism. Hogg sets his novel in an explicitly Calvinist context and demonstrates not only the danger of antinomianism, an exaggerated form of Predestinarian faith that absolved individual subjects of the responsibility to live morally, but also the greater threat of *moderated* Calvinism. *A Simple Story* and *Zofloya* are each set in Roman Catholic contexts: the household of Mr. Dorriforth/Lord Elmwood and the city-state of fifteenth-century Venice. Both texts distinguish between Catholic power as epitomized by literal and figurative Inquisition and Catholic doctrine. In doing so, *A Simple Story* and *Zofloya* suggest the need to revise our understanding of the relationship between Gothic fiction and Catholicism. These novels differ from the Radcliffean Gothic of the 1790s, to which scholars have attributed a sharply anti-Catholic position. Outlining the prehistory of Victorian responses to English Catholicism, Peter O'Malley claims that Ann Radcliffe, Matthew Lewis, and Charles Maturin "displaced the sexual and religious transgressions represented by the Gothic onto the Catholic Continent."[12] A number of scholars agree on this point; from J. M. S. Tompkins to Victor Sage and Robert Miles, literary critics describe the Gothic as an anti-Catholic, enlightenment genre.[13] Even Hoeveler, whose transnational and transmedia approach yields evidence of nostalgia for the Catholicism evoked by residual supernaturalism, in the end affirms this picture. Through the demonization of the Catholic other, she argues, Gothic writers like Radcliffe and Lewis participated in the "unfinished business of Protestant Reformation," as Miles had put it earlier: they attempt to "kill Catholicism" so that the Protestant, modern subject might live.[14] This scholarship reinforces larger intellectual histories in which Catholicism appears as an obstacle to modernization. Elizabeth Hurd describes two articulations of the modern secular imaginary in the West: French "laicism," in which religion is categorically excluded from civic life; and Anglo-American "Judeo-Christian secularism," which synonymizes Judeo-Christian morality and the values of liberal-secular democracy.[15] Both historical versions construct Catholicism in much the same way that the Gothic is supposed to have done, as modernity's backward counterpart—feudal, superstitious, and demonic.

A Simple Story and *Zofloya,* however, represent Catholicism as part of the whirring engine of secularist discipline rather than as a stand-in for premodernity. The semiotic ideology of secularized Calvinism that Hogg invokes explicitly also abides in Inchbald's depictions of an English-Catholic enclave, crossing borders between denominations and cultural domains and aligning Roman Catholic partisans with Reformed Protestant heuristics. Dacre's Venice, similarly, aligns the authority of the early modern Church with the prescripts of liberal modernity. These writers seem to argue, with Gil Anidjar, for the artificiality of denominational schisms. Like the ostensibly more fundamental divisions between "private and public, politics and economics, . . . religious and secular" in the process of crystallizing at the time, distinctions between Catholic and Protestant mask the "corporate institution" of Christianity, a "plastic" and "cumulative" entity that has been "colonizing the world since 1492."[16] Preempting this insight of new secular studies by centuries, *A Simple Story* and *Zofloya* recognize in the insistence of these distinctions, as well as those inscribed on flesh, the discursive operations of power.

Where Inchbald and Dacre oppose Catholic belief to secularism, they do so to refashion transubstantiation as a subversive logic of devotion. Performed spontaneously and aslant of formalized ritual, the rite of communion brings remote objects of reverence into physical proximity—and does so, importantly, at the will of the reverential subject rather than that of the revered object. Complicating the role of Catholicism in secularization histories, one of the key sources of terror in the Gothic, the eccentricity of Catholic theology, becomes an alternative model of mutual intelligibility imbued with erotic and spiritual potential.

"Cameleonic Art": *Confessions of a Justified Sinner*

Radical Scottish Presbyterian Robert Wringhim comes to see himself as an executor of God's judgment. Spurred on by his mysterious coreligionist Gil-Martin, Wringhim commits a series of murders in the name of Providence. *Confessions of a Justified Sinner* tells his story twice, as a found-text memoir from the turn of the eighteenth century and as a contemporary editor's ultimately thwarted investigation of its facticity. Wringhim's religious fanaticism would seem to be the primary target of Hogg's critical energy. Gil-Martin, Wringhim, and other ill-favored characters embody a cherished Anglican bugbear. They are antinomians, Calvinists who exaggerate providential determinism to, or past, the point of logical extremity.[17] Gil-Martin asserts the indefectibility of election with special vehemence, persuading his friend that the predestined elect are not only saved through the operations of grace, but also released from all responsibility to law and conscience. Combined with the disciplinary imperative of gathered-church ecclesiology, to police the borders of the visible church, this conviction sanctions violence against supposed reprobates, including Wringhim's father and brother, the George Colwans. Hogg's satirical crosshairs thus come to rest on Calvinist understandings of individual salvation and social organization—the very features that, articulated within the bounds of doctrinal orthodoxy or wrested from it, helped give shape to early novelistic character from *The Pilgrim's Progress* forward.

An explicit reference to Bunyan's allegory late in the narrative suggests that Hogg took aim at this literary inheritance as well. Having narrowly escaped mob justice, Wringhim finds employment in the Edinburgh shop of real-life printer James Watson. Once there, he redirects his militant religious energy toward publishing a memoir, which he describes to Watson as "a religious parable such as the Pilgrim's Progress."[18] Superficially, Wringhim's homage to Bunyan reinforces the novel's association of Calvinist Protestant theology with psychological and moral perversion. The allusion does more than raise the specter of antinomianism, however; it also signals Hogg's disavowal of a tradition of character-writing that reached from Bunyan's day to the Romantic era while extending, through the variant of secularization this book has been tracking, the exclusionary logic of predestinarianism beyond the culture of dissent. Despite his strict doctrinal commitments, Bunyan actually initiates this project. As I argued in chapter 1, *The Pilgrim's Progress* enacts the complementarity of reason and grace through its unstable emblematic method, and *The Holy War* racializes Calvinist typology. Though brief, the episode in Watson's print shop serves an important purpose, intoning the self-conscious literariness of *Confessions of a Justified Sinner.* Hogg invokes Bunyan to call attention to not only the overt violence of Wringhim's fanaticism but also the more insidious threat of its capacity to be moderated according to liberal-secular prescripts.

Wringhim targets religious tolerationists, like the Colwans and Reverend Blanchard, in what Colin Jager describes as a reflexive expression of resistance to the pluralistic ethos of secular modernity.[19] His impulse to harm those characters, whether internalized or projected outward, onto Gil-Martin, reflects a fuzzy perception of something Hogg's audience and modern readers alike have been conditioned not to see at all: the way that pluralism produces and regulates marginalized subject positions, like that of religious minority. It is difficult to square the designation of Wringhim and Gil-Martin as critics rather than agents of secular violence with the novel's caustic humor; more often than not, they and their pretensions are the butt of the joke. Jager's reading also misses Hogg's interest in the Calvinist character of modernity, the codependency of sectarian religiosity and secularizing discourses like the novel. Hogg aligns Gil-Martin, especially, with secularized Calvinism. Through his "cameleon art," his power to inhabit the characters of other people, Hogg burlesques the hermeneutics that structure communities of Protestant dissent, as well as the natural ease with which this model of reading became the grounds of secular authority.[20]

Gil-Martin's necromantic power negates the anxiety that elsewhere obtains to Calvinist-inflected social taxonomies. What was for Bunyan, George Whitefield, and Henry Fielding an uncertain proposition with high spiritual stakes reappears as a straightforward matter of interest and attentiveness. The explanation for his imitative capacity brings together physiognomic scrutiny and sympathetic identification.

> "My countenance changes with my studies and sensations," said he. "It is a natural peculiarity in me, over which I have not full control. If I contemplate a man's features seriously, mine own gradually assume the very same appearance and character. And what is more, by contemplating a face minutely, I not only attain the same likeness, but, with the likeness, I attain the very same ideas as well as the same mode of arranging them, so that, you see, by looking

at a person attentively, I by degrees assume his likeness, and by assuming his likeness I attain to the possession of his most secret thoughts. . . . I can never be mistaken of a character in whom I am interested."[21]

The process he describes exaggerates and literalizes the emphasis, within Calvinism and the modes of character-writing by which early novels rearticulated its teachings, on examining the surface of character in order to see its depths. Earlier in the narrative, Wringhim attributes to his minister namesake a peremptory authority that obviates discernment: "He knew the elect as it were by instinct," Wringhim writes admiringly, "and could have told you of all those in his own, and some neighbouring parishes, who were born within the boundaries of the covenant, and who were not."[22] Gil-Martin's shapeshifting talent takes Reverend Wringhim's claim to localized omniscience several steps further.

Amalgamated with concepts of Scottish Enlightenment philosophy, Gil-Martin's countenance-reading produces something more than knowledge. Ian Duncan observes that the passage integrates Adam Smith's theory of sympathy with the pseudoscience of countenance reading popularized by Johan Kasper Lavatar's *Essays on Physiognomy* (1789–98).[23] I would add that the two-dimensional model of character and the necessity of patrolling the "boundaries of the covenant" at the core of Gil-Martin's professed faith channel these intellectual currents. Where "interest" and other social "sensations" direct his intense gaze, minute physiognomic attention yields infallible knowledge of interiorized truth. More than that, though, Gil-Martin in this way attains "possession" of other people's character in terms of both surface ("likeness") and depth ("ideas" and their arrangements, "secret thoughts"). This ability to "colonize character," to borrow Duncan's suggestive phrase, associates secularized Calvinism—secularized in the sense that it has been made more flexible, accommodated to a quintessentially modern intellectual tradition—with a form of epistemic mastery that figures imperial ambition. Gil-Martin annexes other subjectivities to his own.

Confessions of a Justified Sinner exemplifies a different genre of response to the discourse of secularism and its ways of reading character than we have thus far encountered. The novel offers a mode of immanent critique

that develops in the several decades immediately preceding the publication of Hogg's work. *A Simple Story* and *Zofloya*, the following sections
of this chapter argue, belong to the same genre. If Inchbald and Dacre
engage more subtly than Hogg does with the specific religious genealogy
of the British novel's secular characters, with English Calvinism, they also
orient their critiques more directly toward the disciplinary bent of the
secularist ideology written into the form and show greater attention to
alternative ways of knowing and being.

Sacrilegious Desire and Postsecular Devotion
in *A Simple Story*

Although it is more frequently cited as an English Jacobin novel, a novel of
manners, or a Romantic psychodrama, *A Simple Story* incorporates a number of tropes typically identified with Gothic fiction: doubling, a dreary
castle, and, united in the same character, a sexually attractive priest and
a "darkly threatening paternal figure."[24] George Haggerty makes a more
nuanced case by measuring the "Gothic dimensions" of the death of Miss
Milner (now Lady Elmwood) at the beginning of the third volume: "Inchbald calls to her aid the conventions of Gothic fiction in order to underline
Lady Elmwood's position as a tragic victim of unfeeling tyranny. . . . Only
in the sublime violence of the Gothic can Lady Elmwood's suffering be
evoked in anything like its full emotional dimensions."[25] In this account,
Inchbald alights on Gothic horror (here, an interpolated mode rather
than a self-contained fictional genre) as ideally suited to represent the
experience of abjection, an irresolvable push-pull between the subject and
object of desire—and, as Haggerty goes on to argue, the only form that
female desire can take under patriarchy. By emphasizing atmospheric and
thematic effects over supernatural elements, Haggerty reveals the importance of Gothic conventions to Inchbald's critique of patriarchy. Evoking
the experience of female abjection does not, however, exhaust the critical
resources of the Gothic.

The Gothic convention that best elucidates the radical potential of this
text and of the genre as a whole is its tendency toward self-thematizing

characterization. Through the character evaluations performed within *A Simple Story*, Inchbald comments on the affordances of the paradigm that traveled from Calvinist soteriology to the pages of the early English novel. The semiotics of character feature in the first two volumes of *A Simple Story* as a formal strategy of subjectivation. Miss Milner recognizes herself, through this lens, as a (bad) secular subject: a "heretic" or "savage" motivated by illegible desires and inadequately submissive to the will of the father. Inchbald takes the familiar preoccupation with inside-outside incongruence in a new direction by inserting God into the machinery of novelistic characterization. When the secular Roman Catholic priest Dorriforth unexpectedly ascends to his cousin's earldom, becoming Lord Elmwood, he lives out the Weberian secularization thesis applied by rise-of-the-novel scholarship, scaled to an individual lifetime. As in this resilient historical metanarrative, ostensibly secular forces (the social and political requirement to extend the earldom to the next generation) displace religious commitments (the vow of celibacy). The effect in this case is to condense the imperatives to discern the content of other people's characters and to produce knowledge of the divine will into a single epistemic crux.

A Simple Story in this way marks a subtle but important shift in the semiotics of character normative to secularism. Eighteenth-century novelists address the precariousness of signification, the disjunction of value and grounding meaning, almost exclusively through questions of character in its intersecting literary and nonliterary definitions. By contrast, in stipulating the content of true religion, contemporary secularism asserts semiotic coherence in the specific context of worshiping the divine. Wendy Brown, Judith Butler, and Saba Mahmood argue that the "Protestantized conception of religion" legitimated through secularist differentiation "enfolds a concomitant semiotic ideology in which signs stand apart from the meanings they signify, objects from subjects, signifiers from signified."[26] The twenty-first-century articulation of secularism discourse, in other words, prescribes a devotional practice in which signs are restricted to the function of communicating prior spiritual meanings. Practices in which phenomenal signs exceed that function (such as veiling in Islam or the Corpus Christi tradition in which the Eucharist embodies the materiality of the deity rather than merely "standing in" for him) count as bad belief, fetishism. Inchbald's work reflects a moment of transition, the point at which systems of interpretation based on signs gather disciplinary pressure by uniting the contexts of devotion and social organization, the acts of character-reading with the representational practices of Protestant devotion. *A Simple Story* thus narrativizes the hardening of semiotic ideology, a process that consigns Miss Milner/Lady Elmwood and her daughter, Lady Matilda, to postures of abject creatureliness. Inchbald's critique is not merely descriptive, however. In addition to illustrating the psychosocial harms of secularist gender inequalities, *A Simple Story* imagines an alternative devotional logic.

Miss Milner, Secular Subject

A synopsis of the plot makes the irony of Inchbald's title readily apparent. Volumes 1 and 2 of *A Simple Story* focus on the tormented, halting love affair between the young Protestant heiress Miss Milner and her Catholic guardian, Dorriforth. Although he promises that it won't be a point of contention between them, the "difference, in their systems of divine faith" accounts in part for Miss Milner's attraction to Dorriforth.[27] If Miss Milner had received a Catholic education and, with it, a proper valuation of the clergy, the narrator reasons, her desire would have met an insuperable "barrier" (74). In fact, her desire is a problem, the cause of various misinterpreted actions and somatic responses, until Dorriforth's cousin dies of a sudden illness. By special dispensation of the Church, Dorriforth renounces his vows and leaves the priesthood, free to marry at his pleasure. A tumultuous courtship ensues, with the couple's mutual inscrutability threatening to prevent and then break their engagement. At the end of the second volume, though, the new Lord Elmwood marries Miss Milner in a hurried Catholic ceremony.

The narrative resumes in volume 3 after a seventeen-year gap. Inchbald's structural choice extends the conflict into the next generation but relegates its crisis to the margins of the narrative. After a brief period of connubial happiness, which includes the birth of Matilda, Lord Elmwood is called away to a mismanaged property in the West Indies, where he falls ill and becomes incommunicative. His unexplained three-year absence provokes Lady Elmwood, and her resentment leads her into an extramarital affair with a nobleman who had courted her before the marriage. Hearing news of her husband's imminent return, she then flees London and exiles herself to a castle on the border with Scotland. Lord Elmwood sends their young daughter after her, but years later he grants Lady Elmwood's posthumous wish to allow Matilda to live with him on his country estate, on the condition that she avoid his presence and affront him with no sign of her own. He makes their daughter a ghost, the absent presence of her mother's guilt and her father's repented weakness. The latter volumes of the novel recount Matilda's unsteady path to reinstatement in her father's favor, a resolution achieved not through activity but passive obedience.

In the parts of the narrative dedicated to Miss Milner, the semiotics of character buttresses structures of domination. Dorriforth embodies the perfect symmetry of inside and outside, while Miss Milner's experience attests to the normative force that this hermeneutic ideal carries. The narrator at first describes Dorriforth's face as a system of reference that, like mimetic visual art or emblem, creates air-tight correspondences between signs and signifieds:

> Many people mistook his face for handsome, and all were more or less attracted by it.—In a word, the charm that is here meant to be described is a countenance—on his countenance you beheld the feelings of his heart— saw its inmost workings—the quick pulses that beat with hope and fear, or the placid ones that were stationary with patient resignation. On his countenance his thoughts were pictured, and as his mind was enriched with every virtue that could make it valuable, so was his honest face adorned with every emblem of those virtues. . . . It was persuasive, it was perfect eloquence, whilst in his looks you beheld his thoughts moving with his lips, and ever coinciding with what he said. (S, 8–9)

Internal truths are easily gleaned where the boundary between outside and inside, world and self, is transparent. Dorriforth's initial characterization establishes a baseline of perfect symmetry, exposing the circuits of legibility into which he later interpolates Miss Milner.

Frustrated in his attempt to ascertain his ward's "real sentiments" about her suitor, Lord Frederick Lawnly, Dorriforth arranges a semipublic interrogation (*S*, 55). He asks Miss Milner to declare her "thoughts in regard to matrimony" before her confidant, Miss Woodley, and his spiritual advisor, Mr. Sandford (55). Dorriforth asks them for their "constructions" on Miss Milner's answers, and they oblige by inspecting her face for evidence of self-contradiction: "Miss Woodley looked hard at her, to discover some lurking wish adverse to all these protestations, but she could not discern one.—Sandford too fixed his penetrating eyes as if he would look through her soul, but [found] it perfectly composed" (58). Miss Woodley and Sandford presume a two-dimensional model of character familiar from Dorriforth's description, as well as from earlier fictions, in which somatic clues lead to knowledge of the "inmost workings" of heart and soul.

Gendered standards of propriety authorize their scrutiny. The expectation of "the world in general" for female modesty permits dissimulation, Dorriforth concedes—within certain bounds: "To what point I may limit, or you may think proper to extend this kind of venial deceit, may so widely differ, that it is not impossible I remain wholly unacquainted with your sentiments, even after you have revealed them to me" (*S*, 55). By classifying the deception licensed by modesty as a "venial" sin, Dorriforth betrays the specifically Catholic moral standard by which he evaluates Miss Milner. Her venial sin would become a mortal one, he implies, if she were to "extend" her deception far enough to contradict his right to the truth of her "sentiments." In addition to coordinating his sexual politics and religious commitments, Dorriforth's rationalization foreshadows the substitution of paternalistic for providential authority in the second half of the novel. He sits in judgment of Miss Milner, and he measures the difference between an excusable and a damning sin entirely by the sinner's disposition toward his epistemic mastery. Miss Milner responds astutely to the exclusionary logic underlying his interpretive practices. "I thought confessions were only permitted in secrecy," she replies. "However, as I am not a member of your church, I submit to the persecution of a heretic, and answer" (56–57). Miss Milner "submits" to their process of collaborative character-reading, but she names it "persecution." She recognizes her public "confession" as a ritual that begins rather than ends with conviction of heresy.

Eventually, though, Miss Milner's *im*penetrability to the piercing gazes of Dorriforth and his agents, the elusiveness of her interiority, confirms even to her that she is a proper subject for discipline.[28] When her as-yet-unspeakable desire for Dorriforth prompts Miss Milner into several falsehoods and retractions, Sandford feels validated in his low "opinion of the lady" and amplifies the stakes of her character evaluation by bracketing religious and racial difference: "Here do I venture like a missionary among savages—but if I can only save you [Dorriforth] from the scalping knives of some of them; from the miseries which that lady is preparing for you, I am rewarded" (S, 87). The metaphysical implications of Sandford's rhetoric sharpen over the course of the second volume, culminating in his (barely) implicit comparison of Miss Milner to Lucifer (117). At this point, he is content with a sublunary comparison; his simile equates the heresy of Miss Milner's Protestant belief to the disfiguring violence of the Indigenous other. British colonialism is generally a marginal presence in this novel focused on English domestic life, with Dorriforth's three-year sojourn in the West Indies the only other explicit reference.[29] Here, the novel associates imperial Christian purpose (i.e., the missionary's dangerous ambition to convert "savages") with secular characterology (the model of legibility Dorriforth typifies and enforces). Sandford's comparison staggers Miss Milner, who interprets the word "miseries" as an unintentional allusion to "the crime" of her desire (87). Having learned to view her desire through the prism of a religiosity not her own, she is suddenly convinced of "all the fatal effects of sacrilegious love" (87). The full force of the comparison exceeds Sandford's conscious control (he does not know that Miss Milner loves Dorriforth) and testifies to the operations of an impersonal, superseding discourse. Secularism translates what the narrator has just described as "real, delicate, and restrained love" into the racializing language of bad belief (81).

Enlarging on the effects of this language in her second novel, *Nature and Art* (1796), Inchbald clarifies secularism's tendency to "conjugate" the flesh of its subjects.[30] Hannah Primrose mistakes the desire of her unfaithful lover, William Norwynne, for divine intervention: "He was a miracle! His unremitting attention seemed the condescension of a superior being, to whom she looked up with reverence, with admiration, with awe, with pride, with sense of obligation."[31] By indulging this evidently religious feeling, Hannah "prepared for her fall" through extramarital sex, which appears to her not as a sin but as a "sacrifice" to the god of her heart (82). The novel punishes Hannah relentlessly for her errant devotion, not only by assigning her a bleak end after William abandons her but also through the narrator's editorializing. In a particularly heavy-handed application of her argument against the poor's "idolatrous worship" of the wealthy, the narrator opines that Hannah is damned by "the magic of her passion," which "like a fatal talisman had enchanted her whole soul" (154, 87, 98). She speaks in this register not for Inchbald, but for the hegemonic discourse that teaches Hannah, like Miss Milner before her, the profanity of her love. Hannah's bad belief racializes her; the labor she performs in elaboration of her original sacrifice to William leaves "her fair skin burnt yellow" (123). Along with more subtle passages in her first novel, Inchbald's characterization of Hannah anticipates a key insight of postsecular scholarship. Sex and race are not simply parallel logics under secularism; they are coformative.[32] *Nature and Art* also carries forward a phenomenon at the center of the latter volumes of *A Simple Story*, which illustrate the harms of self-apotheosizing masculinity.

Fetishism and Feminism

A review later attributed to Mary Wollstonecraft criticizes *A Simple Story* for falling short of a core objective of Jacobin feminism: to advocate for the rational education of women. The review singles out Matilda, who "should have possessed greater dignity of mind. Educated in adversity she should have learned (to prove that a cultivated mind is a real advantage) how to bear, nay, rise above her misfortunes, instead of suffering her health to be undermined by the trials of her patience, which ought to have strengthened her understanding."[33] Matilda's characterization does not "prove" the "real advantage" of rational capacity, and, as a result, the juxtaposition of her education to the finishing-school refinements of her mother carries little prescriptive force—this, despite the novel's stated moral about the value of a "PROPER EDUCATION" (338).

Although less stridently rationalist, recent criticism nevertheless draws its standard of evaluation from the same tradition of feminist thought that Wollstonecraft helped to inaugurate. Influential readings by Terry Castle and Patricia Meyer Spacks take the measure of female liberty in the novel, but they disagree about the scope of the freedoms afforded to Inchbald's heroines.[34] Amplifying the religious echoes of Castle's interpretation, Barbara Judson relates the novel's valorization of "independent judgment" and "free will" to what she sees as its radical critique of Christianity.[35] What Inchbald repudiates in Christian culture and myth, Judson argues, is their failure to grant women the kind of "meaningful freedom" enjoyed by Matilda at the end of the narrative.[36] John Morillo compares the retellings of the story of original sin in *A Simple Story* and Jane Austen's *Persuasion* (1818), concluding that "Inchbald's revision of Eve is more explicit and her critique is more modern in its feminist stance, by making self-determination over sexuality and gendered identity key to a more enlightened and less repressive life in the body politic."[37] Diverging from these celebratory readings, Candace Ward describes Matilda as "the product of reactionary attitudes toward sensibility and sexuality" and contends that she, like her mother, ultimately conforms to expectations of passive femininity.[38]

Assessments of the political upshot of *A Simple Story* rest on polarized readings of its principal female characters. Yet scholars agree upon an evaluative criterion, a theory of agency as active resistance to masculine authority. Applying Saba Mahmood's critique of liberal-secular feminism to Inchbald's novel helps us to see a different conceptualization of agency at work, one that is oblique to both the universalizing definition of feminist literary criticism and the mediating practices of Protestantized religion. In Lady Matilda's devotional practice, phenomenal forms embody rather than emblematize her father-god, Lord Elmwood, closing the gap between reverential subject and revered object. She expresses agency not as a desire to liberate herself from coextensive religious and familial structures of male domination, but as a wish to revise the terms of her subordination, and, with them, the creature-creator dynamic.

As several scholars have observed, Inchbald veils her criticism of Christian myth by "mak[ing] God a fictional character."[39] He is characterized, more precisely, by the arbitrary and "heavy-handed manner" in which he executes his authority.[40] Lady Elmwood's exile not only takes place in a conventionally Gothic setting—she spends her last days confined to "a large gloomy apartment" in "a single house by the side of a dreary heath" (*S,* 199)—but also models the only relation available to a god so disposed. Before her death, Lady Elmwood "declared it was not her intention, to leave a single sentence behind her in the form of a will—She had no will, she said, but what she would wholly submit to Lord Elmwood's; and if it were even his will, her child should live in poverty, as well as banishment, it should be so" (203). One sense of the homonym "will," a legal instrument for transferring property, converges with several further definitions arrayed by the concept of volition: the thing intended (Lord Elmwood's asserted will) and the faculty of deciding on or initiating an action (Lady Elmwood's abdicated will). The effect of the repetition is to specify the nature of Lady Elmwood's repentance, complete and "explicit submission to his lordship" (203). But how can Matilda submit to God's will without knowledge of it?

Matilda understands the creature-creator relationship as, first of all, an epistemic problem. Lord Elmwood's impossible remoteness changes the nature of interpretation at the same time that it raises the spiritual stakes of that labor. Because she cannot see his "honest face" to read it, Matilda frets over the exegesis of his word(s). Informed of his decision to grant her mother's petition, Matilda asks Sandford, "Are you sure he *did* grant it?—Was there nothing equivocal, on which he may ground his displeasure should he hear that I am here?—Oh! do not let me hazard being once again turned out of his house!—Oh! Save me from provoking him perhaps to curse me!" (*S,* 222). Like a photo-negative Eve, Matilda exhibits a pathological aversion to disobedience. Her doubts attest to a self-disciplinary impulse so powerful that it conflicts with belief in authority according to another definition: indirect revelation, or the testimony of God's ministering agents. Matilda finds in Sandford's appeal to another witness—"call Giffard [the steward], and let him inform you;—my lord repeated the same words to him he did to me"—a temporary source of confidence and even, as the narrator puts it, "joy" (233). Yet she subsequently pursues a more immediate relation to her object of worship.

Living a version of Christian myth with the character of Christ omitted, Matilda confronts the deity's retributive judgment without its countervailing mercy.[41] Absent the promise of Christology, and in contrast to her mother's deathbed resignation, Matilda seeks to reconcile human and divine nature through independent pietistic practice. When her father departs for London at the end of her first summer sequestered to a wing of Elmwood House, Matilda performs a spontaneous ritual:

> No sooner was the chariot, with all its attendants, out of sight, than Lady Matilda was conducted by Miss Woodley from her lonely retreat into that part of the house from whence her father had just departed—and she visited every spot where he had so long resided, with a pleasing curiosity that for a while diverted her grief.—In the breakfast and dining rooms she leaned over those seats with a kind of filial piety, on which she was told he had been accustomed to sit. And in the library she took up with filial delight, the pen with which he had been writing; and looked with the most curious attention into those books that were upon his reading desk.—But a hat, lying on one of the tables, gave her a sensation beyond any other she experienced on this occasion—in that trifling article of his dress, she thought she saw himself, and held it in her hand with pious reverence. (S, 245–46)

Matilda projects Lord Elmwood's divine character onto the material environment, transferring her attachment to objects associated with him: favorite chairs, books, a pen, his hat. Like the Catholic rite of communion, Matilda's practice of "filial piety" exceeds the bounds of representation. The items that she regards "with pious reverence" not only betoken Lord Elmwood but also incorporate his presence. Matilda's ritual transubstantiates everyday things into the body of the deity, thereby enabling communion by physical touch. Through her fetishization of phenomenal signs, her piety, too, is embodied: Matilda "leaned over," "looked . . . into," "took up," and "held . . . in her hand" the externalized form of the divine. It may be tempting to interpret this passage through a biographical lens, comparing its adaptation of Catholic doctrine to Inchbald's on-again-off-again commitment to Catholic faith.[42] Yet the novel elsewhere repudiates institutionalized Catholicism through its portrayal of the priests Dorriforth and Sandford. The scales of narrative judgment tilt toward the Protestant Miss Milner wherever those men practice inquisitorial rigor. This ambivalence points us away from the straightforward matter of pastoral difference and toward Catholicism's paradoxical relationship to secularism. Catholic belief serves, alternately, to codify and reconfigure its sexual asymmetries.

In reading the passage for this latter potential rather than for pathology, I read it against the grain of recent criticism. Speaking for a wide cross-section of scholars, Haggerty interprets this episode as an expression of Matilda's incestuous attraction to Lord Elmwood: "'Filial delight' hardly needs a gloss in a novel which has eroticized authority and rendered it problematic. Lady Matilda fetishizes these leavings and plays with his pen because patriarchy itself has made any other relation to power utterly pointless."[43] While Haggerty emphasizes the pen, grounding his claim to that object's erotic meaning on an implied, universal association with the phallus and a "gloss" on the novel's presentation of authority in general, the narrator of this passage clearly distinguishes Lord Elmwood's hat as the most affecting object. As an "article of dress," the hat is the item on the list that is most proximate and particular to his body. No wonder, then, that the object inspires her with especially acute and explicitly religious feeling: a conviction of presence that conveys "a sensation beyond any other." On my reading, the overarching logic of the passage is that of metonymic rather than erotic substitution—not the pen for the phallus but the hat for the person who wears it. For Haggerty's application of the concept to work, religious affects must be reinterpreted as coded erotic desire. Why do Matilda's somatic responses to her father's proximity necessarily indicate "Oedipal absorption"?[44] Such an interpretation presumes rather than demonstrates the replacement of religion with sex, suggesting the reach of secularist ideology in contemporary criticism. Viewed through that prism, Matilda's felt experience of filial piety is only comprehensible as rerouted sexual desire, which is unassimilable on its own terms because phenomenological and spiritual experience belong to mutually exclusive domains.

Neither mere play nor "pointless," Matilda's ritual in fact creates a novel association to power. Intensifying the phenomenological signs of Lord Elmwood's divinity beyond the semiotic framework brings the human and the divine into direct contact. Matilda's "fetishism" in this way repairs a severance that Lord Elmwood creates by arbitrary command and transforms the "sensations" of religious submission from fear and uncertainty to "delight" and "reverence." Matilda's relation to her/ the father remains one of subordination, as circumspect readers from Wollstonecraft onward have taken pains to demonstrate. But we need not think of subordination as monolithic, nor as antithetical to either agency or happiness. Mahmood warns against generalizing desire as the wish to be "free from relations of subordination and, for women, from the structures of male domination."[45] In her research on the Islamic revival in postcolonial Egypt, Mahmood shows that by affixing this notion of desire to the analytical category of agency a priori, feminist scholarship enforces "normative liberal assumptions."[46] She writes, "To analyze people's actions in terms of realized or frustrated attempts at social transformation is to necessarily reduce the heterogeneity of life to the rather flat narrative of succumbing to or resisting relations of domination."[47]

Whereas the context for Mahmood's argument is a contemporary, nonliberal culture, Inchbald writes nearer, historically and culturally, to the inception of the liberal hegemony that Mahmood sees in Western feminist responses to the Egyptian women's mosque movement. As we have seen, the "flat narrative" of succumbing or resisting has been imposed on the novel from its earliest reviews, making it a simpler story than the one Inchbald wants to tell. However normative these ideas of agency and desire have proven in the work's critical reception, they nevertheless fail to comprehend the range of possibilities entertained by the novel itself, including a form of devotional agency defined by rather than against hierarchical social arrangements. Matilda's pietistic practice cannot be said to bring about a reconciliation with her father directly—that cannot happen until Lord Elmwood learns to "take personal responsibility for her deliverance," Judson rightly points out—but it does clarify that the "summit of her wishes" is an immediate, felt affiliation to the figure of authority rather than freedom from his control (S, 331).[48]

Although "true" and "complete," Matilda's happiness is also short lived (S, 331). A Simple Story finally concedes its fantasy of feminine devotional agency to ways of character-reading and character-writing that make pity, and the heteronormativity it enshrines, mandatory. Shortly after the reconciliation with Lord Elmwood, Matilda's cousin, Harry Rushbrook, proposes marriage. Rushbrook, who effuses sentimentality and whose love originates in "sympathy" and "pity" for Matilda, looks at first like a foil to the stinting, authoritarian Lord Elmwood (250). There is no religious content either to his professions nor his self-understanding, so far as Inchbald grants access to it, and he couches his proposal in an acknowledgment of Matilda's autonomy. Lord Elmwood, Rushbrook tells her, "has yielded to you alone, the power over my happiness or misery.— Oh! Do not doom me to the latter" (337). His appeal to Matilda's twofold authority (her power of individual choice, and her power over his own happiness) veils the compulsory nature of the proposal, the inevitability of her acceptance created in part by his framing and in part by our interpretation of her character. We have been told, rather definitively, that Matilda does not reciprocate Rushbrook's feelings: "She loved him as her friend, her cousin, her softer brother, but not as a lover" (S, 334). At this point, the narrator obtrudes and forecloses her response: "Whether the heart of Matilda, such as it has been described, *could* sentence him to misery, the reader is left to surmise—and if he supposes that it did not, he has every reason to suppose their wedded life was a life of happiness" (337). Through seams in the fourth wall, readers glimpse the workings of a malign sociability in which we are made complicit. At stake is not the fact of Matilda's compassionate nature but a supposition based on its description. Where she pities, she could deny nothing that would abate suffering. Readers who accept this characterization and, by extension, Rushbrook's tacit claim would have "every reason" to imagine a "life of happiness" because they omit the question of Matilda's own desire.

In the refracted light of political modernity, the conclusion of *A Simple Story* takes on a prophetic quality. Passing between patriarchal regimes, from a model grounded in overtly religious rationales to one that disguises power as the effect of social passion, Matilda epitomizes the arc of the liberal subject in the centuries proceeding Inchbald's literary career. The projected marriage between Matilda and Rushbrook represents secularism's codification as "sentimental liberalism," a tradition of political thought in which "women's supposed innate preference for sentiment led them to voluntarily take up their domestic roles" and through which domesticity became "symbolically associated with freedom of individual choice."[49] In "yielding" this illusory rational autonomy to Matilda, Inchbald's fictionalization of God (Lord Elmwood) perpetuates the aegis of patriarchy in a new form. Rushbrook represents the new, liberal paradigm when he redescribes compulsion as volition and exchanges the bald claims of providentially ordained (or, more properly, providential) absolutism for the feints of sentimental politics. Moreover, by reassigning agency from Matilda to her readers, Inchbald's double-conditional ending implicates the form of the novel in this secularizing discourse.

Satan and Secular Modernity in *Zofloya*

Zofloya literalizes a relationship briefly implied by Mr. Sandford and echoed, in the rather different key of valorization, by modern feminist readers of *A Simple Story:* affinity between non-normative femininity and satanic psychology. Taking the form of the titular enslaved Moor, Satan abets Victoria in her relentless pursuit of sexual self-determination and political mastery. Their relationship is similar, superficially, to the dynamic between Wringhim and Gil-Martin in *Confessions of a Justified Sinner,* though Dacre sets her infernal agent in a different relation to secular modernity. Gil-Martin, I have argued, personifies the harms of the emergent liberal-secular order and espouses its familiar justifications. Zofloya stands opposed to secularism's disciplinary structures and for alternative subjectivities—at least in rhetoric and self-presentation. Until his big reveal in the penultimate paragraph, Zofloya embodies the radical potential that energizes Dacre as well as Victoria: the capacity to destroy the coherence of the secular body, its sex and its signifying qualities. The text conveys this desire well before Zofloya makes his first appearance almost exactly halfway through the narrative.

Set in early modern Venice and pervaded by stylistic and thematic homages to *The Monk, Zofloya* narrates the progressive degeneration of Victoria and her brother Leonardo, scions of a fallen aristocratic house. Victoria's story receives most of the narrator's attention. Anne K. Mellor recapitulates her arc with enviable concision:

Victoria de Loredani's mother elopes with her lover Count Ardolph when Victoria is 15; her father is subsequently killed in a duel with Ardolph. The beautiful, dark-haired Victoria's dawning sexuality is then aroused by the older libertine, Count Berenza; her mother tries to prevent this liaison by imprisoning Victoria with her aunt; Victoria escapes to Berenza, initiates their sexual affair, seduces him into marrying her, only to discover that Berenza cannot sexually satisfy her. She then becomes enamored of Berenza's younger, more virile brother Henriquez, who rejects her advances because he is engaged to the delicate, pale-skinned Lilla. At this point Henriquez' servant, Zofloya, a Moor, appears, first in Victoria's dream, then in fact, and offers her his services in gaining Henriquez's love. Victoria, overcome with frustrated sexual passion, first poisons her husband and then, when Henriquez still rejects her, chains Lilla in a cave and drugs Henriquez with a love-potion. But her longed-for sexual consummation with Henriquez proves disappointing. Henriquez commits suicide, Victoria kills Lilla, and escapes with Zofloya to a cave of bandits. When these bandits are surrounded by the army, Victoria flees with the Moor's help, only to learn at last that he is the Devil; he hurls her to her death from a cliff.[50]

Parallels with the heroines of *A Simple Story* abound. Insofar as Victoria lives out the "curse" of her mother's original sin, and the narrator attributes her evil to the dual causes of natural "propensities" and bad education, she combines the worst attributes of Miss Milner with the object lesson of Matilda's story.[51] Both novels rewrite the trajectory of Eve's character in *Paradise Lost* in ways that interrogate the gendering of fallen experience in Genesis and in Milton's epic.[52] *Zofloya* makes its point through a tension between overt moral didacticism—here, as in *A Simple Story,* the lesson is about the importance of educating women properly—and lurid descriptions of the criminal desires it supposedly denounces.[53]

The consequent ambiguity has fomented debate among modern readers, with recent criticism tending either to revise or reaffirm the nominal conservatism of text and author. With few exceptions, these readings treat *Zofloya* as representative of the politics of the Gothic genre. Where the Gothic in general is supposed to normalize the political dominant, *Zofloya* plays upon the reactionary fears of early nineteenth-century Britons, fears of women's sexual agency or revolutionary violence in the metropole and in the colonies. Hoeveler argues that Victoria's status as villain is tantamount to a condemnation of non-normative femininity and, further, that the relationship between Victoria and Zofloya represents the "threat of dispossessed subject populations working together, recognizing their mutual alienation and objectification and banding as one in a maniacal and deadly pursuit of the great white father and his property."[54] Stephanie Burley and Sara D. Schotland offer similar interpretations, locating the source of terror in the possibility of insurrection by enslaved people.[55] Each of these scholars applies to Zofloya H. L. Malchow's definition of Gothic fiction as a literary analogue to nineteenth-century "racist discourse."[56] For them, as for Malchow, the Gothic exploits anxiety about (often sexual) contamination by nonwhite, non-Christian bodies and, thus, legitimizes the violence of slavery and colonialism.

A second school of thought distinguishes the narrator's moralizing commentary from the novel's subversive effects. According to Mellor, Dacre's representation of interracial desire in Zofloya illustrates the capacity of the Gothic to imagine "culturally outlawed" subjectivities.[57] Jennifer L. Airey agrees with Hoeveler that Dacre demonizes Victoria, but she puts a different construction on the character's villainy. Victoria is evil less because she deviates from a bourgeois capitalist ideal of femininity than because she participates in an extreme form of homosocial competition in which there are no winners except patriarchy, Airey writes.[58] Adriana Craciun elucidates the "either/or limitations" of previous scholarship, rightly cautioning that such readings reproduce a gender polarity that Dacre herself wishes to interrogate. More specifically, it conducts a "radical critique of the subject," unsexing and destabilizing the key analytical category of modernity.[59] My own interpretation hews most closely to Craciun's Foucauldian approach, in that I seek to understand Dacre's "resistance" within rather than outside of structures of domination. I agree with Craciun that Zolfloya neither achieves nor aims at liberation from those structures but challenges the integrity and the legibility of its conception of subjecthood. My contribution is to situate these challenges in relation to the broader phenomenon, secularization, that defines both the subject and the social arrangements in which they are entangled.

Dacre, on my reading, takes aim at the representational practices through which earlier novels naturalize secularist disciplinary practices.

Unmaking the Secular Body

Disciplinary pressures on Victoria, and particularly the forces working to convert her "masculine spirit" and "masculine features" into expressions of properly feminine subjectivity, at first assume the guise of religious reform (Z, 190, 211). Count Ardolph, her de facto stepfather, arranges for Victoria's imprisonment at the remote estate of an elderly and out-wardly devout aunt. For Signora di Modena, pious motives justify Victoria's incarceration. The Signora explains that, by confining Victoria to her bedchamber,

> I merely wished to evince to you that softness, humility, and obedience, are indispensable requisites here, and that nothing can be tolerated that shews an overbearing, haughty, or ferocious spirit. You are by this time, I trust, properly convinced of your error. . . . I shall likewise expect that you peruse such religious books as I shall put into your hands, and which, I humbly hope, will tend to amend the stubbornness of your proud heart. Moreover, that you abjure the vanities of dress, and meekly comply with every requisition, that, as a good and pious catholic, anxious for the salvation of your soul, I shall think it my duty to make of you. (76)

Her speech relates Catholic piety to normative gender expression in two ways. First, it prescribes effeminacy, drawing on the same vocabulary that Berenza later uses to juxtapose Victoria to ideal femininity while lever-aging rote Christian moralism. Victoria's "overbearing, haughty, [and] ferocious spirit" must be replaced with virtues that are at once typically feminine and essentially Christian—"softness, humility, and obedience." Secondly, because Victoria's soul is at stake in the substitution of femi-nine for masculine attributes, meek compliance for ferocity, the Signo-ra's own devotion authorizes "every requisition" she might impose on her prisoner. According to the narrator, who is usually unsympathetic to Vic-toria, Signora di Modena's commands amount to a "system of torments," the "tyranny of a discontented bigot" (74, 92). Tracking Dacre's critique of hegemony often means prioritizing the novel's "figural discourse" over the fronted moralism of the narrator.[60] In this case, though, narrative sympathy helps to clarify the object of her criticism. Dacre homes in on the interrelation of gender identity ideology and secularist distinction in di Modena's rationalization, a logic that makes adherence to normative femininity a kind of good belief and, thus, a matter of eternal salvation rather than social performance.

In *Zofloya,* as in *A Simple Story,* the semiotics of character support this disciplinary program. Dacre's novel also features an avatar of patriarchy enforcing his ideas about sex and gender by practicing this way of reading. Il Conte Berenza travels to Venice out of "an investigating spirit, to analyse its inhabitants, and to discover, if possible, from the result of his own observation, whether the mischief they had caused, and the conduct they pursued, arose from a self-depravity of heart, or was induced by the force of inevitable circumstances: he came to investigate character, and to increase his knowledge of the human heart" (*Z*, 58). How can we explain the causation of evil, as an expression of innate character or the product of external forces? Berenza poses one of the questions that ramifies from the theological controversy of the late seventeenth century, between followers of Calvin and followers of Arminius, but, in keeping with his own character type, "the liberal philosopher," he isolates the query from religious contexts (58). When Berenza meets Victoria, the will to power veiled by his moral-philosophical inquiry becomes explicit.[61] He appraises her "beauties" and "defects" by repeatedly scrutinizing her facial features, as well as her speech and actions, and then resolves to "restrain and correct the improper bias of her character" (90, 89). The "bias" Berenza wishes to correct is toward the masculine: "her *fierte* he would have softened, and her boldness checked," and he classes the "violence" of her spirit among the counterpoises to her conventional "attractions" (58, 90). His aversion to Victoria's masculine qualities foreshadows Henriquez's preference for Lilla, the teenaged orphan whom several scholars see as Dacre's exemplary woman: meekly passive, asexual, and almost translucent.[62] Before he can mold Victoria to this pattern, however, Berenza must first measure the force of her attachment to him. He desires her "absolute, her exclusive affection," and explicitly as a guarantee of influence: "Oh! could I but penetrate her thoughts; could I but discover her actual *feelings,* my mind would be at rest; were I only convinced of her love, I could easily new model her character, because the precepts and the wishes of those we love sink deep into the heart" (92). Berenza's wish echoes Dorriforth's desire for epistemic mastery over Miss Milner, but it makes the equation of knowledge of character with power over it more explicit, underscoring the regulatory ambition of heteropatriarchy: to "new model" the feminine subject according to its own erotic ideal.

As the similarities between Berenza's desire and Signora di Modena's "duty" attest, erotic and salvific ideals of femininity overlap. But they are not merely parallel, with carceral and courtship episodes reproducing secularism's false dichotomy of religious and extra- or anti-religious contexts. Berenza does more than translate religious discipline into the language of heterosexual romance; he literally embodies the threat of semiotic ideology, concretizing the menace of secularism's representational mode in the shape of the Venetian Inquisition. When Berenza finally succumbs to the poison gradually administered by Victoria, a priest with medical training attempts to treat him with bloodletting. Berenza's blood spurts onto Victoria's face, marking her crime: "The avenging blood of Berenza had fixed upon its murderer, and hung its flaming evidence upon her cheek! She dared not lift her eyes, lest those of others should read in them the self-written characters of guilt" (Z, 187). Even in death, Berenza constrains Victoria to his semiotic system. For a brief moment their bodies are a unified physiognomic text, with the "flaming evidence" of his blood and the legibility of her eyes combining to testify to her "guilt." What's more, because it betrays his cause of death, Berenza's flesh is forensic evidence in potential. First in a dream and then by the light of day, Victoria "beheld his countenance and various parts of his body discoloured and disfigured by livid marks" (190). Zofloya acknowledges that "whoever beholds the Conte will clearly ascertain" the "fact" of his poisoning, then hides the body to protect Victoria from suspicion (192). Corinna Wagner presents this passage as evidence of widespread anxiety about emerging scientific-medical discourses that presuppose the one-to-one correspondence of body to self and paved the way for increasingly technocratic forms of surveillance and control.[63] The text is more specific than that about the source of Victoria's terror, however.

She imagines that the interpreters of Berenza's posthumous body language will be agents of the Consiglio dei Dieci, governing body of Venice and local outpost of the "terrible Inquisition" (Z, 190). It is their "lynx-eyed scrutiny" and "horrid torments" that she dreads when she first sees Berenza's corpse, and, later, when a servant rediscovers the body in an uninhabited wing of the castle, the vivid image of their public executions between the Pillars of St. Mark motivates her to flee with Zofloya (190, 223–24). Beyond strengthening Victoria's dependence on Zofloya, the disfigured body ties inside-outside symmetry to an institution with unmistakable associations, for British readers, with state violence and religious bigotry. Contrary to its status in histories of secularization in Europe and the United States, where it functions as one of secular modernity's proliferating religious counterparts, Catholicism appears in Dacre's novel as itself a secularist discourse. *Zofloya* elsewhere abstracts features of Catholic doctrine that militate against the models of selfhood and representation prescribed by secularism, as I discuss below. The juridical machinery of the Inquisition, however, iterates eighteenth-century secularism, a corporate and imperial Christianity that has not yet come to call itself "secularity" but that already grounds its legitimacy—and rationalizes its violence—by insisting on the distinction between true religion and false belief.

Throughout the narrative, Victoria rejects semiotic coherence and, with that, the sexual and racial coding of her body. Despite the vehemence of her passions, the vaguely defined but frequently cited violence of her nature, Victoria shows tremendous self-command. For example, she dissimulates the rage provoked by Signora di Modena's haranguing beneath a tranquil facade:

> To attempt to describe the indignant feelings of Victoria at this treatment, or the struggle it cost her, amounting almost to phrensy, to subdue the expression of the violent rage that fermented in her bosom, would be indeed vain; yet she bore all, and was determined sooner to die than betray the smallest symptom of vexation or impatience.
>
> But desire of revenge, deep and implacable, was nurtured in her heart's core, and gave to her character an additional shade of harshness and

ferocity: thus she became like the untameable hyaena, that confinement renders only more fierce. (Z, 75)

The narrator describes Victoria's dissimulation as an exhausting yet successful effort to stifle every "symptom" of her interior disorder, disjoining somatic sign from emotional signified. The darkening of her inward character to "shades" of "harshness and ferocity" anticipates (but does not yet find expression as) the "increasing physical masculinization" and racialization observed by Craciun, the way Victoria's features dilate and darken over the course of the narrative.[64] By comparing Victoria to "the untameable hyaena," the narrator underlines the brutal, implacable nature she couples with masculine-feminine inversion.

More subtly, she aligns Victoria's semiotic disruption with sexual indeterminacy. Hyenas were widely thought to be hermaphroditic, and, like them, Victoria undermines not only gender but also its supposedly anatomical basis in sex.[65] Horace Walpole's description of Wollstonecraft as a "hyaena in petticoats," Craciun points out, reflects a wider satirical endeavor to "unsex" advocates of Jacobin feminism: Walpole and Richard Polwhele, author of The Unsex'd Females (1798), create the category of the "notfemale," which, "like the hermaphrodite suggested by the hyena, points to the limits of the two-sex model" that had been naturalized by the Enlightenment.[66] For Walpole and Polwhele, this fluidity makes writers like Wollstonecraft and Mary Robinson into monsters, subjects incomprehensible within mirrored natural and political orders. Zofloya seems more sympathetic toward Victoria's destabilization of sex, as Craciun observes. I would add that the passage synthesizes this challenge to the two-sex model with a challenge to the secularist prescript that the exterior surfaces of the body convey interior meanings. The conjunctive adverb "thus" introducing the final clause of the passage establishes a direct relationship between Victoria's untamed aggression and her figurative transformation into a hyena. But its position at the end of a chain of coordinating conjunctions–it follows "yet," "and," "but"–implies the accretion of causal force. The grammar of these two sentences suggests that Victoria's likeness to the hyena, her "notfemale" character, results as much from her capacity to suppress its external signifiers, to prevent the signs of violent rage from surfacing, as it does from her increasing ferocity itself.

Through her seduction of Berenza and then his younger brother Henriquez, Victoria demonstrates further mastery of the signs that comprise sexual character. Having learned the "secret" of Berenza's search for proof of her love by making him the object of her own physiognomic investigation–"she watched, with scrutinizing eye, every movement, every look" for evidence of "the workings of his mind" (Z, 96)–Victoria settles on a plan to exploit his egotism. She feigns a passion calibrated particularly to Berenza's melancholic disposition, confident that his "self-love" will make her virtuosic performance still more effective: "Her eyes, no longer full of a wild and beautiful animation, were taught to languish, or to fix for hours with musing air upon the ground; her gait, no longer firm and elevated, became hesitating and despondent. She no longer engrossed the conversation; she became silent, apparently absent, and plunged in thought" (97–98). Manipulating physiognomic signs and body language, Victoria curates the expression of a properly Romantic subjectivity (abstracted, engrossed, even "oppressed" by feeling) in order to assert her eligibility as an object of romantic attachment. Berenza has underestimated Victoria's ability to "new model" her own character after his self-image. Along with this protean quality, Victoria shows acute perceptiveness of the nature of heterosexual desire. Comparing Dacre's last novel, *The Passions* (1811), to Percy Bysshe Shelley's poem "Alastor" (1816), Airey contends that Dacre satirizes the narcissism of the greater Romantic lyric, in which the "ideal woman" is an "externalized version of the poet's own self, a manifestation of intense solipsism."[67] Applying Airey's reasoning to Dacre's first novel, we can see the success of Victoria's performance as confirmation of the same solipsistic tendency: "so well did she support the character she had assumed"—again, *his* character—that Berenza "became convinced, that he possessed the first pure and genuine affection of an innocent and lovely girl" (99). Dacre thus exposes sexual difference, evoked here through one extreme of virginal girlhood, as fantasy, the product of narcissistic masculine desire rather than a reflection of prior biological truth.

The success of her imitation briefly secures not only freedom from the meanings attached to her sexed body—freedom, we could say, from gender—but a version of sexual mastery that resembles godhead. While Victoria's command over the outward signs of emotion "convince" Berenza of the nature and intensity of her attachment to him, a more spontaneous exertion of masculine energy extends her power from persuasion to domination (Z, 137). Victoria deflects the thrust of a stiletto meant for her lover, saving his life and sustaining a minor injury in the process. Her gesture of self-sacrifice not only eradicates Berenza's residual doubt, but also prompts a fundamental change in the way he reads character.

> Longer to doubt the truth, the romantic ardour of her attachment, would, he esteemed, be sacrilege; his ideas underwent a wonderful, but natural revolution—no more the haughty Berenza, proud of his noble, his unsullied blood, fearing to dash it with a tincture of disgrace!—no more looking *down,* with protecting air, a high and superior being, upon a mistress beloved indeed, but not considered as an *equal,* because, though innocent in reality, in his eyes she was a scion of infamy and shame;—no, his heart now throbbed with excessive tenderness, and now ached with compunctious pangs, that he could ever have deemed unworthy of his honorable love the creature before him, shining superior in a glory emanating from *herself!* (137)

Combined with her assumed character, Victoria's muscular devotion foments a "revolution" of "ideas" in Berenza's mind, in which faith deposes evidential reasoning. The new, extrarational paradigm makes skepticism "sacrilege," Berenza a penitent devotee, and Victoria a god—a being who, in her refulgent superiority, generates rather than receives glory. Behind the enlightened pretensions of Dacre's narrator lies a fantasy of erotic reenchantment, the conversion of the "liberal," "calculating philosopher" to "doating and idolatrous love" (Z, 58, 137). Victoria achieves not equality but an inversion of the relations of sexual mastery. Berenza once looked "down" from a position of social and moral elevation, but now looks up to Victoria as belonging to a higher order of being and, therefore, as a fit object of reverence. She now enjoys a "complete and powerful . . . dominion" over him. The sensuality of Dacre's language ("his heart now throbbed . . . and now ached") undercuts the narrator's tone of lament by conveying the erotic charge of reverence and repentance. It is only from the entrenched vantage of patriarchy, the position served by rendering sexual difference as a political struggle between absolutes, that Berenza's immanent experience of the feminine divine looks like cause for grief.

Victoria's performance of Berenza's personality foreshadows her impersonation of Lilla in the third volume. She articulates their difference of character, and her wish to collapse it, in terms of binary sex: "Would that this unwieldy form could be compressed into the fairy delicacy of hers, these bold masculine features assume the likeness of her baby face!—Ah! what would I not submit to, to gain but one look of love from the pitiless Henriquez" (Z, 211). Lest we mistake Victoria's motive for the pursuit of an ego-ideal more closely allied to bourgeois femininity, the closing exclamation of her speech clarifies that the wished-for exchange of "bold masculine features" for ethereal, infantile beauty is merely strategic. Personifying innocence in this way is something Victoria "submits to" as the cost of obtaining sexual possession of Henriquez. Zofloya provides a "drug" that confuses Henriquez's perception, substituting the image of his object of desire for "every female" he sees. The shock of recognition Henriquez experiences when these effects wear off bespeaks, at once, the disparity between Victoria and Lilla and the extent of Zofloya's necromantic power: "Scarce could his phrenzied gaze believe the sight which presented itself.—Not the fair Lilla, the betrothed and heart-wedded wife of his bosom, but Victoria! appearing Lilla no longer, blasting his trained eyes with her hated image!—Sleep still overpowered her senses, unconscious of the horror she inspired—those black fringed eyelids, reposing upon a cheek of dark and animated hue—those raven tresses hanging unconfined—oh, sad! Oh, damning proofs!—Where was the fair enamelled cheek—the flaxen ringlets of the delicate Lilla?" (217). The horrified juxtaposition of present and absent metonymic signs inserts Victoria and Lilla into the familiar Christian aesthetic hierarchy that layers black/white and good/evil binaries. In one of the novel's echoes of *A Simple Story*, Victoria's deviance from sexual propriety manifests as racial difference in the eyes of proponents, like Henriquez, of hegemonic gender ideology. Her "black fringed eyelids" suggest non-European cosmetic practices, while her "dark and animated hue" evoke fears of miscegenation. These racialized markers are "damning proofs" of Victoria's true identity, her reprobation, and her exclusion from a standard of beauty based on childlike diminutiveness and porcelain whiteness.

By manipulating the overlaid markers of racial, sexual, and spiritual character, Zofloya's potion also disorders the body-self correspondence that is supposed to preserve individual identity. Sedgwick's gloss on the titular protagonist of Maturin's *Melmoth, the Wanderer* (1820) has relevance here, as well. Melmoth "specializes in horizontal slippage toward other characters," Sedgwick writes, dissolving boundaries between "self-contained character and self-contained character" (*GC*, 31–32). The episode in *Zofloya* appears in previous scholarship as an example of material transmutation, something akin to Melmoth's or Gil-Martin's shapeshifting: Victoria "materializes as Lilla," and in the process unfixes all of identity, biological sex, and gender-as-culture.[68] To be sure, the substitution of Lilla's features (childlike, blonde, translucent) for Victoria's (blackened by sin, enlarged by her masculine spirit) argues at a certain level of abstraction for a performative model of sex and gender. But the exchange occurs only within Henriquez's mind, the result of a "delusion" or drug-induced "partial mania," as Zofloya describes it (*Z*, 212). The other-directedness of Dacre's fantasy makes it primarily epistemological rather than ontological; it is a fantasy of control over the knowledge produced by and about her body. Victoria's flesh is unruly, less because of an actual protean property than its refusal to signify within the system of reference by which sexual and racial differences are made to appear real, corporeal.

Demonic Communion

Victoria's sexual attraction to Zofloya can be understood in the same terms—they, too, offer escape from semiotic order. The first meaningful encounter between the characters includes an act of erotic fetishization. Already moved to condescension by Zofloya's beauty, Victoria extends her hand to receive his proffered rose:

> when, as she did so, a thorn ran deep into one of her fingers, and the blood issued in a large drop. Zofloya, in apparent consternation, opened his vest, and, tearing some linen from his bosom, cast himself upon his knees, and applied it with trembling eagerness to the wound. Victoria felt

too surprised—almost gratified to repulse him, and the Moor continued, unchecked, to press the blood from her finger, and to absorb it with the linen, as it flowed. At length, it ceased to do so: Zofloya pressed the crimsoned linen to his heart, and tearing from it every particle that remained unstained, he folded it up as a sacred relic, and placed it in his bosom. Then seeming suddenly to recollect himself, he appeared struck with confusion at his own audacity: he dared not raise his eyes to Victoria; and a dark-red blush animated with lurid colour his expressive countenance. (Z, 154)

The frisson of this description stems from an excess of signification. Symbol and sign intensify toward materialization as the logics of religious devotion and interracial desire merge. The rose, popular symbol of eros, literally penetrates Victoria and, since Zofloya's blush brings his own blood to the surface, leaves only one layer of skin to prevent the mingling of their bodily fluids. Several Gothic tropes combine through the creation of this "sacred relic," including vampirism and transfusion.[69] Above all, though, the blood-soaked linen calls to mind the doctrine of transubstantiation, with Zofloya expressly relating the object's value to its synecdochic meaning: "it is of equal value to me with yourself," he explains, "for it is a part of you—your precious blood! chary will I be of it; and, safely placed upon my bosom, no earthly power shall tempt me to resign it" (155). In *A Simple Story*, Matilda's revision of the rite of communion provides the idiom for otherwise incommunicable devotion—incommunicable, in her case, because of the physical remoteness of the object. Here, too, Catholic doctrine undergoes translation as a language for an otherwise inarticulate attachment.

The extensibility of that doctrine beyond codified ritual suggests Catholicism's double relation to secularism within Gothic fiction. It is also the most striking point of contrast to Lewis's fiction. If, as Hoeveler suggests, there is a scholarly "controversy" over the valence of the Gothic's depiction of Catholicism, the disagreement does not extend to works like *The Monk*.[70] Indeed, critics agree that Lewis, Radcliffe, and Maturin all "capitalized on the vogue for anti-Catholic hysteria," as Hoeveler puts it.[71] Joseph Crawford has recently issued a dissenting opinion with respect to the Gothic as a whole, but his revision of the consensus interpretation of Lewis's best-known contribution to the genre goes only so far. In *The*

Monk, Crawford argues, the Madrid Inquisition functions as a lesser terror compared to the depraved monk Ambrosio's unrealized potential to incite the proletariat to revolutionary violence.[72] The attenuation of anti-Catholic feeling suggests to Crawford sympathies with Edmund Burke's reactionary politics rather than sympathy with Catholic people or traditions. *Zofloya* manifests a stronger ambivalence. The novel dwells with the expected level of anxiety on carceral and sexual violence perpetrated in the name of converting young women to Catholic sisterhood, and it underscores the arbitrary power of the Inquisition. But *Zofloya* omits another familiar target of anti-Catholic Gothic writers, the sexual perversion of the Catholic priest, and instead explores the insurgent potential of transubstantiation with undisguised interest. An analysis of Dacre's text that foregrounds discursive machinery rather than stylistic influences reveals a stronger resemblance to Inchbald's writings than to the Radcliffean British Gothic fictions to which it is usually compared.

Zofloya's ritual differs from Matilda's pietistic praxis in several important ways, however. He clearly eroticizes the object of reverence, in part because his relic pushes semiotic correspondence even further than the items in Lord Elmwood's study. The fabric is suffused with sacral meaning as it soaks up Victoria's blood, concretely a part of the body that Zofloya reverences above "any earthly power." The linen facilitates direct, physical contact rather than symbolic association with the divine. Building sexual tension (euphemized as Zofloya's "trembling eagerness") and postcoital embarrassment (his "confusion," averted gaze, and "lurid colour") testify to the phenomenal immediacy of their connection. Like the protagonist of *The Woman of Colour,* published two years later, Victoria finds her character appraised through a sexual-spiritual framework that functions outside of semiotic parameters. Zofloya's appeal places contrary emphasis on embodied meaning over abstract value, and it meets with greater success. Where Olivia Fairfield feels repulsed, Victoria feels "flattered" and "irresistibly impelled" (Z, 155). The characters' responses match their contrasting attitudes toward the ideal of secular legibility.

To appraise the novel's response to secularism discourse, we must attend not only to how Zofloya represents Victoria but also to the ways in which the novel represents him. The character has two referents: the titular "Moor" and Lucifer, the quintessential other of early modern Christendom and the incarnation of evil. Despite the tendency of scholarship to neglect the infernal truth of Zofloya's character or to overlay it with his performed racial and ethnic identity, these meanings are not so easily disentangled. In fact, the irresolvable tension between enslaved Moor and Satan helps to illustrate the limits of postsecular critique in Dacre's time and our own.

The specificity of the subject position that Satan assumes remains an understudied feature of the text. Even scholarship that foregrounds the novel's relationship to contemporary racial constructs tend to assign blanket categories, like "black slave" or "black male," and, from there, to place Zofloya within histories of literary representations of enslaved people of African or Caribbean origins.[73] One exception is Ian Kim Michasiw's work, which anchors a postcolonial analysis to Zofloya's explicitly avowed cultural background as an Iberian Moor.[74] Born in the Nasrid kingdom of Granada, the last Muslim state in Spain, Zofloya was among the hundreds of thousands of residents expelled when the city fell to Spanish Catholic forces in 1492: "Though a Moor, and by a combination of events, and the change of war, (in the final victory of the Spaniards over the Moors of Granada), reduced to a menial situation, [he] was yet of noble birth, of the race of Abduhlrahmans" (Z, 150). Zofloya's family name is a variant transcription of the Arabic phrase *abd al-rahman,* or "servant of the most gracious." Beyond indicating his class status, and thereby activating the associations of the "noble savage" and "royal slave" traditions, Zofloya's genealogy strengthens his religious identification. Is it possible that continued adherence to Islam after "the unhappy defeat of my countrymen, in Granada" exacerbated Zofloya's hardships? The details of his biography are scant, but we know this much: first, that the defeat of Moorish forces and Zofloya's subsequent enslavement by a Spanish nobleman are indirectly rather than causally related, outcomes separated by "a combination of events" and "severe vicissitudes"; and, second, that Ferdinand and Isabella forced Muslims to choose between conversion and exile after the fall of Granada (150).[75] The novel leaves readers to infer what relationship, if any, links the two scales of history operative in Zofloya's backstory, the personal and the geopolitical. As a displaced Muslim, Dacre's "Moor" represents, in any case, an imperial rival laid low by Euro-Christian violence in the year of global racial cataclysm.[76]

This representation flirts with the line between orientalism and genuine autocritique. If, as Michasiw contends, Dacre constructs Zofloya partly by reviving early modern stereotypes of Moorish character and capacity, she nevertheless reverses the polarity of clash-of-civilizations rhetoric.[77] For example, Zofloya's mysterious pharmacological expertise may conjure the figure of the moor-as-mad-scientist, but it also bestows on that figure a genuinely radical potential. Zofloya carries the power to topple the epistemological bulwarks of a discourse, secularism, that this novel persistently identifies with psychic and physical violence—with, variously, colonial expansion, slavery, incarceration, patriarchal domination, and public execution. The "secrets of art and nature" that confer this power derive, in turn, from his avowed cultural legacy; he learned them, he tells Victoria, from "an ancient Moor of Granada" (Z, 160–61).

Of course, the speaker who makes the avowal, the Zofloya we meet at the novel's halfway point, claims this backstory as a mode of deception. Burley stresses that there are really two Zofloyas in this text.[78] Zofloya the Moor drowns in the margins of the narrative, shoved into a canal by a jealous fellow servant. Satan subsequently possesses his body and assumes his identity, but the fact is implied rather than revealed until the conclusion of the novel. For Burley, the demonic Zofloya erases Zofloya the Moor, signaling the text's refusal to imagine a revolutionary theo-racial other. In other words, Dacre bifurcates the title character in the service of her reactionary politics. She softens the threat of patrio-colonial dispossession by substituting the uncanny powers of the Devil for the even more menacing (because real) agency of the subaltern. Burley's argument presupposes that there is no authentic or original content to the title character of the now-dead human Zofloya. His personal history demonstrates otherwise. Though told in outline, Zofloya's story contours a religious and ethnic character which Dacre's Satan appropriates to entrap Victoria, a subject position that is seductive to the same extent that it is unassimilable. The enslaved Moor who might have spoken from that perspective undergoes colonization, but not erasure. The final pages of Zofloya furnish evidence of Dacre's repudiation of this formal violence.

In the heightened allegorical register of Gothic Romance, the end of the novel condemns the secularist equation of colonized other with incarnate evil. The anticlimax of Satan's declaration (by this time, Zofloya's true identity can come as a surprise only to Victoria) conveys something of the rote inevitability with which anti-Christianity became recognizable under the sign of blackness and as a particular system of bad faith—Islam. Instead of ameliorating a threat to white European patriarchy, Satan's unmasking underscores how naturally the mutually enforcing, conservative energies of Christian myth and patriarchy contain the liberatory potential epitomized by Zofloya. Stripped of that character's beauty and external referents, Satan appears as an appropriate emblem of both hegemonic discourses. He is as ugly as he is evil, and the sudden return of semiotic congruity jars Victoria back into horrified subjection to Christian moral absolutism. In place of Zofloya–Muslim, black, desirable and desirous, openly rebellious—"stood a figure, fierce, gigantic, and hideous to behold," a figure, here as in Victoria's premonitory dream, "monstrous and deformed" according to his position within Christianity's binary frame (*Z*, 254, 238). Satan manifests in his true form to assert the claim of a husband. Dacre, Craciun writes, "deliberately describes Victoria's eventual submission to Zofloya's will as a marriage, and his attempts to convince her to depend on him are expressed in the language of romantic courtship."[79] When he casts her into the "abyss," Victoria plummets into a marriage allegory, a nightmare of sociolegal annihilation, or "the loss of social identity, mobility, and independence that a woman suffers in marrying her lover, who then becomes her master after having acted the part of her devoted and enthralled servant."[80] Elaborating this interpretation, I propose that the self-legitimizing mode of secularism escalates the source of terror, signaling the novel's rejection of secularist ideology. By splitting Zofloya's character, the novel represents the tendency of secularism to conjure sexual, political, and theological alternatives as a way to tighten its control, in this case circumscribing Victoria's deviant sexual agency within the form of the conjugal couple.

Zofloya, in the end, refuses to ratify its own emancipatory fantasies. Like Lady Matilda in Inchbald's novel, Victoria's story ends in submission to liberal-secular forms, in what appears to be either affirmation of or acquiescence to heteropatriachal authority. Feminist scholarship attributes this unsatisfying feature to a failure of critical vision. Donna Heiland states that "Dacre's strength as a writer of gothic fiction is that she can imagine a radical assault against the patriarchal structures that trap women; her limitation is that she cannot imagine that assault succeeding. [Her heroines] can neither claim the status of patriarch, nor change the patriarchy, nor eliminate it. . . .The only way out is through death."[81] Dacre espouses without fully realizing the politics of the Gothic genre, in other words. Heiland's assessment is both perceptive and limiting. She sees that the novel's critique operates more cogently through description than prescription, denouncing hegemonic discourses without charting a retraceable way out of them. In describing this feature as a failure to reach escape velocity, however, Heiland also applies a universalizing definition of resistance so often imposed on eighteenth- and nineteenth-century women writers, with the effect of narrowing the possibilities of engagement with the discursive operations of power. Neither Inchbald nor Dacre depict the liberation of their characters—not from the material constraints of marriage, nor from the epistemological fetters of novelistic secularism. As I discuss in the following conclusion, their novels nevertheless contribute to the critical legacy of Gothic fiction, its anticipation of the self-interrogatory method and subjunctive mood of postsecular scholarship today.

Subjunctive Criticism

THE EIGHTEENTH-CENTURY NOVEL'S Calvinist semiotics consistently reproduces distinctions between good and bad faith. It begins as a paradigm for differentiating the two taxa of Calvinism's doctrine of salvation, the saved and the damned. The unpredictability that inheres to semiotic activity in that instance reflects the challenges of recognizing authentic, inward motions of grace from the outside and shapes Bunyan's surprisingly unstable allegorical method. Knowledge is probabilistic or conjectural, at best, where we depend on exterior evidence of the contents of character because those signs perpetually threaten to detach from their referents or to accumulate instead of signifying in a straightforward way. This epistemic model is quickly extended, through the process of secularization, to confrontations between Christianity and other religions. There, misalignments of interior and exterior sometimes mark the incursion of a theo-racial other, and sometimes the false Christianity of white European colonizers and enslavers. We can see these secularist mechanics of distinction operate in, for example, Aubin's strategic application of Calvinist heuristics to distinguish between the latent Christianity of virtuous Muslims and the absolute alterity of people of African descent, or in Sterne's deployment of the model to contrast the true religion of liberal-Anglican Protestantism from its counterparts inside and outside of Christendom. But we can also see it in ameliorationist and abolitionist novels like *Oroonoko* and *The Woman of Colour.* Even in *Obi,* where the semiotic paradigm serves antiracist interpretations of religious character or helps to level Obeah with "white obi," imperial Christianity, it reinforces the secular dialectic and maps the good faith/bad faith dyad onto colonizers and colonized subjects.

This regime of character doesn't always establish simple correspondences between somatic signs, like epidermal race, and the inner meaning of religious character. It does, however, presume that some kind of referential relationship exists between surface and essence, and it demands of those who would redirect this tendency away from racist conclusions the task of constructing precarious representational structures. Hence, Cugoano's fictive encounter between the white man and the black man, which entails a triangulation of somatic signs to hold racial and spiritual blackness in a strictly emblematic relationship and requires the black man to bear the emblem of shared depravity on his skin. Hence, too, Olivia Fairfield's efforts to abstract markers of racial difference from secular circuits of legibility that she otherwise defends. They evince different relationships to Calvinist theology, but both Cugoano's jeremiad and *The Woman of Colour* develop their theories of race entirely within this character system. And, within this system, the burden of representation falls heaviest on black authors and characters. They must in certain important respects mean *for* their white counterparts: signifying to their moral benefit; in their physical presence; and, in Cugoano's example, on their behalf.

Early novels present no obvious alternative to this way of thinking about religious character, in which the question is not whether bodies and beliefs are associated but which bodies and beliefs are viable, and which are errant. In stressing the secular character of the eighteenth-century British novel, its propensity to enact through form the embodied distinction between good and bad faith, I do not intend to vilify overtly colonialist authors, nor do I regard antislavery or antiracist writers who also reveal secularist tendencies with "teleological pity." Novelist Zadie Smith uses this phrase to name a form of condescension toward the literary past, a presentist mood that combines calls for patience with the limitations of historical texts and figures with the claim that today's societies are morally superior, enlightened.[1] *If only they knew what we know.* This attitude toward history sustains itself on the false assumption of linear progress, Smith explains, and a blinkered analysis of the current situation. Although she writes most immediately in response to contemporary

readers' impatience with Georgian attitudes toward slavery, Smith's lesson applies just as aptly to analyses of eighteenth-century secularism. The
pervasiveness, so well documented in Talal Asad's work and the scholarship that has followed in its wake, of secularist premises and prescriptions
within contemporary institutions and academic disciplines dedicated to
their study militates against the assumption of moral superiority. We are
still very much in the thrall of the liberal-secular hegemony that was taking shape during the long eighteenth century.

While following the afterlife of Calvinism's taxonomy in novelistic
characterization and imperial race-making, I have tried to avoid sorting
authors or texts into my own moral categories. My goal has not been to
identify heroes and villains, in other words. Rather, I have attempted to
elucidate the complex formal machinery and the expansiveness of the
formation of the secular that defines this period. The telos of nineteenth-
and twentieth-century liberal-secular ideology looms over my analyses
of moderate and even radical writers, it's true. But it's also the case that
I see a way forward in their complex negotiations of secularist discourse.
Especially in chapters 4 and 5, I am interested in writers who struggle
productively against the discursive constraints of secularism, whether by
attempting to hold apart racialization and Christian imperialism or by
redirecting the regulatory, disciplinary force of secularism toward Anglican Protestant excesses. Even as I point out the impossibility of fully or
finally breaking the fetters of secularist ideology, I want to convey my
optimism about the possible renewal of their project.

The metadeployment of Calvinist semiotics in Gothic fictions strikes
me as an especially promising gesture since it exemplifies the kind of self-
interrogation for which scholars like John Modern advocate.[2] Viewed
through the lens of zero-sum conflict between normalization and resistance instantiated by modern criticism, the novels discussed in my final
chapter appear to fall within the boundary of Christian secularism. Inchbald and Dacre imagine subjects or subjectivities askew of secularist
prescriptions, but they cannot imagine them outside of secularism's
ever-expanding perimeter. The narrative of A Simple Story stops short of
definitively pronouncing Lady Matilda's subjection, but it forecloses the
conditions of her flourishing at almost the same moment that it defines

them. The counterpossiblities entertained by *Zofloya* are reintegrated, finally and violently, within secular modernity's foundational myth and its fundamental unit of social organization. Victoria descends into a hellish version of the same structure, marriage, imposed conditionally on Matilda. With her goes any optimism that transgressive femininity—muscular, self-insisting, irrepressibly sexual, racially ambiguous—might have a place in the impersonal orders of God and empire. The agent of her downfall, Zofloya, likewise proves assimilable. Colonized by the biblical antagonist, his beauty, agency, and knowledge are in the end instruments of rather than challenges to hegemony.

My objective in pointing out the characters' incapacity to disentangle themselves from secularist ideology is not to hold their authors accountable to an ahistorical standard for radical politics, nor to despair at the unavailingness of critique in the face of secular recursivity. The point, rather, is to show Gothic fiction's capacity to map, if not always to extend, the possibilities of being and believing. *A Simple Story* and *Zofloya* perform this cartographic labor in starts and stops, with what can look, from our vantage, like incompleteness. To adopt such a valuation is to perpetuate the secularist equation of historical alterity with inferiority and, at the same time, to misconstrue the goal of postsecular scholarship in the present. Contributors to this interdisciplinary field encounter the same dilemma that faced Inchbald and Dacre at the turn of the nineteenth century. Given secularism's tendency to produce its own outside, and thereby contain the potential for its own critique, to what extent is it possible to generate cosmological, erotic, political, or formal conditions under a new sign?

While critique is necessarily secular, its tools are still useful—as long as we recognize the tendency within critical thought to define our fields and their key categories against cultural and temporal others. This is one way to describe the aspirations of postsecular criticism: to develop analytical methods and historical models that make the fewest possible concessions to the claims of secularization, while at the same time cultivating a posture of self-interrogation that never lets us forget our tendency to reproduce a hierarchized globality in the name of knowledge production. Within the immanent critique of Gothic fiction, two-dimensional characters serve an analogous function. Elsewhere a technology of naturalization, novelistic characterization recurs in the Gothic as a strategy of "disaggregation," to adopt Orlemanski's term.[3] Hogg, Inchbald, and Dacre use character not only to describe the constructed reality of secular modernity (and the role that novels played in its construction) but also to deligature the binaries that provide its structure. If the alternatives that appear in these writings appear only in the process of domestication, as subject to disciplinary force rather than as generative of liberatory potential, they are nevertheless visible.

NOTES

Introduction

1. Bunyan, *Pilgrim's Progress,* 7; hereafter cited parenthetically as *P.*
2. Forster, *Aspects of the Novel.*
3. For Bunyan's views on church membership and conversion, see Greaves, *Glimpses of Glory,* 66, 271–77, 301–9. See also Nuttall, *Visible Saints,* 110–14.
4. See Hill, *Turbulent, Seditious, and Factious People,* for background on the Bedford congregation. Where John Calvin imagined the visible church as a "mixed body" composed of both elect and reprobate, churches in the Congregationalist tradition attempted to "make the visible church a more accurate spiritual approximation of the invisible church." Hindmarsh, *Evangelical Conversion Narrative,* 47–50.
5. Damrosch, *God's Plot and Man's Stories,* 37.
6. Eco, *Semiotica e filosophia del linguaggio.*
7. Boelhower, *Through a Glass Darkly,* 10.
8. Boelhower, 20.
9. For a comprehensive yet concise survey of this body of scholarship, see Coviello, *Make Yourselves Gods,* 23–47.
10. Taylor, *Secular Age,* 299.
11. Taylor, 303–4.
12. Asad, *Formations of the Secular;* Anidjar, "Secularism." Anidjar writes, "Secularism is a name Christianity gave itself when it invented religion, when it named its other or others as religions" (62).
13. Coviello, *Make Yourselves Gods,* 38.
14. Coviello, 38.
15. Cragg, *Puritanism;* Rivers, *Reason, Grace, and Sentiment.*
16. Rivers, 1:1. The same is true of the more radical Latitudinarians and deists, who figure in Rivers's narrative as successors to the rationalist turn in Protestant theology. See also Wallace, *Shapers of English Calvinism.*
17. Wallace, 18.
18. Weber, *Protestant Ethic;* Watt, *Rise of the Novel;* Starr, *Defoe and Spiritual Autobiography.*
19. Rivett, *Science of the Soul.*

20. Rivett, 23. Dewey Wallace similarly proposes in *Shapers of English Calvinism* that radical forms of religious thought moderated Calvinist theology rather than simply supplanting it, contradicting the dominant narrative and his own conclusions from an earlier study. See *Puritans and Predestination*.

21. Bunyan, *Holy War*, 183, 9.

22. Throughout this book, I follow La Marr Jurelle Bruce's in writing "lowercase blackness," a practice that accords with the fluid race-thinking of the long eighteenth century. The texts I discuss exhibit what Bruce describes as "a blackness that is ever-unfurling rather than rigidly fixed; a blackness that is neither capitalized nor propertized via the protocols of Western grammar." *How to Go Mad*, 6.

23. Cugoano, *Thoughts and Sentiments*, 40.

24. For the Calvinist strain of eighteenth-century black antislavery writing, and its influence on twentieth- and twenty-first-century Afropessimism, see Stewart, "Cugoano and Hermeneutics." While Stewart emphasizes the distinctiveness of the Calvinism developed by black writers, I am interested in the features of Cugoano's religious thought and representational practice that link him to novelists of the period.

25. Cugoano, *Thoughts and Sentiments*, 42.

26. Wheelock, *Barbaric Culture and Black Critique*, 45.

27. Cugoano, *Thoughts and Sentiments*, 40.

28. Boelhower, *Through a Glass Darkly*, 38.

29. Lynch, *Economy of Character*.

30. Gallagher, "Rise of Fictionality," 350.

31. Gallagher, 346.

32. Orlemanski, "Who Has Fiction?," 146.

33. Aravamudan, *Enlightenment Orientalism*.

34. Frow, *Character and Person*, 95.

35. Frow, xi.

36. Hershinow, *Born Yesterday*, 4.

37. For an example of the contrary approach, see Blakey Vermeule, *Why Do We Care about Literary Characters?* Vermeule accepts Gallagher's definition of fictionality, but not her periodization. She suggests that the suspension of disbelief that enables us to identify with literary characters is not, as Gallagher argues, "historically particular" nor idiosyncratic to the novel but a universal psychological capacity, a feature of human "evolutionary heritage," that shapes all cultural forms (9).

38. Hersinow, *Born Yesterday*, 6.

39. Said, *Orientalism*.

40. Conway and Harol, "Toward a Postsecular Eighteenth Century," 569.

41. Anderson, *Imagining Methodism*; Codr, *Raving at Usurers*; Sider Jost, *Prose Immortality*; Rosenberg, *Critical Enthusiasm*; Weiss Smith, *Empiricist Devotions*.

42. Codr, *Raving at Usurers*, 23.

43. Codr, 23.

44. For reflections on this methodological shift, see Holsinger, "Literary History and the Religious Turn."

45. Jager, *Unquiet Things*.

46. Seidel, *Rethinking the Secular Origins of the Novel*.

47. Anidjar, "Secularism," 58.
48. Coviello and Hickman, "Introduction," 645.
49. In addition to the literary-critical work cited at the head of this section, historians of enlightenment cultures have executed a "religious turn." Among the most influential of these accounts are Clark's *English Society,* Pocock's *Barbarism and Religion,* and Sorkin's *Religious Enlightenment.*
50. Taylor, *Secular Age.*
51. Branch, "Bunyan, Theory, and Theology," 502.
52. Branch, 516.
53. Block, *Colonial Complexions,* 3.
54. See, for instance, Wheeler, *Complexion of Race;* and Boulukos, *Grateful Slave.* Wheeler and Boulukos draw on Williams's arguments in *Capitalism and Slavery.*
55. See Block, *Colonial Complexions,* 1–9, and especially Block's gloss of Wheeler's argument (3).
56. Heng, *Invention of Race,* 3.
57. Heng, 3.
58. Heng, 3.
59. Heng, 3. An outlier among scholars who identify race with modernity, Hickman also observes the inseparability of religion and race. For Hickman, race is a phenomenon of the global convulsion of 1492 rather than a nineteenth-century telos. Hickman and Heng ultimately define race differently—Hickman, as an "immanentization" or ontological solidification of religio-cultural difference, and Heng as a more abstract, superseding metalanguage that subsumes an array of social relations (*Black Prometheus,* 43).
60. Coviello, *Make Yourselves Gods,* 38. See also Modern, *Secularism in Antebellum America;* and Scott, *Sex and Secularism.*

Chapter 1. Character Detection

1. Watt, *Rise of the Novel,* 76.
2. Watt, 76.
3. Damrosch, *God's Plot and Man's Stories,* 13.
4. Damrosch, 19.
5. Davies, "Spirit in the Letters," 324.
6. See also Gribben, "Lay Conversion and Calvinist Doctrine."
7. For the conversion narrative as the defining genre of the gathered church tradition, see Caldwell, *Puritan Conversion Narrative.* For the social role of spiritual self-examination, see Lynch, *Protestant Autobiography,* 27.
8. Literary critics often flatten distinctions between Calvinist sects, assigning a term that best describes a reformist political movement within English Protestant culture to a religious aesthetic, an economic paradigm, or a generic pattern. Wallace has shown that the label "Puritan" needs careful parsing. *Puritans and Predestination.*
9. Bunyan, *Holy War,* 171, 183; hereafter cited parenthetically as *HW.*
10. Hunter, *Reluctant Pilgrim,* 96.
11. For Bunyan's work as a course in Christian strategies of interpretation, see Damrosch, *God's Plot and Man's Stories,* 159–60; and Haskin, "Burden of Interpretation," 261, 272.

12. Wallace, *Puritans and Predestination*; Beeke, *Assurance of Faith*. For the origin of Puritan "introspective piety," see Winship, "Weak Christians."

13. Calvinist introspective discipline plays an important role in Watt's teleological account of individualism and narrative interiority in *Rise of the Novel*. For the "aggressively private" nature of Nonconformist spiritual practices, see also Ellenzweig, *Fringes of Belief*, 76.

14. Bunyan, *Grace Abounding*, 8; hereafter cited parenthetically as *GA*.

15. *Minutes of the First Independent Church*, 23.

16. *Minutes of the First Independent Church*, 24.

17. For Bunyan's influence on spiritual autobiography in the Nonconformist and later evangelical traditions, see Hindmarsh, *Evangelical Conversion Narrative*, 50–51; and Lynch, *Protestant Autobiography*, 182–206.

18. Bunyan, *Doctrine of the Law and Grace*, 220, 304–13.

19. For Christian's conspicuously nonlinear "progress," see Fish, "Progress in *The Pilgrim's Progress*."

20. OED Online, "Conversation, n."

21. Davies argues that the church community insulated its members against the alienating effects of Calvinist theology. Personal salvation became a matter of collective conscience ("Spirit in the Letters," 325–26, 336).

22. OED Online, "Character, n." Insofar as these detailed reports do circulate, "character," here, carries the sense of an "estimate formed of a person's qualities; reputation," as well.

23. Dorothy Van Ghent defines "proper" allegory as a system of emblematic images that are endowed with the "power of symbols." Such emblems evoke feelings and associations "spontaneously" and "naturally," reinforcing the allegory's larger conceptual framework (*English Novel*, 25).

24. Fletcher, *Allegory*, 8, 60–63.

25. Fletcher, 8.

26. Knapp, *Personification and the Sublime*.

27. Damrosch, *God's Plot and Man's Stories*, 179.

28. Haskin, "Burden of Interpretation," 265.

29. McKeon, *Origins of the English Novel*, 297.

30. McKeon, 312. McKeon echoes Martin Battestin, who argues that eighteenth-century novels differ from conventional allegories insofar as they preserve the "illusion of reality" and the integrity of their literal narratives. Battestin, *Providence of Wit*, 148.

31. Rita Felski points out that Ricoeur used this phrase retrospectively to describe his work and not, as it is widely thought, in *Freud and Philosophy*; see Felski, *Limits of Critique*, 31.

32. Felski, 31.

33. Felski, 32–33.

34. Ginzburg, "Clues."

35. Ginzburg, 105.

36. Felski, *Limits of Critique*, 32.

37. Felski, 32.

38. Ginzburg, "Clues," 102.

39. Bunyan, *Life and Death of Mr. Badman*, 120.

40. Branch, "Bunyan, Theory, and Theology," 502.
41. Branch, 516.
42. Branch, 516.
43. Branch, 514.
44. Brown, "Bunyan and Empire."
45. Spargo, *Writing of John Bunyan;* Hofmeyr, *Portable Bunyan.*
46. Pahl, *Empire of Sacrifice.*
47. Brown, "Bunyan and Empire," 667.
48. Aravamudan, *Tropicopolitans,* 3.
49. Modern editor James F. Forrest compares Bunyan's descriptions of combat to those in M. H. Keen's *Laws of War in the Late Middle Ages* and concludes that Bunyan writes "within the framework of accepted conventions of war" and describes "late medieval military practice" accurately. *Holy War,* 81n1. More recent scholarship draws connections to the English Civil War. See, for example, Greaves, "Bunyan and The Holy War"; and Walker, "Militant Religion and Politics."
50. Forrest, 7n10; OED Online, "Complexion," 4a. The citations for this definition span 1569 to 1865.
51. For the relation of "complexion" to epidermal race in British literature before 1800, see Wheeler, *Complexion of Race;* and Coles, *Bad Humor.*
52. Gen. 9.20–27 (KJV). See Goldenberg, *Curse of Ham;* and Whitford, *Curse of Ham in the Early Modern Era.*
53. Willbewill's use of spies resembles the phenomenon that Ginzburg places at the turn of the twentieth century, when, he argues, the evidential paradigm that had traveled from medical-scientific discourse to conjectural humanistic disciplines found its way into systems of identification and surveillance that support state control. "Clues," 119.
54. Rev. 19.10 (KJV).
55. Rev. 19.8 (KJV).
56. Gronniosaw, *Narrative,* 1. Hereafter cited parenthetically as *N.*
57. For Gronniosaw's Dutch Reformed and British Calvinist social networks, see Hanley, *Slavery and Abolition,* 99–119. Hanley emphasizes the "recalcitrant proslavery" position of the prominent white Calvinists in Gronniosaw's circle (102). My reading focuses on the way, in the text of the *Narrative* itself, Calvinist semiotics at first uphold and then undercut a popular justification for the practice: the predestined damnation of people of African descent.

Chapter 2. Empire of Types

1. Frow, *Character and Person,* 107.
2. Frow, 107, 122; my emphasis.
3. Frow, 107.
4. Heng, *Invention of Race,* 6.
5. Aubin, *Noble Slaves,* 6; hereafter cited parenthetically as *NS.*
6. Brown, "Romance of Empire"; Aravamudan, *Tropicopolitans;* Doyle, *Freedom's Empire;* Mallipeddi, *Spectacular Suffering.*

7. Aravamudan, *Tropicopolitans*, 30.

8. McKeon, *Origins of the English Novel*, 113.

9. Behn, *Oroonoko*, 49; hereafter cited parenthetically as *O*.

10. See Guffey, "Aphra Behn's *Oroonoko*," 17, 22.

11. Aravamudan argues that Oroonoko becomes threatening when he transgresses the bounds of the "ludic kingship" offered him and makes "a claim to actual political authority" (*Tropicopolitans*, 42–43).

12. Pacheco, "Royalism and Honor," 500; see also Pacheco, "'Little Religion' but 'Admirable Morals.'"

13. For a prominent example of scholarship that perpetuates the religious-secular dialectic, see McKeon's discussion of *Oroonoko* in *Origins of the English Novel*. He argues that Oroonoko's experience converts him to "Western Skepticism," and that his violent and ignoble death shortly thereafter conveys Behn's nostalgic endorsement of the "native simplicity" that Oroonoko at first shares with the Indigenous people of Suriname (*Origins of the English Novel*, 113).

14. Ellenzweig, *Fringes of Belief*, x.

15. Ellenzweig, 58.

16. Ellenzweig, 58.

17. Ellenzweig, x.

18. Aravamudan, *Tropicopolitans*, 59.

19. Aravamudan, 59–60.

20. McKeon, *Origins of the English Novel*, 113.

21. Rosenthal, "Reception, Ideology, and Narrative Strategy," 152.

22. Guffey, "Aphra Behn's *Oroonoko*"; Brown, "Romance of Empire."

23. Pincus's *1688* shows how the politicized debates about emergent capitalist institutions fomented revolution in the years leading to the revolution of 1688–89.

24. Doyle, *Freedom's Empire*, 98.

25. Doyle, 98.

26. Mallipeddi, *Spectacular Suffering*, 37.

27. Applying the paradoxical logic of fetishism to Oroonoko's body, Mallipeddi writes that Behn's hero is the "living incarnation" of gold bullion; "his royalism and his splendor are measures of all the other commodified bodies of his fellow countrymen," yet he transcends the undifferentiated mass of "common slaves" in the colony. Like the precious metal, he is both "inside and outside the circuits of exchange" (39).

28. Aravamudan, *Tropicopolitans*, 69–70.

29. Frow, *Character and Person*, 114.

30. Doyle, *Freedom's Empire*, 104.

31. Aravamudan, *Tropicopolitans*, 48.

32. Aravamudan, 45.

33. 1 Cor. 11.24 (KJV).

34. Other critics have observed *Oroonoko*'s generic hybridity. Doyle calls it a blend of "courtly romance, historical memoir, colonial ethno-history, and Restoration drama" (*Freedom's Empire*, 97). Mallipeddi shows Behn's debts to the mercantilist spectacle of the lord mayor's civic pageants, in which "Africa, Asia, and Europe were routinely emblematized and their stereotypical attributes personified," as well as to plays that

functioned as "imperialist fantasies for aristocratic coterie" (*Spectacular Suffering*, 27–28).

35. Beach, "Aubin's *The Noble Slaves*," 584. For a discussion of enlightenment-era "Islamic republicanism," see Garcia, *Islam and the English Enlightenment*.
36. Beach, "Aubin's *The Noble Slaves*," 588.
37. O'Quinn, *Engaging the Ottoman Empire*, 2.
38. O'Quinn, 3.
39. Nussbaum, "Slavery, Blackness, and Islam," 159–60.
40. Bannet, *Transatlantic Stories*.
41. Gollapudi, "Virtuous Voyages," 671.
42. Gollapudi, 671.
43. Gollapudi, 684.
44. Aubin, *The Strange Adventures of the Count Vinevil and His Family* (London, 1721); quoted in Gollapudi, 682.
45. Gollapudi, 683.
46. Gollapudi, 684.
47. For the frequency of "scenes of violence perpetrated *by* women rather than *on* them" in Aubin's novels, see Gollapudi, 676.
48. Kim, "Penelope Aubin's Novels Reconsidered."
49. For biographical evidence of Aubin's religious orientation, see Welham, "Particular Case of Penelope Aubin."
50. Heng, *Invention of Race*, 3–5.
51. According to Yoojung Choi, the confused geography of *The Noble Slaves* reflects the limits of contemporary cartographic knowledge rather than Aubin's personal ignorance ("Between Japan and California").
52. Aubin is among the writers of travel fiction who incorporate a "narrative voice who tries to see in the random and the coincidental the mysterious workings of Providence." Richetti, *Popular Fiction before Richardson*, 62.
53. Gollapudi, "Virtuous Voyages," 681.
54. Ellenzweig, *Fringes of Belief*, x.
55. Richetti, *Popular Fiction before Richardson*, 217.
56. Gollapudi, "Virtuous Voyages," 673.

Chapter 3. Novels and the Nova Effect

1. Asad, *Formations of the Secular*; Modern, *Secularism in Antebellum America*.
2. Taylor, *Secular Age*, 299.
3. I borrow this term from Melvyn New, who writes that Sterne "demonstrates a commitment to Christian belief as defined by the centrist Anglicanism of his age and taught in the Cambridge of the 1730s. His sermons are typically balanced appeals to reason and emotion, the head and the heart, and to religion (the institution) and revelation (scripture). He is rarely if ever innovative, certainly not about doctrine or truth, nor would he have wanted to stray from established positions" ("Editor's Introduction," xli).
4. Rosengarten, *Henry Fielding and the Narration of Providence*, 8.

5. Battestin, *Moral Basis of Fielding's Art* and *Providence of Wit.*

6. Rawson, *Henry Fielding and the Augustan Ideal;* Hunter, *Occasional Form.* Rawson and Hunter both relate local disruptions in Fielding's fiction to the volatility of their intellectual backdrop, which on their accounts precluded affirmations of faith.

7. Damrosch, *God's Plot and Man's Stories*, 8, 71.

8. For the elements of the mainline secularization theory, see Casanova, *Public Religions in the Modern World;* and Asad, *Formations of the Secular.*

9. Rosengarten provides a helpful survey of polarized approaches to religion in Fielding criticism. For his part, Rosengarten seeks a middle way. Fielding's novels, he writes, present a "view of Christian belief that acknowledges the challenges of realism and compromises in response, but is by no means brittle in its overarching commitment" (*Henry Fielding and the Narration of Providence*, 8). My readings focus on this property, pliability, as well. It applies not only to Fielding's specific theological positions, as Rosengarten suggests, but also to his attempt to define the horizons for religion as a category of thought.

10. *Johnsonian Miscellanies*, 1.282.

11. See Watt, *Rise of the Novel.*

12. Battestin, *Providence of Wit*, 181. Battestin weaves together different lines of argument developed by Sheldon Sacks and Hunter, respectively. Sacks describes Fielding's characters as personifications of specific virtues and vices (*Fiction and the Shape of Belief*). Hunter identifies Puritanism with emblematic representation in *Reluctant Pilgrim.*

13. Damrosch, *God's Plot and Man's Story*, 265, 267.

14. Lynch, *Economy of Character*, 76.

15. Lynch, 5.

16. Lynch, 29.

17. See Rader, "*Tom Jones*," 57–60.

18. Fielding's objections to the Calvinist thinking manifest in Whitefield's sermons are not limited to its attenuation of human agency. Damrosch outlines a range of contrasts between Calvinist-inflected literature and Fielding's "Augustan" imagination (*God's Plot and Man's Stories*, 265). They differ in their choice of central image (the prison vs. the road) and the principles the images evoke (life as threat vs. life as possibility); in their attitudes toward the social order (extirpation vs. justification); and in their responses to both humor and desire (abstinence vs. toleration).

19. Insofar as Fielding targets the specifically Calvinist elements of Whitefield's thought, his critique departs from his own satiric practice and the general cultural response to Methodism. On Fielding's confrontation with Methodism and especially with transformative religious enthusiasm that shared a permeable boundary with erotic desire, see Anderson, *Imagining Methodism*, 29–30, 70–129.

20. Fielding, *Joseph Andrews*, 64–65; hereafter cited parenthetically as *JA.*

21. Judith Stuchiner challenges the consensus that Adams's denunciations of Whitefield and Methodism are representative of Fielding's views ("Fielding's Latitudinarian Doubt"). While I maintain that Adams speaks for the author, here I second Stuchiner's assertion that Fielding's stance on works-based Arminianism is more precarious than scholarship generally allows.

22. Whitefield, *Doctrines of the Gospel*, 4.13–14, 23; hereafter cited parenthetically by sermon and page number and abbreviated *D*.

23. Fielding, *Miscellanies*, 1:167.

24. Fielding, 1:55, 1:172.

25. Fielding, 1:154.

26. Fielding, *Tom Jones*, 92–93; hereafter cited parenthetically as *T*.

27. For the coordination of accidents as an expression of providential design, see Battestin, *Providence of Wit*, 151–63. Leo Braudy argues to the contrary that the narrative architecture of *Tom Jones* evokes a post-Christian understanding of history as dictated by pure chance. *Narrative Form*.

28. Sarah Rivett regards the doubt inherent to the task of spiritual discernment as the connective tissue between English Calvinism and experimental philosophy. *Science of the Soul*, 16, 23–70.

29. Battestin, *Providence of Wit*, 181.

30. Battestin, 182–83.

31. On the significance of the name "Sophia," see Battestin, *Providence of Wit*, 181–85. Sophia's visible moral and spiritual perfection contradicts Thomas G. Pavel's recent argument that Fielding's method of characterization tends toward comic anti-idealism (*Lives of the Novel*, 141). This generalization fits an Abraham Adams or even a Tom Jones, but it neglects Fielding's fascination with female exemplarity.

32. Gen. 2.23–24 (KJV).

33. On the identification, within Christian theology, of marriage with the logic of substitution, see Song, "Love against Substitution," 682.

34. Fielding, *Amelia*, 190; hereafter cited parenthetically as *A*.

35. Fielding, *Miscellanies*, 1:164.

36. Damrosch, *God's Plot and Man's Stories*, 37–40.

37. Damrosch, 267.

38. Booth's gesture of using childbirth to structure the episode, not the episode itself, reminds Miss Mathews of a "News-paper." This is because newspapers, too, overlay the quotidian with an artificial eventfulness. Miss Mathews evidently makes the comparison to newspapers by way of complaint, but Fielding may be using irony to reinforce the immediacy of this lost era of Booth's history. Lennard J. Davis explains that journalism "requires a special sense of time" that makes the past feel proximate to readers, its events almost continuous with the present (*Factual Fictions*, 72–74). It is possible that Fielding grasps journalism's sense of time and intends to draw a parallel with the temporality of Booth's earthly paradise.

39. Hunter, *Occasional Form*, 199–206.

40. The phenomenon resembles a process that Modern understands as inherent to secularism, in which religion is inscribed with the "mark of the real" (*Secularism in Antebellum America*, 45). That inscription, on his account, conduces to invisible forms of seizure and control. *Amelia*, though, presents its effects as salubrious. The entanglement of religion with the real transposes salvific stakes onto the domain of action.

41. Conway and Harol, "Toward a Postsecular Eighteenth Century," 567.

42. Seidel, "Beyond the Religious and the Secular," 640–42. See also Pecora, *Secularization without End,* 1–17.

43. Lynch, *Economy of Character,* 37, 76.

44. Watt, *Rise of the Novel,* 291; Keymer, *Sterne, the Moderns, and the Novel.*

45. Schlovsky, "Parodying Novel."

46. Fawcett, "Creating Character in '*Chiaro Oscuro,*'" 141–61, 143.

47. Fawcett, 147.

48. Fawcett, 143.

49. Sterne, *Tristram Shandy,* 67; henceforth cited parenthetically as *TS.*

50. New, "Editor's Introduction," xli; Parnell, "Swift, Sterne, and the Skeptical Tradition," 227.

51. New, xlvii.

52. Parnell, "Swift, Sterne, and the Skeptical Tradition," 231.

53. Parnell, 226.

54. Parnell, 222.

55. Mallipeddi, *Spectacular Suffering,* 84–108.

56. See Parnell, "Swift, Sterne, and the Skeptical Tradition." Parnell complains that scholars miss Sterne's religious conservatism because they are "too quick to celebrate a modern voice that breaks out from the supposed shackles of an imagined neoclassicism" (225).

57. Jordy Rosenberg references this frisson in his postmodern rewriting of the Jack Sheppard myth, *Confessions of the Fox.* In Rosenberg's novel, the fictional editor of Sheppard's as-yet-undiscovered memoir quotes this passage in full and concludes: "So, one thing comes into contact with another over and over again–*maybe in an . . . excitable place on the body*–and that friction, over time: that's character" (107).

58. See Fawcett, "Creating Character in '*Chiaro Oscuro,*'" 150. Rosenberg's fictional Dr. R. Voth also refers to Sterne's "rather infamous theory of obsession (as figured in the hobby-horse) as the fundament of character" (*Confessions of the Fox,* 107). Melanie D. Holm glosses Sterne's theory as an exploration of an errant but pleasurable (and, thus, widespread) form of associationist psychology ("Laughter, Skepticism," 362).

59. Sterne, *Works,* 4.83; hereafter cited parenthetically as *W.*

60. Benedict, "Reading Faces," 323.

61. Parnell, "Swift, Sterne, and the Skeptical Tradition," 231.

62. See also Wehrs, "Sterne, Cervantes, Montaigne," to which Parnell responds.

63. For Sterne's debts to comic romance and Cervantes in particular, see Black, "*Tristram Shandy*'s Strange Loops of Reading."

64. See Stewart, *Eighteenth-Century Novel,* 94–96. Holm describes "On Conscience" as an argument for the relativism of conscience and against "faith in the rectitude of moral judgment" ("Laughter, Skepticism," 370). Holm misconstrues the sermon's application of Matthew 7, glossing the sentiment as "we know our moral quality by the feelings it effects." In fact, Sterne quotes this verse as support for his claim that we can distinguish correct from false positions by evaluating cause and effect.

65. For secularism's semantic masking of imperial Christianity, see Anidjar, "Secularism," 62. For the role of Islam in Western liberal-secular self-conception, see Asad, *Formations of the Secular;* and Massad, *Islam in Liberalism.*

Chapter 4. The "True Religion" of Abolitionist Fiction

1. Earle, *Obi*, 156; hereafter cited parenthetically as *OBI*.
2. Layne, "Re-evaluating Religion and Superstition," 51.
3. Layne, 61.
4. In his indispensable Broadview edition of *Obi*, Srinivas Aravamudan points out Earle's debts to the House of Commons Sessional Papers on "Obiah Practice" and "Obiah Trials" in Jamaica during and after Tacky's Rebellion of 1760 ("Introduction," 25). Kelly Wisecup ("Knowing Obeah") examines the novel's extensive use of three colonial histories: Edward Long's *History of Jamaica* (1774), Bryan Edwards's *History, Civil and Commercial, of the British Colonies in the West Indies* (1793), and Benjamin Moseley's *A Treatise on Sugar* (1799).
5. For Lyndon J. Dominique, the novel's radical potential hinges on the plausibility "that a woman of color wrote *The Woman of Colour*" and thus represents a genre of black critique ("Introduction," 32). A similar focus on the author's subject position leads to qualifications in appraisals of *Obi*'s politics. Katherine G. Charles writes that Amri's tale, "though written by a white author and embedded in the fictional correspondence of a white narrator, nonetheless purports to speak for an enslaved person" ("Speaking Across," 292). Following this line of argument, the most that Earle (and, if Dominique's speculation is unfounded, the author of *The Woman of Colour*) can do is interrogate their own appropriation of black peoples' stories.
6. Richardson, "Romantic Voodoo," 5.
7. Wisecup, "Knowing Obeah," 418.
8. Wisecup, 408.
9. For excerpts from the Sessional Papers, see Aravamudan, *Obi*, 168–81.
10. Earle, *Obi* (1800), 73. To preserve Earle's emendations, I cite the first edition, here.
11. Earle, 173.
12. Earle, 73–74.
13. Earle, 74–75.
14. Wisecup, "Knowing Obeah," 410.
15. Earle, *Obi* (1800), 75.
16. Earle, 79.
17. *Obi* (2005), 171.
18. Earle, *Obi* (1800), 73.
19. Rivers, *Reason, Grace, and Sentiment*, 1:24.
20. Rivers, 2:13.
21. In a footnote to this scene, Aravamudan speculates that Amri and Makro, identified in the text as "Feloops," may be members of the Fulani ethnic group of present-day Northwest Nigeria and, therefore, Muslims (*OBI*, 77n1). However, Earle seems to identify Jack's parents as "pagan natives" in a note on Amri's gift of an amulet to Harrop, which indicates that she believes "in the virtues of the Saphie," but not the "Mahomedan" religion (81).
22. *Collection of Papers*, 13.
23. Anonymous, *Female American*, 115.

24. Burnham and Freitas observe that *The Female American,* while opposed to "capitalist accumulation, colonial conquest, and political imperialism" and engaged in "fantasies of feminist utopianism and cross-racial community, both of which are enabled, however, by a specifically religious form of imperialism" ("Introduction," 12).

25. Rivers, *Reason, Grace, and Sentiment,* 2:9.

26. Gen. 3:17–19 (KJV).

27. OED Online, s.v. "flattering."

28. Charles, "Speaking Across," 292.

29. Dominique, *Imoinda's Shade,* 259.

30. Dominique, 252.

31. Barnett-Woods, "Models of Morality," 622.

32. De Vere Brody, *Impossible Purities,* 25. For similar lines of argument, see Salih, *Representing Mixed Race;* and Reed, "Moving Fortunes."

33. Van Renen also seeks a middle ground, though he bypasses the novel's evident concern with religion and racialization and overstates the extent to which "the novel urges the British to welcome the contributions of West Indian peoples and fosters a transatlantic community" ("Temple of Folly,"162).

34. Anonymous, *Woman of Colour,* 92; hereafter cited parenthetically as *WOC.*

35. Moten, *In the Break,* 18.

36. Moten, 7.

37. Moten, 13–14, 16. See also Spillers, "Mama's Baby, Papa's Maybe."

38. Fielder, "Black Atlantic Movement," 175.

39. Fielder, 175.

40. Fielder, 178.

41. It's John Donne and not John Suckling who articulates it. Dominique traces the reference to Donne's "A Funeral Elegy" (1610). See *Woman of Colour,* 102n2.

42. Hickman, *Black Prometheus,* 33–73.

43. See Van Renen, "Temple of Folly," 149–56, for an extended discussion of the novel's denunciation of the Inglots as East India Company officers.

44. For the use of this stereotype to exclude people of African and African-Caribbean descent from British rational sociability and its undergirding "values of liberty and independence," see Boulukos, *Grateful Slave,* 22.

45. Dominique, *Imoinda's Shade,* 253.

46. Reed, "Moving Fortunes," 525.

47. Brown, Butler, and Mahmood, "Preface," xiv.

48. Fielder, "Black Atlantic Movement," 183.

49. Caretta, "Introduction," xxi.

50. Cugoano, *Thoughts and Sentiments,* 66–67; hereafter cited parenthetically as *ES.*

51. Hole, "Sentiment to Security," 177. For an alternative interpretation of Cugoano's relation to empire, see Tacuma Peters, "Anti-Imperialism of Ottobah Cugoano."

52. Hole, "Sentiment to Security," 177.

53. Hole, 180.

54. Wheelock, *Barbaric Culture and Black Critique,* 5.

55. Wheelock, 10.

56. Wheelock, 11, 15.

57. Wheelock, 24, 34.
58. Wheelock, 21.

Chapter 5. Gothic Postsecularism

1. This term comes from Ian Duncan's description of Gil-Martin's shape-shifting abilities ("Introduction," xxxii).
2. For *Zofloya*'s debts to Lewis's *The Monk*, see Miles, *Gothic Writing*, 167–75. For the relationship between gender and Gothic conventions in Dacre's fiction, see Hoeveler, *Gothic Feminism*; Davidson, "Getting Their Knickers in a Twist"; and Airey, "Male Narcissism."
3. Modern, "Conversion Diptych."
4. Orlemanski, "Who Has Fiction," 153.
5. Clery, *Rise of Supernatural Fiction*, 35.
6. Clery, 35.
7. Hoeveler, *Gothic Riffs*, 6.
8. Milbank, *God and the Gothic*, 1.
9. Compare Eugenia Delamotte's reading of the Gothic as an illustration of the failure of the larger movement of Romanticism to transcend mortality (*Perils of the Night*).
10. Sedgwick, *Coherence of Gothic Conventions*, vi; hereafter cited parenthetically as *GC*.
11. The complete sentence shows the influence of progressivist literary historicism on Sedgwick's understanding of Gothic character: "The issue of what constitutes the character—what internecine superposition of a length of words, the image of a body, a name, and, on a countenance, an authentic graphic stamp—had *never before the Gothic* been confronted so energetically in those terms" (my emphasis).
12. O'Malley, *Catholicism, Sexual Deviance*, 72.
13. Thompkins, *Popular Novel in England*; Sage, *Horror Fiction*; Miles, "Europhobia." Diverging from this consensus, Maria Purves seeks to recover Catholic sympathies in Gothic literature (*Gothic and Catholicism*). She does so, however, by curating a more inclusive archive rather than offering an alternative interpretation of texts like *The Italian* or *The Monk*.
14. Miles, "Europhobia," 84; Hoeveler, "Demonizing the Catholic Other," 90.
15. Hurd, *Politics of Secularism*. For a synopsis and application of Hurd's argument, see Scott, *Sex and Secularism*, 32–34.
16. Anidjar, "Secularism," 58–60.
17. For Hogg's representation of Scottish Calvinism, see Mack, "Hogg's Religion"; Bligh, "Doctrinal Premises"; and Crawford Gribben, "James Hogg, Scottish Calvinism."
18. Hogg, *Confessions of a Justified Sinner*, 165.
19. Jager, *Unquiet Things*, 153–77.
20. Hogg, *Confessions of a Justified Sinner*, 95.
21. Hogg, 95. For a discussion of the relationship between Gil-Martin's preternatural power and Scottish literary nationalism, see Duncan, "Upright Corpse."
22. Hogg, *Confessions of a Justified Sinner*, 78.
23. Duncan, "Introduction," xxxii–iv. For more extensive discussions of Hogg's engagement with Scottish Enlightenment philosophy, see Duncan, "Sympathy, Physiognomy" and "Fanaticism and Enlightenment."

24. Haggerty, "Female Abjection," 656. For the relationship of Inchbald's fiction to English Jacobinism, see Kelly, *English Jacobin Novel*, 65–113. For Inchbald's use of the novel of manners to screen her radical critique of Christianity, see Judson, "Psychology of Satan," 603. Terry Castle suggests that in the novel's second half "we see the outlines of classic Romantic psychodrama, from *Prometheus Unbound* to *Wuthering Heights*" (*Masquerade and Civilization,* 319).

25. Haggerty, 664.

26. Brown, Butler, and Mahmood, "Preface," xiii.

27. Inchbald, *Simple Story,* 74; hereafter cited parenthetically as *S*.

28. The failure of supposedly perspicuous signs to communicate meaning in *A Simple Story,* and particularly in the vexed intercourse between Miss Milner and Dorriforth, has been well documented. See Nachumi, "Those Simple Signs"; Osland, "Heart-Picking"; and Judson, "Psychology of Satan," 606.

29. *A Simple Story* shares this feature with early nineteenth-century literature, like Austen's *Mansfield Park* (1814), that embeds without erasing colonial violence. See Said, *Culture and Imperialism,* 80–96.

30. I borrow this suggestive term for secularism's inherently sexualizing and racializing logic from Peter Coviello. *Make Yourselves Gods,* 38.

31. Inchbald, *Nature and Art,* 82; hereafter cited parenthetically.

32. See Coviello, *Make Yourselves Gods,* 42–47.

33. *Analytical Review* 10 (1791), 101–2, quoted in Spencer, "Introduction," xiv.

34. Castle, *Masquerade and Civilization;* Meyer Spacks, *Desire and Truth.* Castle interprets the novel as celebratory of Miss Milner's and Lady Matilda's rebelliousness, whereas Spacks stresses that they are punished for their transgressions of patriarchal commandment.

35. Judson, "Psychology of Satan," 616.

36. Judson, 616.

37. Morillo, "Editing Eve," 201.

38. Ward, "Inordinate Desire," 13.

39. Judson, "Psychology of Satan," 613. See also Morillo, "Editing Eve," 215.

40. Judson, 603.

41. Earlier criticism that reads the novel as a religious allegory informs my interpretation here. See, for example, Castle, *Masquerade and Civilization,* 325; Morillo, "Editing Eve," 215; and Judson, "Psychology of Satan," 618–19. These readings help us to see Inchbald's dissatisfaction with Christian myth, and particularly with the Abrahamic characterization of God, but they are less alert to the alternative she develops through Matilda's arc.

42. For Inchbald's religious orientation and its influence on her fiction, see Wilcox, "Idols and Idolaters"; Keegan, "Bred a Jesuit"; Tomko, *British Romanticism and the Catholic Question;* and Carnes, "Let Not Religion Be Named."

43. Haggerty, "Female Abjection," 666. See also Castle, *Masquerade and Civilization,* 319; Ward, "Inordinate Desire," 13–15; Judson, "Psychology of Satan," 618; and Morillo, "Editing Eve," 217.

44. Haggerty, "Female Abjection," 664.

45. Mahmood, "Feminist Theory," 206. Mahmood expands her argument in *Politics of Piety.*

46. Mahmood, 203.
47. Mahmood, 222.
48. Judson, "Psychology of Satan," 618.
49. Scott, *Sex and Secularism,* 48. To explain the synonymy of secularism and liberalism, Scott draws on Dillon's arguments in *Gender of Freedom.*
50. Mellor, "Interracial Sexual Desire," 171–72.
51. Dacre, *Zofloya,* 143; hereafter cited parenthetically as *Z.*
52. For the relationship between *Zofloya* and *Paradise Lost,* see Brewster, "Monstrous Philosophy."
53. Miles and Kelly argue that the narrator's editorializing is incoherent or self-contradictory on its own. Miles, *Gothic Writing,* 181; Kelly, *English Fiction of the Romantic Period,* 106.
54. Hoeveler, "Charlotte Dacre's *Zofloya,*" 191.
55. Burley, "Death of Zolfoya"; Schotland, "Slave's Revenge." DeLamotte discusses *Zofloya,* briefly, in similar terms in "White Terror, Black Dreams," 22.
56. Malchow, *Gothic Images of Race,* 5. See also Schmitt, *Alien Nation.*
57. Mellor, "Interracial Desire," 173.
58. Airey, "Male Narcissism," 223–41.
59. Craciun, *Fatal Women,* 131, 153.
60. Mellor, "Interracial Desire," 172. Miles, *Gothic Writing,* and Craciun, *Fatal Women,* are additional examples of scholarship that foregrounds the effects of Dacre's compositional practices rather than the narrator's explicit sentiments.
61. Airey argues that the focus of modern critics on Victoria distracts from Dacre's anger toward figures of patriarchal authority. Victoria's status as the novel's antiheroine "does not make [Berenza] less morally dubious in his treatment of her" ("Male Narcissism," 235).
62. Cynthia Murillo describes Lilla as Victoria's döppelganger, the "perfect specimen" of femininity as it was defined by early nineteenth-century "patriarchal ideology" and travestied by Victoria's ungovernable passions ("Haunted Spaces and Powerful Places," 78). Craciun emphasizes their antagonism, as well, though she reads it as an illustration of the novel's double-edged critique of bourgeois femininity (*Fatal Women,* 134).
63. Wagner, "Dream of a Transparent Body."
64. Craciun, *Fatal Women,* 150–51.
65. Laqueur, *Making Sex,* 19.
66. Craciun, *Fatal Women,* 120.
67. Airey, "Male Narcissism," 238.
68. Craciun, *Fatal Women,* 150. Applying Judith Butler's theories, Craciun attributes to Dacre a postmodern understanding of sex and gender, one that prioritizes "performance over essence" (151).
69. For the cultural work that blood performs in nineteenth-century British literature, see Kibbie, *Transfusion.*
70. Hoeveler, "Demonizing the Catholic Other," 83.
71. Hoeveler, 90.
72. Crawford, "'Terror in Inquisition,'" 203–9.

73. Craciun, *Fatal Women,* 148; Hoeveler, "Charlotte Dacre's *Zofloya,*" 189. Hoeveler, Mellor, and Schotland identify *Oroonoko* as a key source text for *Zofloya.* Schotland argues that the hero of *Oroonoko* is Zofloya's "prototype," and that Dacre's character figures "in particular the Caribbean threat" of violent revolution ("Slave's Revenge," 127, 129). Mellor contends that the novel draws inspiration from depictions of "sexual liaisons" between white enslavers and enslaved Africans in the British Atlantic ("Interracial Sexual Desire," 169).
74. Michasiw, "Charlotte Dacre's Postcolonial Moor."
75. Members of Granada's sizeable Jewish population were subject to similar treatment, suggesting a possible identification between Zofloya and the author, beyond the sexual alliance between him and Victoria. Several critics have proposed that Dacre inherited the stigma of religious difference from her father, John King, the infamous "Jew King of London" (Craciun, "Introduction," 12).
76. Wynter ("1492") dates the eruption of a new, racialized world order to 1492. For the role of religious—or, to use his term, cosmographic—variety in this historical convulsion, see Hickman's *Black Prometheus.*
77. Michasiw, "Charlotte Dacre's Postcolonial Moor." See also Craciun's explanatory note (*Zofloya,* 160n1).
78. Burley, "Death of Zofloya."
79. Craciun, *Fatal Women,* 147.
80. Craciun, *Fatal Women,* 147.
81. Heiland, *Gothic and Gender,* 49.

Conclusion: Subjunctive Criticism

1. Smith, "Foreword," xviii.
2. Modern, "Conversion Diptych."
3. Orlemanski, "Who Has Fiction?," 153.

BIBLIOGRAPHY

Airey, Jennifer L. "'He bears no rival near the throne': Male Narcissism and Early Feminism in the Works of Charlotte Dacre." *Eighteenth-Century Fiction* 30, no. 1 (Winter 2017–18): 223–41.

Anderson, Misty G. *Imagining Methodism in 18th-Century Britain: Enthusiasm, Belief, and the Borders of the Self.* Baltimore, MD: Johns Hopkins University Press, 2012.

Anidjar, Gil. "Secularism." *Critical Inquiry* 33, no. 1 (2006): 52–77.

Aravamudan, Srinivas. Introduction to *Obi; or, The History of Three-Fingered Jack.* Petersborough, ON: Broadview, 2005.

———. *Enlightenment Orientalism: Resisting the Rise of the Novel.* Chicago: University of Chicago Press, 2011.

———. *Tropicopolitans: Colonialism and Agency, 1688–1804.* Durham, NC: Duke University Press, 1999.

Asad, Talal. *Formations of the Secular: Christianity, Islam, Modernity.* Stanford, CA: Stanford University Press, 2003.

Aubin, Penelope. *The Noble Slaves.* London: J. Darby, 1722. Eighteenth Century Collections Online. Accessed 30 August 2023. https://link.gale.com/apps/doc/CW0109218236/ECCO?u=uga&sid=bookmark-ECCO&xid=664ffde7&pg=1.

Bannet, Eve Taylor. *Transatlantic Stories and the History of Reading, 1600–1850: Migrant Fictions.* Cambridge: Cambridge University Press, 2011.

Barnett-Woods, Victoria. "Models of Morality: The Bildungsroman and Social Reform in *The Female American* and *The Woman of Colour.*" *Women's Studies* 45 (July–December 2016): 613–23.

Battestin, Martin. *The Moral Basis of Fielding's Art.* Middletown, CT: Wesleyan University Press, 1959.

———. *The Providence of Wit: Aspects of Form in Augustan Literature and the Arts.* Charlottesville: University of Virginia Press, 1989.

Beach, Adam R. "Aubin's *The Noble Slaves,* Montagu's Spanish Lady, and English Feminist Writing about Sexual Slavery in the Ottoman World." *Eighteenth-Century Fiction* 29, no. 4 (2017): 583–606.

Beeke, Joel R. *Assurance of Faith: Calvin, English Protestantism, and the Dutch Second Reformation.* New York: Peter Lang, 1991.

Behn, Aphra. *Oroonoko, or The Royal Slave*. 1688. Edited by Janet Todd. New York: Penguin, 2003.

Benedict, Barbara M. "Reading Faces: Physiognomy and Epistemology in Late Eighteenth-Century Sentimental Novels." *Studies in Philology* 92, no. 3 (1995): 311–28.

Black, Scott. "*Tristram Shandy*'s Strange Loops of Reading." *ELH* 82, no. 3 (Fall 2015): 869–96.

Bligh, John. "The Doctrinal Premises of Hogg's *Confessions of a Justified Sinner*." *Studies in Scottish Literature* 19 (1984): 148–64.

Block, Sharon. *Colonial Complexions: Race and Bodies in Eighteenth-Century America*. Philadelphia: University of Pennsylvania Press, 2018.

Boelhower, William. *Through a Glass Darkly: Ethnic Semiosis in American Literature*. 2nd ed. Oxford: Oxford University Press, 1987.

Boulukos, George. *The Grateful Slave: The Emergence of Race in Eighteenth- and Nineteenth-Century British and American Culture*. Cambridge: University of Cambridge Press, 2008.

Branch, Lori. "Bunyan, Theory, and Theology: A Case for Post-Secular Criticism." In *The Oxford Handbook of John Bunyan*, edited by Michael Davies and W. R. Owens, 502–20. Oxford: Oxford University Press, 2018.

Braudy, Leo. *Narrative Form in History and Fiction: Hume, Fielding, and Gibbon*. Princeton, NJ: Princeton University Press, 1970.

Brewster, Glen. "Monstrous Philosophy: Charlotte Dacre's *Zofloya, or The Moor* and John Milton's *Paradise Lost*." *Literature Compass* 8, no. 9 (2011): 609–19.

Brody, Jennifer De Vere. *Impossible Purities: Blackness, Femininity, and Victorian Culture*. Durham, NC: Duke University Press, 1998.

Brown, Laura. "The Romance of Empire: *Oroonoko* and the Trade in Slaves." In *Early Women Writers: 1600–1720*, edited by Anita Pacheco, 197–221. London: Longman, 1998.

Brown, Sylvia. "Bunyan and Empire." In *The Oxford Handbook of John Bunyan*, edited by Michael Davies and W. R. Owens, 665–82. Oxford: Oxford University Press, 2018.

Brown, Wendy, Judith Butler, and Saba Mahmood. Preface to *Is Critique Secular? Blasphemy, Injury, and Free Speech*, edited by Talal Asad, Wendy Brown Brown, Judith Butler, and Saba Mahmood, n.p. Berkeley: University of California Press, 2009.

Bruce, La Mar Jurelle. *How to Go Mad without Losing Your Mind: Madness and Black Radical Creativity*. Durham, NC: Duke University Press, 2020.

Bunyan, John. *The Doctrine of the Law and Grace Unfolded*. London: M. Wright, 1659. Early English Books Online. Accessed 30 August 2023. https://www.proquest.com/books/doctrine-lavv-grace-unfolded-discourse-touching/docview/2240950364/se-2.

———. *Grace Abounding to the Chief of Sinners*. 1666. *Grace Abounding with Other Spiritual Autobiographies*, edited by John Stachniewski and Anita Pacheco. Oxford: Oxford University Press, 2008.

———. *The Holy War*. 1682. Edited by James F. Forrest. New York: New York University Press, 1967.

———. *The Life and Death of Mr. Badman*. 1680. Edited by James F. Forrest and Roger Sharrock. New York: Oxford University Press, 1988.

———. *The Pilgrim's Progress*. 1678. Edited by Cynthia Wall. New York: Norton, 2007.

Burley, Stephanie. "The Death of Zolfoya; or, The Moor as Epistemological Limit." In *The Gothic Other: Racial and Social Constructions in the Literary Imagination*, edited by Ruth Bienstock Anolik and Howard L. Douglas, 197–211. Jefferson, NC: MacFarland, 2004.

Burnham, Michelle, and James Freitas. Introduction to *The Female American,* by Anonymous, 9–32. 2nd ed. Peterborough, ON: Broadview, 2014.

Caldwell, Patricia. *The Puritan Conversion Narrative: The Beginnings of American Expression.* Cambridge: Cambridge University Press, 1983.

Carnes, Geremy. "'Let Not Religion Be Named between Us': Catholic Struggle and the Religious Context of Feminism in *A Simple Story.*" *Eighteenth-Century Novel* 9 (2012): 193–235.

Carretta, Vincent. Introduction to *Thoughts and Sentiments on the Evil of Slavery,* by Quobna Ottobah Cugoano, ix–xxviii. New York: Penguin, 1999.

Casanova, José. *Public Religions in the Modern World.* Chicago: University of Chicago Press, 1994.

Castle, Terry. *Masquerade and Civilization: The Carnivalesque in Eighteenth-Century English Culture.* Stanford, CA: Stanford University Press, 1986.

Charles, Katherine G. "Speaking Across: Literary Form and Speech in *Obi; or, The History of Three-Fingered Jack.*" *Eighteenth Century* 61, no. 3 (2020): 289–312.

Choi, Yoojung. "'Between Japan and California': Imaginative Pacific Geography and East Asian Culture in Penelope Aubin's *The Noble Slaves.*" *Eighteenth-Century Fiction* 34, no. 1 (2021): 33–60.

Clark, J. C. D. *English Society, 1688–1832: Ideology, Social Structure, and Political Practice during the Ancien Regime.* Cambridge: Cambridge University Press, 1985.

Clery, E. J. *The Rise of Supernatural Fiction, 1762–1800.* Cambridge: Cambridge University Press, 1999.

Codr, Dwight. *Raving at Usurers: Anti-Finance and the Ethics of Uncertainty in England, 1690–1750.* Charlottesville: University of Virginia Press, 2016.

Coles, Kimberley Anne. *Bad Humor: Race and Religious Essentialism in Early Modern England.* Philadelphia: University of Pennsylvania Press, 2022.

A Collection of Papers, Printed by Order of the Society for the Propagation of the Gospel in Foreign Parts. London: Joseph Downing, 1706.

Conway, Alison, and Corinne Harole. "Toward a Postsecular Eighteenth Century." *Literature Compass* 12, no. 11 (2015): 565–74.

Coviello, Peter. *Make Yourselves Gods: Mormons and the Unfinished Business of American Secularism* Chicago: University of Chicago Press, 2019.

Coviello, Peter, and Jared Hickman. "Introduction: After the Postsecular." *American Literature* 86, no. 4 (2014): 645–54.

Craciun, Adriana. *Fatal Women of the Romantic Period.* Cambridge: Cambridge University Press, 2003.

———. Introduction to *Zofloya* by Charlotte Dacre, 9–32. Petersborough, ON: Broadview, 1997.

Cragg, Gerald R. *From Puritanism to the Age of Reason: A Study of Changes in Religious Thought within the Church of England, 1660–1700.* Cambridge: Cambridge University Press, 1950.

Crawford, Joseph. "Terror in Inquisition." In *Terrorism and Literature,* edited by Peter C. Herman, 196–211. Cambridge: Cambridge University Press, 2018.

Cugoano, Quobna Ottobah. *Thoughts and Sentiments on the Evil of Slavery.* 1787. Edited by Vincent Caretta. New York: Penguin, 1999.

Dacre, Charlotte. *Zofloya, or The Moor.* 1806. Edited by Adriana Craciun. Petersborough, ON: Broadview, 1997.

Damrosch, Leopold, Jr. *God's Plot and Man's Stories: Studies in the Fictional Imagination from Milton to Fielding.* Chicago: University of Chicago Press, 1985.

Davies, Michael. "Spirit in the Letters: John Bunyan's Congregational Epistles." *Seventeenth Century* 24, no. 2 (2009): 323–60.

Davidson, Carole Margaret. "Getting Their Knickers in a Twist: Contesting the 'Female Gothic' in Charlotte Dacre's *Zofloya*." *Gothic Studies* 11, no. 1 (2009): 32–45.

Davis, Lennard J. *Factual Fictions: The Origins of the English Novel*. New York: Columbia University Press, 1983.

Delamotte, Eugenia. *Perils of the Night: A Feminist Study of Nineteenth-Century Gothic*. Oxford: Oxford University Press, 1990.

———. "White Terror, Black Dreams: Gothic Constructions of Race in the Nineteenth Century." In *The Gothic Other: Racial and Social Constructions in the Literary Imagination*, edited by Ruth Bienstock Anolik and Howard L. Douglas, 17–31. Jefferson, NC: MacFarland, 2004.

Dillon, Elizabeth Maddock. *The Gender of Freedom: Fictions of Liberalism and the Literary Public Sphere*. Stanford, CA: Stanford University Press, 2007.

Dominique, Lyndon J. *Imoinda's Shade: Marriage and the African Woman in Eighteenth-Century British Literature, 1759–1808*. Columbus, OH: Ohio State University Press, 2012.

———. Introduction to *The Woman of Colour, A Tale*, by Anonymous, 11–42. Petersborough, ON: Broadview, 2008.

Doyle, Laura. *Freedom's Empire: Race and the Rise of the Novel*. Durham, NC: Duke University Press, 2007.

Duncan, Ian. "Fanaticism and Enlightenment in *Confessions of a Justified Sinner*." In *James Hogg and the Literary Marketplace*, edited by Sharon Alker and Holly Faith Nelson, 57–69. Farnham: Ashgate, 2009.

———. Introduction to *The Private Memoirs and True Confessions of a Justified Sinner* by James Hogg, ix–xxxiv. Oxford: Oxford University Press, 2010.

———. "Sympathy, Physiognomy, and Scottish Romantic Fiction." In *Recognizing the Romantic Novel: New Histories of British Fiction, 1780–1830*, edited by Jillian Heydt-Stevenson and Charlotte Sussman, 285–305. Liverpool: Liverpool University Press, 2008.

———. "The Upright Corpse: Hogg, National Literature, and the Uncanny." *Studies in Hogg and His World* 5 (1994): 29–54.

Earle, William, Jr. *Obi; or, The History of Three-Fingered Jack*. Edited by Srinivas Aravamudan. Petersborough, ON: Broadview, 2005.

———. *Obi; or, The History of Three-Fingered Jack in a Series of Letters from a Resident in Jamaica to his Friend in England*. London: Earle & Hemet, 1800.

Eco, Umberto. *Semiotica e Filosophia del Linguaggio*. Turin: Einaudi, 1984.

Ellenzweig, Sarah. *The Fringes of Belief: English Literature, Ancient Heresy, and the Politics of Freethinking, 1660–1760*. Stanford, CA: Stanford University Press, 2008.

Fawcett, Julia. "Creating Character in '*Chiaro Oscuro*': Sterne's Celebrity, Cibber's *Apology*, and the Life of *Tristram Shandy*." *Eighteenth Century* 53, no. 2 (2012): 141–61.

Felski, Rita. *The Limits of Critique*. Chicago: University of Chicago Press, 2015.

The Female American. 1667. Edited by Michelle Burnham and James Freitas. Petersborough, ON: Broadview, 2014.

Fielder, Brigitte. "*The Woman of Colour* and Black Atlantic Movement." In *Women's Narratives of Early America and the Formation of Empire*, edited by Mary McAleer Balkun, Susan C. Imbarrato, and Marion Rust, 175–85. Basingstoke: Palgrave Macmillan, 2016.

Fielding, Henry. *Amelia*. 1751. Edited by Linda Bree. Peterborough, ON: Broadview, 2010.

———. "An Essay on the Knowledge of the Characters of Men." 1743. In *Miscellanies by Henry Fielding, Esq.*, vol. 1, edited by Henry Knight Miller, 153–78. *The Wesleyan Edition of the Works of Henry Fielding*. Oxford: Clarendon, 1972.

———. *Joseph Andrews*. 1742. Edited by Homer Goldberg. New York: Norton, 1987.

———. *Tom Jones*. 1749. 2nd ed. Edited by Sheridan Baker. New York: W. W. Norton, 1995.

Fish, Stanley. "Progress in *The Pilgrim's Progress*." *English Literary Renaissance* 1 (1971): 261–93.

Fletcher, Angus. *Allegory: The Theory of a Symbolic Mode*. Ithaca, NY: Cornell University Press, 1964.

Forster, E. M. *Aspects of the Novel*. London: Edward Arnold, 1927.

Frow, John. *Character and Person*. Oxford: Oxford University Press, 2014.

Gallagher, Catherine. "The Rise of Fictionality." In *The Novel, Vol. 1: History, Geography, Culture*, edited by Franco Moretti, 336–63. Princeton, NJ: Princeton University Press, 2007.

Garcia, Humberto. *Islam and the English Enlightenment, 1670–1840*. Baltimore, MD: Johns Hopkins University Press, 2011.

Ginzburg, Carlo. "Clues: Roots of an Evidential Paradigm." In *Clues, Myths, and the Historical Method*, translated by John and Anne C. Tedeschi, 87–113. Baltimore, MD: Johns Hopkins University Press, 1989.

Goldenberg, David M. *The Curse of Ham: Race and Slavery in Early Judaism, Christianity, and Islam*. Princeton, NJ: Princeton University Press, 2005.

Gollapudi, Aparna. "Virtuous Voyages in Penelope Aubin's Fiction." *SEL: Studies in English Literature, 1500–1900* 45, no. 3 (2005): 669–90.

Greaves, Richard L. "Bunyan and the Holy War." In *The Cambridge Companion to Writing of the English Revolution*, edited by N. H. Keeble, 268–85. Cambridge: Cambridge University Press, 2001.

———. *Glimpses of Glory: John Bunyan and English Dissent*. Stanford, CA: Stanford University Press, 2002.

Gribben, Crawford. "James Hogg, Scottish Calvinism, and Literary Theory." *Scottish Studies Review* 5, no. 2 (2004): 9–26.

———. "Lay Conversion and Calvinist Doctrine." In *The Rise of the Laity in Evangelical Protestantism*, edited by Deryck W. Lovegrove, 36–46. London: Routledge, 2002.

Gronniosaw, James Albert Ukawsaw. *A Narrative of the Most Remarkable Particulars in the Life of James Albert Ukawsaw Gronniosaw, an African Prince, As Related by Himself*. Bath: W. Gye, ca. 1772. Eighteenth Century Collections Online. Accessed 30 August 2023. https://link.gale.com/apps/doc/CB0129877062/ECCO?u=uga&sid=bookmark-ECCO& xid=de837605&pg=1.

Guffey, George. "Aphra Behn's *Oroonoko*: Occasion and Accomplishment." In *Two English Novelists, Aphra Behn and Anthony Trollope: Papers Read at a Clark Library Seminar*, edited by Guffey and Andrew Wright, 3–41. Los Angeles: William Andrews Clark Memorial Library, 1975.

Haggerty, George. "Female Abjection in Inchbald's *A Simple Story*." *SEL: Studies in English Literature, 1500–1900* 36, no. 3 (Summer 1996): 655–71.

Hanley, Ryan. *Beyond Slavery and Abolition: Black British Writing, c. 1770–1830*. Cambridge: Cambridge University Press, 2018.

Haskin, Dayton. "'The Burden of Interpretation in *The Pilgrim's Progress*." *Studies in Philology* 79, no. 3 (1982): 256–78.

Heiland, Donna. *Gothic and Gender: An Introduction*. Malden, MA: Blackwell, 2004.

Heng, Geraldine. *The Invention of Race in the European Middle Ages*. Cambridge: Cambridge University Press, 2018.

Hershinow, Stephanie Insley. *Born Yesterday: Innocence in the Early Realist Novel*. Baltimore, MD: Johns Hopkins University Press, 2020.

Hickman, Jared. *Black Prometheus: Race and Radicalism in the Age of Atlantic Slavery*. Oxford: Oxford University Press, 2017.

Hill, Christopher. *A Turbulent, Seditious, and Factious People: John Bunyan and His Church, 1628–1688*. Oxford: Oxford University Press, 1988.

Hill, George Birkbeck, ed. *Johnsonian Miscellanies*, 2 vols. New York: Harper, 1897.

Hindmarsh, D. Bruce. *The Evangelical Conversion Narrative: Spiritual Biography in Early Modern England*. Oxford: Oxford University Press, 2005.

Hoeveler, Diane Long. "Charlotte Dacre's *Zofloya*: A Case Study in Miscegenation as Sexual and Racial Nausea." *European Romantic Review* 8, no. 2 (1997): 185–99.

———. "Demonizing the Catholic Other: Religion and the Secularization Process in Gothic Literature." In *Transnational Gothic: Literary and Social Exchanges in the Long Nineteenth Century*, edited by Monika Elbert and Bridget M. Marshall, 83–96. Burlington, VT: Ashgate, 2013.

———. *Gothic Feminism: The Professionalization of Gender from Charlotte Smith to the Brontës*. State College: Pennsylvania State University Press, 1998.

———. *Gothic Riffs: Secularizing the Uncanny in the European Imaginary, 1780–1820*. Columbus: Ohio State University Press, 2010.

Hofmeyr, Isabel. *The Portable Bunyan: A Transnational History of* The Pilgrim's Progress. Princeton, NJ: Princeton University Press, 2004.

Hogg, James. *The Private Memoirs and True Confessions of a Justified Sinner*. 1824. Edited by Ian Duncan. Oxford: Oxford University Press, 2010.

Hole, Jeffrey. "From Sentiment to Security: Cugoano, Liberal Principles, and the Bonds of Empire." *Criticism* 59, no. 2 (Spring 2017): 175–99.

Holsinger, Bruce. "Literary History and the Religious Turn: Announcing the New *ELN*." *English Language Notes* 44, no. 1 (2006): 1–3.

Holm, Melanie D. "Laughter, Skepticism, and the Pleasures of Being Misunderstood in Laurence Sterne's *Life and Opinions of Tristram Shandy, Gentleman*." *Eighteenth Century* 55, no. 4 (2014): 355–75.

Hunter, J. Paul. *Occasional Form: Henry Fielding and the Chain of Circumstance*. Baltimore, MD: Johns Hopkins University Press, 1975.

———. *The Reluctant Pilgrim: Defoe's Emblematic Method and the Quest for Form in* Robinson Crusoe. Baltimore, MD: Johns Hopkins University Press, 1966.

Hurd, Elizabeth. *The Politics of Secularism in International Relations*. Princeton, NJ: Princeton University Press, 2008.

Inchbald, Elizabeth. *Nature and Art*. 1796. Edited by Shawn Lisa Maurer. Petersborough, ON: Broadview, 2005.

———. *A Simple Story*. 1791. Edited by J. M. S Thompkins. Oxford: Oxford University Press, 2009.

Jager, Colin. *Unquiet Things: Secularism in the Romantic Age*. Philadelphia: University of Pennsylvania Press, 2014.

Judson, Barbara. "The Psychology of Satan: Elizabeth Inchbald's *A Simple Story*." *ELH: English Literary History* 76, no. 3 (Fall 2009): 595–624.

Keegan, Bridget. "'Bred a Jesuit': *A Simple Story* and Late Eighteenth-Century Catholic Culture." *Huntington Library Quarterly* 71, no. 4 (2008): 687–706.

Kelly, Gary. *English Fiction of the Romantic Period*. London: Longman, 1989.

———. *The English Jacobin Novel, 1780–1805*. Oxford: Oxford University Press, 1976.

Keymer, Thomas. *Sterne, the Moderns, and the Novel*. Oxford: Oxford University Press, 2005.

Kibbie, Ann Louise. *Transfusion: Blood and Sympathy in the Nineteenth-Century Literary Imagination*. Charlottesville: University of Virginia Press, 2019.

Kim, Elizabeth S. "Penelope Aubin's Novels Reconsidered: The Barbary Captivity Narrative and Christian Ecumenism in Early Eighteenth-Century Britain." *Eighteenth-Century Novel* 8 (2011): 1–29.

Knapp, Stephen. *Personification and the Sublime: Milton to Coleridge*. Cambridge, MA: Harvard University Press, 1985.

Laqueur, Thomas. *Making Sex: Body and Gender from the Greeks to Freud*. Cambridge, MA: Harvard University Press, 1992.

Layne, Jhordan. "Re-evaluating Religion and Superstition: Obeah and Christianity in Marlon James's *The Book of Night Women* and William Earle Jr.'s *Obi, or The History of Three-Fingered Jack*." *Journal of West Indian Literature* 26, no. 2 (2018): 50–65.

Lynch, Deidre Shauna. *The Economy of Character: Novels, Market Culture, and the Business of Inner Meaning*. Chicago: University of Chicago Press, 1998.

Lynch, Kathleen. *Protestant Autobiography in the Seventeenth-Century Anglophone World*. Oxford: Oxford University Press, 2012.

Mack, Douglas S. "Hogg's Religion and *Confessions of a Justified Sinner*." *Studies in Scottish Literature* 7 (1970): 272–75.

Mahmood, Saba. "Feminist Theory, Embodiment, and the Docile Agent: Some Reflections on the Egyptian Islamic Revival." *Cultural Anthropology* 16, no. 2 (Spring 2001): 202–36.

———. *The Politics of Piety: The Islamic Revival and the Feminist Subject*. Princeton, NJ: Princeton University Press, 2011.

Malchow, H. L. *Gothic Images of Race in Nineteenth-Century Britain*. Stanford, CA: Stanford University Press, 1996.

Mallipeddi, Ramesh. *Spectacular Suffering: Witnessing Slavery in the Eighteenth-Century British Atlantic*. Charlottesville: University of Virginia Press, 2016.

Massad, Joseph A. *Islam in Liberalism*. Chicago: University of Chicago Press, 2015.

McKeon, Michael. *The Origins of the English Novel: 1600–1740*. Rev. ed. Baltimore, MD: Johns Hopkins University Press, 2002.

Mellor, Anne K. "Interracial Sexual Desire in Charlotte Dacre's *Zofloya*." *European Romantic Review* 13, no. 2 (2002): 169–73.

Meyer Spacks, Patricia. *Desire and Truth: Functions of Plot in Eighteenth-Century English Novels*. Chicago: University of Chicago Press, 1990.

Michasiw, Ian Kim. "Charlotte Dacre's Postcolonial Moor." In *Empire and the Gothic: The Politics of Genre*, edited by Andrew Smith and William Hughes, 35–55. Basingstoke: Palgrave MacMillan, 2003.

Milbank, Alison. *God and the Gothic: Religion, Romance, and Reality in the English Literary Tradition*. Oxford: Oxford University Press, 2018.

Miles, Robert. "Europhobia: The Catholic Other in Horace Walpole and Charles Maturin." In *European Gothic: A Spirited Exchange*, edited by Avril Horner, 84–103. Manchester: Manchester University Press, 2002.

———. *Gothic Writing, 1750–1820: A Genealogy*. London: Routledge, 1993.

Milton, John. *Paradise Lost*. 1667–74. In *The Complete Poems and Major Prose*, edited by Merritt Y. Hughes, 173–470. Indianapolis, IN: Hackett, 2003.

Modern, John Lardas. "Conversion Diptych." In *The Immanent Frame: Secularism, Religion, and the Public Sphere*. 18 October 2017. https://tif.ssrc.org/2017/10/18/conversion-diptych/.

———. *Secularism in Antebellum America*. Chicago: University of Chicago Press, 2010.

Morillo, John. "Editing Eve: Rewriting the Fall in Austen's *Persuasion* and Inchbald's *A Simple Story*." *Eighteenth-Century Fiction* 23, no. 1 (Fall 2010): 195–223.

Murillo, Cynthia. "'Haunted Spaces and Powerful Places': Reconfiguring the Doppelganger in Charlotte Dacre's *Zofloya*." *Studies in the Humanities* 32, no. 1 (2005): 74–92.

Moten, Fred. *In the Break: The Aesthetics of the Black Radical Tradition*. Minneapolis: University of Minnesota Press, 2003.

Nachumi, Nora. "'Those Simple Signs': The Performance of Emotion in Elizabeth Inchbald's *A Simple Story*." *Eighteenth-Century Fiction* 11, no. 3 (Spring 1999): 317–38.

New, Melvyn. Editor's Introduction to *The Life and Opinions of Tristram Shandy* by Laurence Sterne, xxxiii–xlix. London: Penguin, 1997.

Nussbaum, Felicity. "Slavery, Blackness, and Islam: *The Arabian Nights* in the Eighteenth Century." In *Slavery and the Cultures of Abolition: Essays Marking the Bicentennial of the British Abolition Act of 1807*, 150–72. Cambridge: D. S. Brewer, 2007.

Nuttall, George. *Visible Saints: The Congregational Way, 1640–1660*. Oxford: Blackwell, 1957.

O'Malley, Peter. *Catholicism, Sexual Deviance, and Victorian Gothic Culture*. Cambridge: Cambridge University Press, 2006.

O'Quinn, Daniel. *Engaging the Ottoman Empire: Vexed Mediations, 1660–1815*. Philadelphia: University of Pennsylvania Press, 2019.

Orlemanski, Julie. "Who Has Fiction? Modernity, Fictionality, and the Middle Ages." *New Literary History* 50, no. 2 (2019): 145–70.

Osland, Dianne. "Heart-Picking in *A Simple Story*." *Eighteenth-Century Fiction* 16, no. 1 (October 2003): 79–101.

Pacheco, Anita. "'Little Religion' but 'Admirable Morals': Christianity and Honor in Aphra Behn's *Oroonoko*." *Modern Philology* 111, no. 2 (2013): 252–80.

———. "Royalism and Honor in Aphra Behn's *Oroonoko*." *SEL: Studies in English Literature, 1500–1900* 34, no. 3 (Summer 1994): 491–506.

Pahl, John. *Empire of Sacrifice: The Religious Origins of American Violence*. New York: New York University Press, 2010.

Parnell, J. T. "Swift, Sterne, and the Skeptical Tradition." *Studies in Eighteenth-Century Culture* 23 (1994): 221–41.

Pavel, Thomas G. *The Lives of the Novel: A History*. Princeton, NJ: Princeton University Press, 2013.

Pincus, Steven C. *1688: The First Modern Revolution*. New Haven, CT: Yale University Press, 2009.

Pecora, Vincent. *Secularization without End: Beckett, Mann, Coetzee.* Notre Dame, IN: University of Notre Dame Press, 2015.

Peters, Tacuma. "The Anti-Imperialism of Ottobah Cugoano: Slavery, Abolition, and Colonialism in *Thoughts and Sentiments on the Evil of Slavery.*" *CLR James Journal* 23, nos. 1–2 (Fall 2017): 61–82.

Pocock, J. G. A. *Barbarism and Religion.* 6 vols. Cambridge: Cambridge University Press, 1999–2015.

Purves, Maria. *The Gothic and Catholicism: Religion, Cultural Exchange and the Popular Novel, 1785–1829.* Cardiff: University of Wales Press, 2009.

Rader, Ralph W. "*Tom Jones:* The Form in History." In *Ideology and Form in Eighteenth-Century Literature,* edited by David H. Richer, 47–74. Lubbock: Texas Tech University Press, 1999.

Rawson, C. J. *Henry Fielding and the Augustan Ideal Under Stress.* London: Routledge, 1972.

Reed, Jennifer. "Moving Fortunes: Caribbean Women's Marriage, Mobility, and Money in the Novel of Sentiment." *Eighteenth-Century Fiction* 31, no. 3 (Spring 2019): 509–28.

Richardson, Alan. "Romantic Voodoo: Obeah and British Culture, 1797–1807." *Studies in Romanticism* 32, no. 1 (1993): 3–28.

Richetti, John. *Popular Fiction before Richardson.* Oxford: Clarendon, 1969.

Rivers, Isabel. *Reason, Grace, and Sentiment: A Study of the Language of Religion and Ethics in England, 1660–1780.* 2 vols. Cambridge: Cambridge University Press, 1991.

Rivett, Sarah. *The Science of the Soul in Colonial New England.* Chapel Hill: University of North Carolina Press, 2012.

Rosenberg, Jordy. *Confessions of the Fox.* New York: One World, 2018.

———. *Critical Enthusiasm: Capital Accumulation and the Transformation of Religious Passion.* Oxford: Oxford University Press, 2011.

Rosengarten, Richard A. *Henry Fielding and the Narration of Providence: Divine Design and the Incursions of Evil.* Basingstoke: Palgrave Macmillan, 2000.

Rosenthal, Laura J. "*Oroonoko:* Reception, Ideology, and Narrative Strategy." In *The Cambridge Companion to Aphra Behn,* edited by Derek Hughes and Janet Todd, 151–65. Cambridge: Cambridge University Press, 2004.

Sacks, Sheldon. *Fiction and the Shape of Belief: A Study of Henry Fielding, with Glances at Swift, Johnson, and Richardson.* Berkeley: University of California Press, 1964.

Sage, Victor. *Horror Fiction in the Protestant Tradition.* London: Macmillan, 1988.

Said, Edward W. *Culture and Imperialism.* New York: Vintage, 1993.

———. *Orientalism.* New York: Pantheon, 1978.

Salih, Sarah. *Representing Mixed Race in Jamaica and England from the Abolition Era to the Present.* New York: Routledge, 2011.

Schlovsky, Viktor. "A Parodying Novel: Sterne's *Tristram Shandy.*" In *Laurence Sterne: A Collection of Critical Essays,* edited by John Traugott, 66–89. Englewood Cliffs, NJ: Prentice Hall, 1968.

Schmitt, Cannon. *Alien Nation: Nineteenth-Century Gothic Fictions and English Nationality.* Philadelphia: University of Pennsylvania Press, 1997.

Scott, Joan Wallach. *Sex and Secularism.* Princeton, NJ: Princeton University Press, 2017.

Sedgwick, Eve Kosofsky. *The Coherence of Gothic Conventions.* New York: Arno, 1980.

Seidel, Kevin. "Beyond the Religious and the Secular in the History of the Novel." *New Literary History* 38, no. 4 (2007): 637–47.

———. *Rethinking the Secular Origins of the Novel: The Bible in English Fiction, 1678–1767.* Cambridge: Cambridge University Press, 2021.

Schotland, Sara D. "'The Slave's Revenge: The Terror in Charlotte Dacre's *Zofloya*." *Western Journal of Black Studies* 33, no. 2 (2009): 123–31.

Sider Jost, Jacob. *Prose Immortality, 1711–1819.* Charlottesville: University of Virginia Press, 2015.

Smith, Zadie. Foreword to *Black England: A Forgotten Georgian History* by Gretchen Gerzina, xi–xix. London: John Murray, 2022.

Song, Eric B. "Love against Substitution: John Milton, Aphra Behn, and the Political Theology of Conjugal Narratives." *ELH: English Literary History* 80, no. 3 (2013): 681–714.

Sorkin, David. *Religious Enlightenment: Protestants, Jews, and Catholics from London to Vienna.* Princeton, NJ: Princeton University Press, 2008.

Spargo, Tamsin. *The Writing of John Bunyan.* Aldershot: Ashgate, 1997.

Spencer, Jane. Introduction to *A Simple Story* by Elizabeth Inchbald, vi–xx. Oxford: Oxford World Classics, 2009.

Spillers, Hortense. "Mama's Baby, Papa's Maybe: An American Grammar Book." *Diacritics* 17, no. 1 (1987): 65–81.

Starr, George. *Defoe and Spiritual Autobiography.* Princeton, NJ: Princeton University Press, 1965.

Sterne, Laurence. *The Florida Edition of the Works of Laurence Sterne, Vol. 4: The Sermons,* edited by Melvyn New. Gainesville: University Press of Florida, 1996.

———. *The Life and Opinions of Tristram Shandy, Gentleman.* 1759–67. Edited by Melvyn New. New York: Penguin, 1997.

Stewart, Carole. *The Eighteenth-Century Novel and the Secularization of Ethics.* Farnham: Ashgate, 2010.

Stewart, Dustin S. "Cugoano and the Hermeneutics of Black Calvinism." *ELH: English Literary History* 88, no. 3 (2021): 629–59.

Stuchiner, Judith. "Fielding's Latitudinarian Doubt: Faith 'versus' Works in *Joseph Andrews.*" *Studies in Philology* 114, no. 4 (2017): 875–94.

Taylor, Charles. *A Secular Age.* Cambridge, MA: Belknap Press of Harvard University Press, 2007.

Tibutt, H. G., ed. *Minutes of the First Independent Church (Now Bunyan Meeting) at Bedford, 1656–1766.* Bedford: Bedfordshire Historical Record Society, 1976.

Tomko, Michael. *British Romanticism and the Catholic Question: Religion, History, and National Identity, 1778–1829.* Basingstoke: Palgrave Macmillan, 2010.

Tompkins, J. M. S. *The Popular Novel in England, 1770–1800.* London: Methuen, 1969.

Vermeule, Blakey. *Why Do We Care about Literary Characters?* Baltimore, MD: Johns Hopkins University Press, 2010.

Wagner, Corinna. "The Dream of a Transparent Body: Identity, Science, and the Gothic Novel." *Gothic Studies* 14, no. 1 (2012): 74–92.

Wallace, Jr., Dewey D. *Puritans and Predestination: Grace in English Protestant Theology, 1525–1695.* Chapel Hill: University of North Carolina Press, 1982.

———. *Shapers of English Calvinism, 1660–1714: Variety, Persistence, and Transformation.* Oxford: Oxford University Press, 2011.

Walker, David. "Militant Religion and Politics in *The Holy War*." In *The Cambridge Companion to Bunyan*, edited by Anne Dunan-Page, 107–19. Cambridge: Cambridge University Press, 2010.

Ward, Candace. "Inordinate Desire: Schooling the Senses in Elizabeth Inchbald's *A Simple Story*." *Studies in the Novel* 31, no. 1 (Spring 1999): 1–18.

Watt, Ian. *Rise of the Novel: Studies in Defoe, Richardson and Fielding*. 2nd ed. Berkeley: University of California Press, 2001.

Weber, Max. *The Protestant Ethic and the Spirit of Capitalism*. 1904. Edited and translated by Peter Baer and Gordon C. Collins. New York: Penguin, 2002.

Wehrs, Donald R. "Sterne, Cervantes, Montaigne: Fideistic Skepticism and the Rhetoric of Desire." *Comparative Literature Studies* 25, no. 2 (1988): 127–51.

Weiss Smith, Courtney. *Empiricist Devotions: Science, Religion, and Poetry in Early Eighteenth-Century England*. Charlottesville: University of Virginia Press, 2016.

Welham, Debbie. "The Particular Case of Penelope Aubin." *British Journal for Eighteenth-Century Studies* 31, no. 1 (2008): 63–76.

Wheeler, Roxann. *The Complexion of Race: Categories of Difference in Eighteenth-Century British Culture*. Philadelphia: University of Pennsylvania Press, 2000.

Wheelock, Stefan M. *Barbaric Culture and Black Critique: Black Antislavery Writers, Religion, and the Slaveholding Atlantic*. Charlottesville: University of Virginia Press, 2015.

Whitefield, George. *The Doctrines of the Gospel Asserted and Vindicated*. London: C. Davis, 1739. Eighteenth Century Collections Online. Accessed 30 August 2023. https://link.gale.com/apps/doc/CW0123211719/ECCO?u=uga&sid=bookmark-ECCO&xid=80d23616&pg=1.

Whitford, David M. *The Curse of Ham in the Early Modern Era: The Bible and the Justifications for Slavery*. Farnham: Ashgate, 2009.

Wilcox, Lance. "Idols and Idolaters in *A Simple Story*." *Age of Johnson* 17 (2006): 297–316.

Williams, Eric. *Capitalism and Slavery*. 3rd ed. Chapel Hill: University of North Carolina Press, 2021.

Winship, Michael P. "Weak Christians, Backsliders, and Carnal Gospelers: Assurance of Salvation and the Pastoral Origins of Puritan Practical Divinity in the 1580s." *Church History* 70 (2001): 462–81.

Wisecup, Kelly. "Knowing Obeah." *Atlantic Studies* 10, no. 3 (2013): 406–25.

The Woman of Color, A Tale. 1808. Edited by Lindon J. Dominique. Petersborough, ON: Broadview, 2008.

Wynter, Sylvia. "1492: A New World View." In *Race, Discourse, and the Origin of the Americas: A New World View*, edited by Vera Lawrence Hyatt and Rex Nettleford, 6–56. Washington, DC: Smithsonian Institution, 1995.

Van Ghent, Dorothy. *The English Novel: Form and Function*. New York: Harper & Row, 1961.

Van Renen, Denys. "'Temple of Folly': Transatlantic 'Nature,' Nabobs, and Environmental Degradation in *The Woman of Colour*." In *Romantic Sustainability: Endurance and the Natural World, 1780–1830*, edited by Ben P. Robertson, 147–68. Lanham, MD: Lexington, 2016.

INDEX

Printed in the USA
CPSIA information can be obtained
at www.ICGtesting.com
CBHW031330200324
5619CB00002B/52

9 780813 950891